THIS RECORD WAS GIVEN AWAY FREE WITH THE PURCHASE OF TYKES COMICS, WHO CLAIMS NO OWNERSHIP OVER ITS CONTENTS
TYKES
RECORD NO.
99-29571
(43-DB-N 99)
(2:29)
UNBREAKABLE
45 RPM
RECORD
Fox Trot
"SWEET" CHUBBY
CHEEKS
(S. Weissman-M. Weems)
Recorded By Grampa

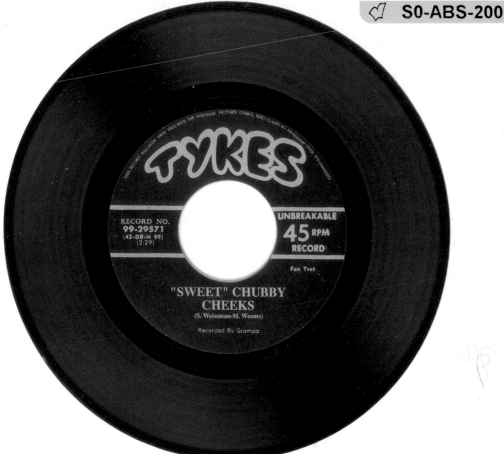

"DON'T CALL ME STUPID"

by Steven Weissman

FANTAGRAPHICS BOOKS

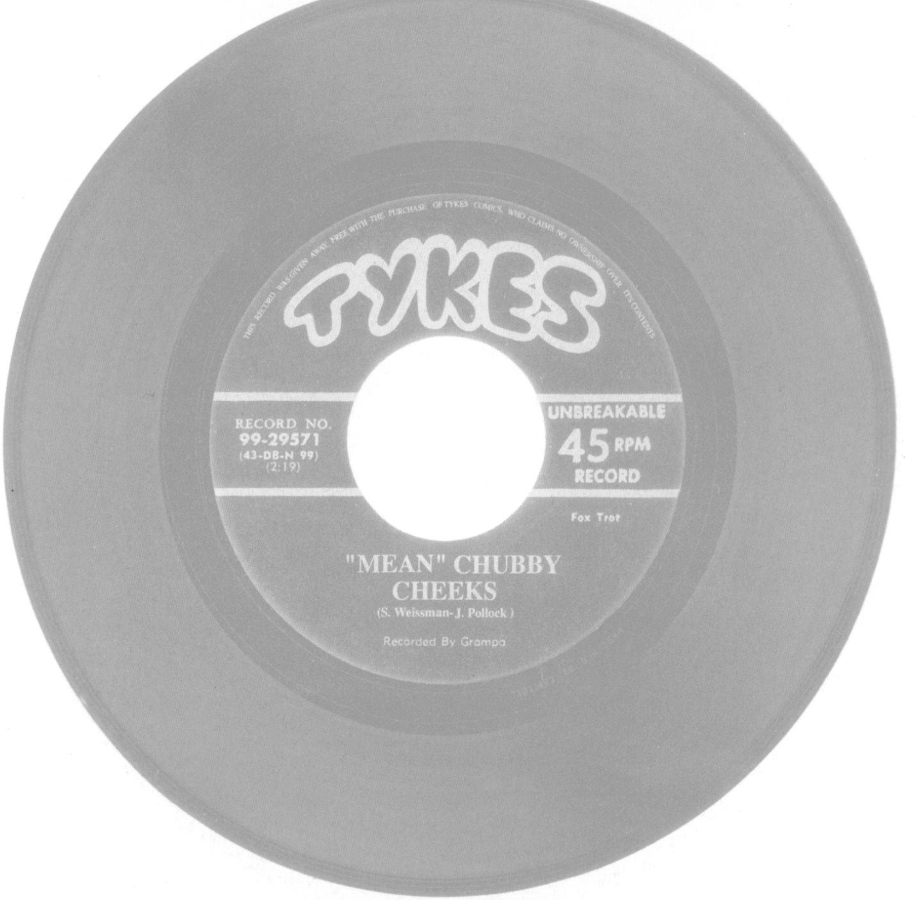
THIS RECORD WAS GIVEN AWAY FREE WITH THE PURCHASE OF TYKES COMICS, WHO CLAIMS NO OWNERSHIP OVER ITS CONTENTS
TYKES
RECORD NO.
99-29571
(43-DB-N 99)
(2:19)
UNBREAKABLE
45 RPM
RECORD
Fox Trot
"MEAN" CHUBBY
CHEEKS
(S. Weissman-J. Pollock)
Recorded By Grampa

Editorial coordinator: Gary Groth Book Design: Steven Weissman Production: Ryan Frederiksen Promotion: Eric Reynolds Publishers: Gary Groth and Kim Thompson Dedicated to: Charissa Chu Special acknowledgements: Jeff Mason, Jordan Crane, Doug Erb, Ron Rege, Jr.

 Fantagraphics Books, 7563 Lake City Way NE, Seattle WA 98115. Call out toll-free number for a free full-color catalogue of comics 'n' related pop culture. 1.800.657.1100. Or visit on-line at fantagraphics.com.

ISBN 1.56097.568.8
PRINTED IN KOREA

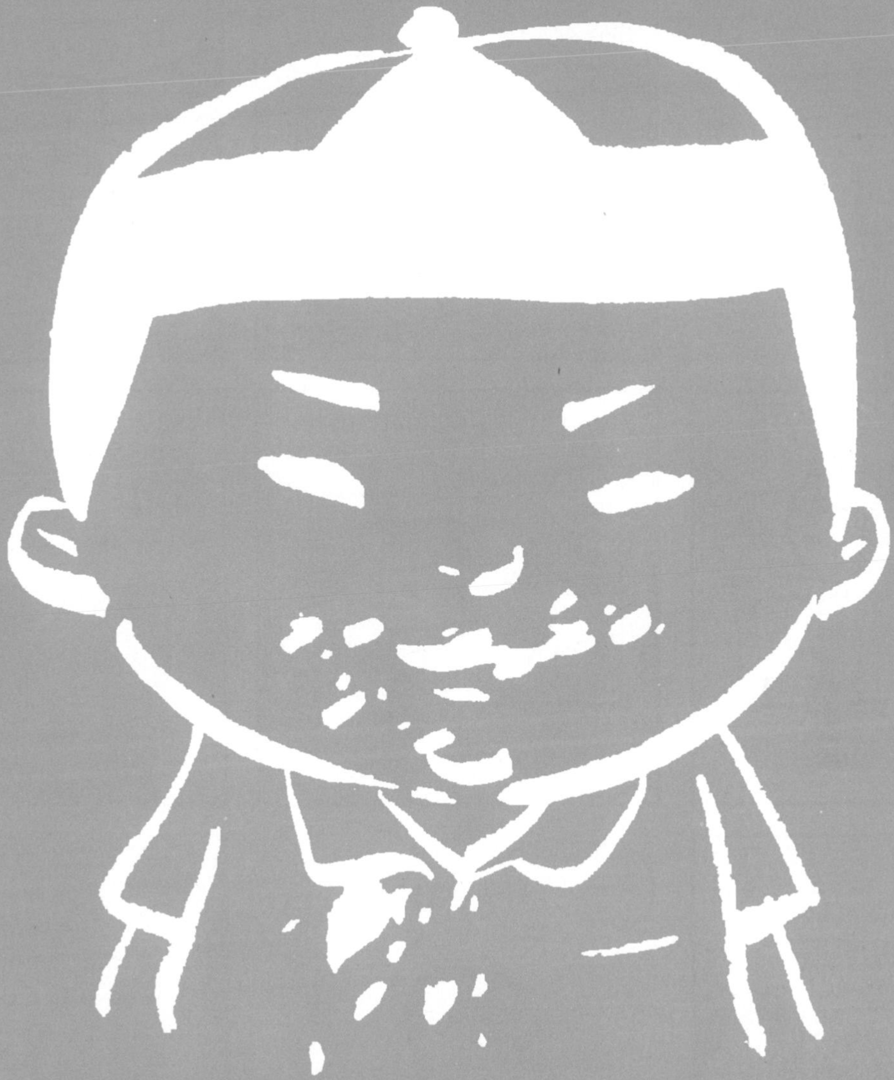

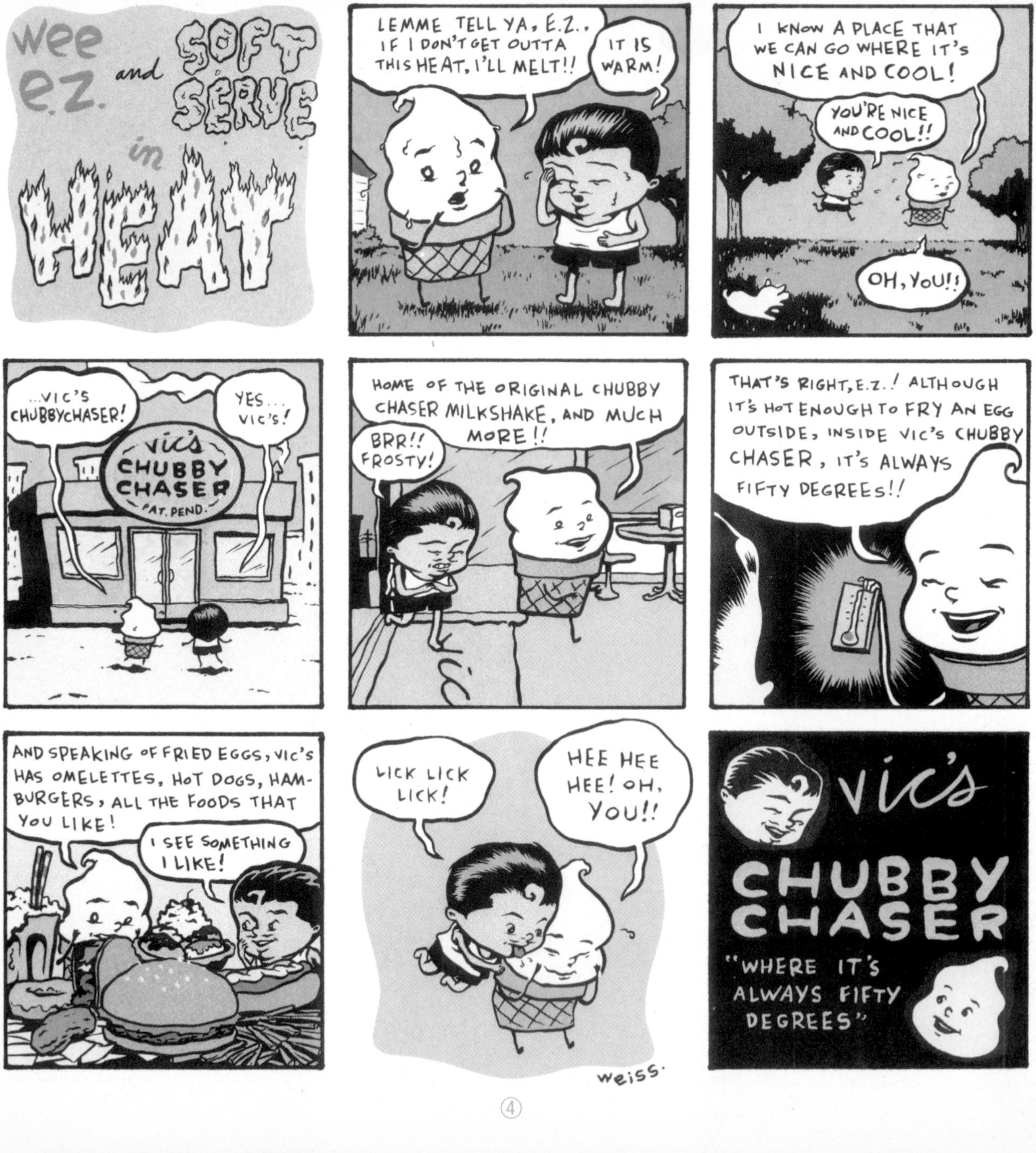
wee e.z. and SOFT SERVE in HEAT
LEMME TELL YA, E.Z., IF I DON'T GET OUTTA THIS HEAT, I'LL MELT!!
IT IS WARM!
I KNOW A PLACE THAT WE CAN GO WHERE IT'S NICE AND COOL!
YOU'RE NICE AND COOL!!
OH, YOU!!
...VIC'S CHUBBYCHASER!
YES... VIC'S!
Vic's CHUBBY CHASER PAT. PEND.
HOME OF THE ORIGINAL CHUBBY CHASER MILKSHAKE, AND MUCH MORE!!
BRR!! FROSTY!
THAT'S RIGHT, E.Z.! ALTHOUGH IT'S HOT ENOUGH TO FRY AN EGG OUTSIDE, INSIDE VIC'S CHUBBY CHASER, IT'S ALWAYS FIFTY DEGREES!!
AND SPEAKING OF FRIED EGGS, VIC'S HAS OMELETTES, HOT DOGS, HAMBURGERS, ALL THE FOODS THAT YOU LIKE!
I SEE SOMETHING I LIKE!
LICK LICK LICK!
HEE HEE HEE! OH, YOU!!
Vic's CHUBBY CHASER "WHERE IT'S ALWAYS FIFTY DEGREES"
weiss.

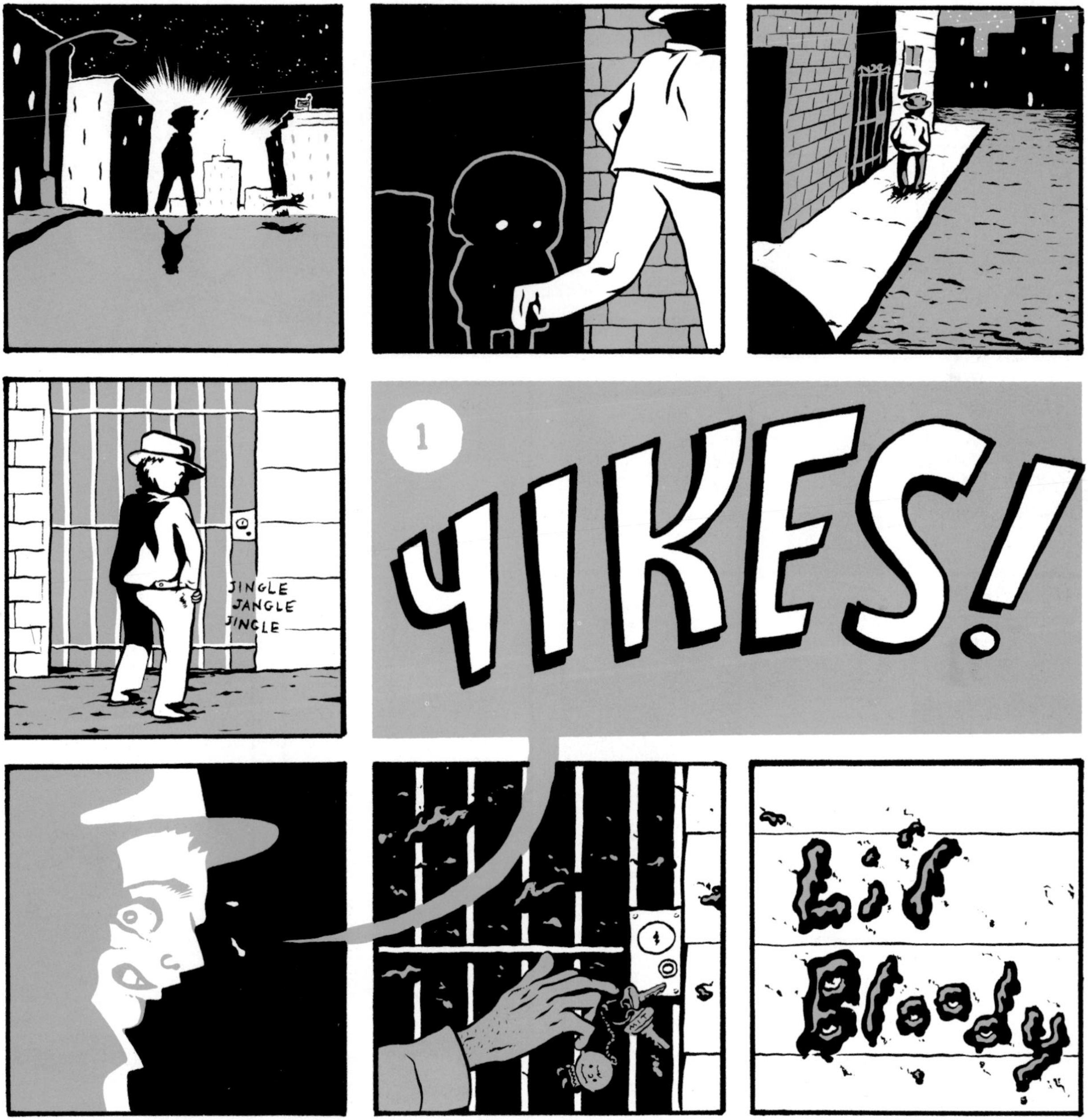
JINGLE
JANGLE
JINGLE
1
YIKES!
Lil
Bloody

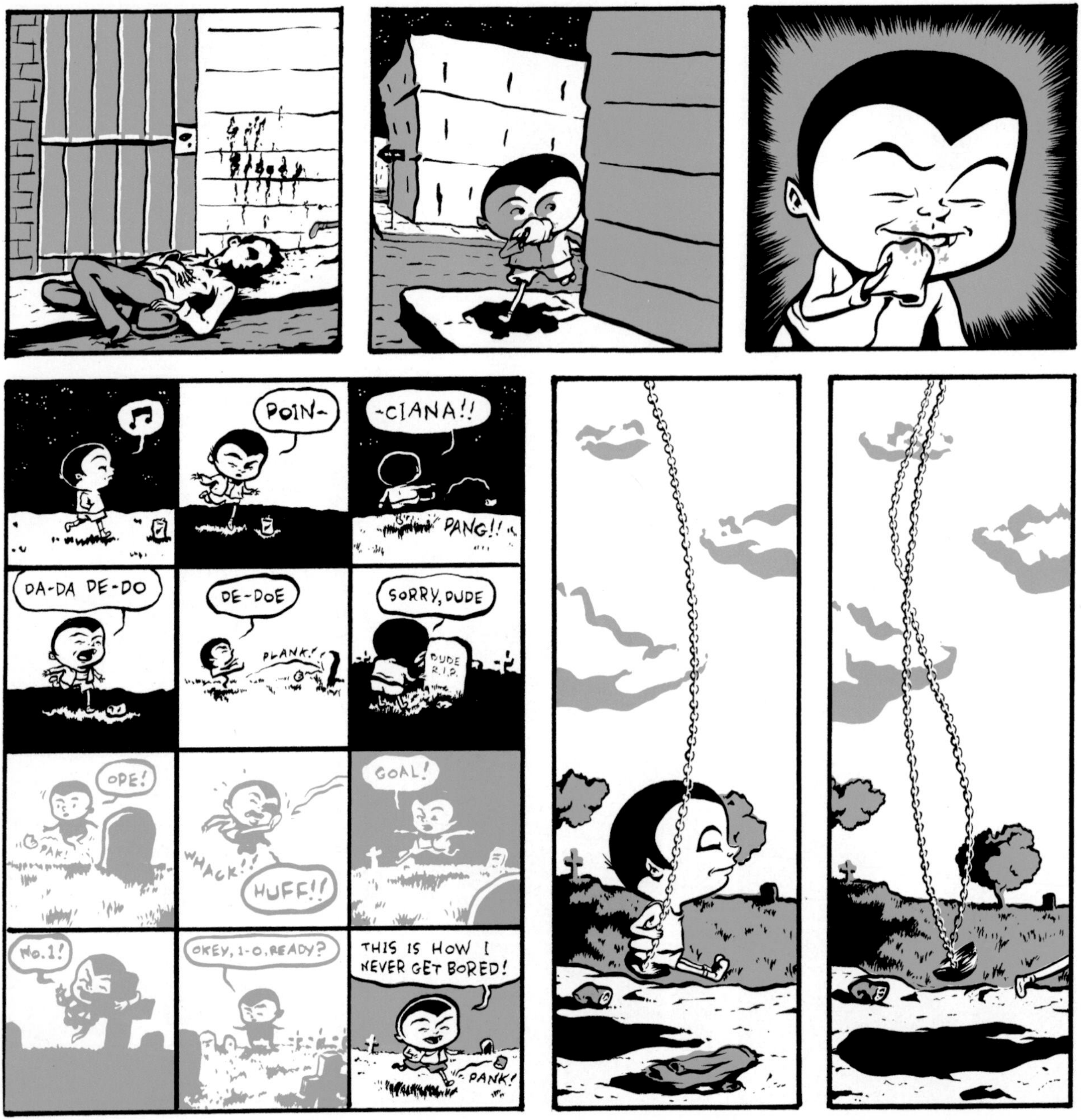
POIN-
-CIANA!!
PANG!!
DA-DA DE-DO
DE-DOE
PLANK!
SORRY, DUDE
DUDE R.I.P.
OPE!
PAK!
WHACK!!
HUFF!!
GOAL!
No.1!
OKEY, 1-0, READY?
THIS IS HOW I NEVER GET BORED!
PANK!

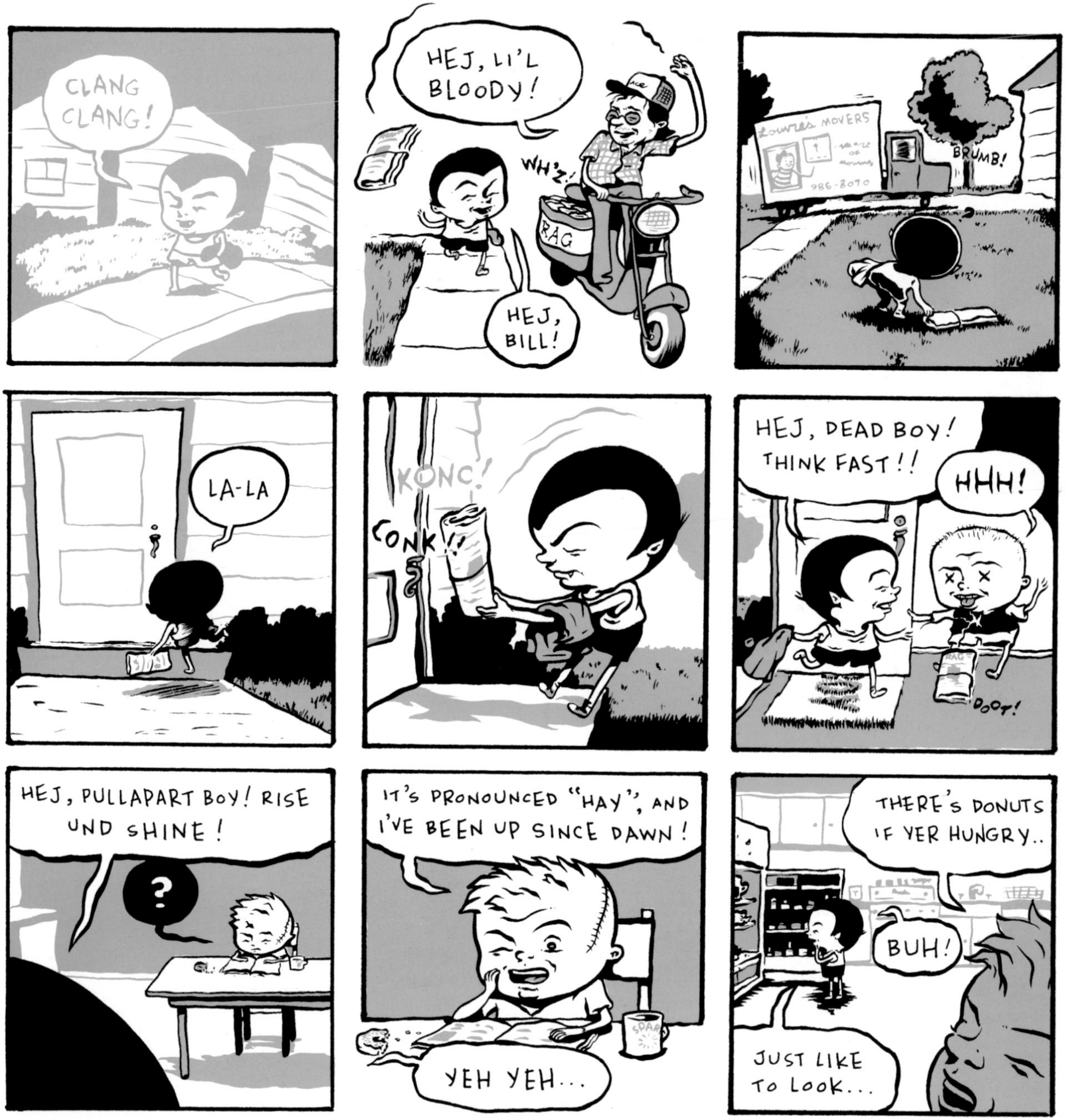
CLANG CLANG!
HEJ, LI'L BLOODY!
WH'Z!
HEJ, BILL!
RAG
LOWRIE'S MOVERS
986-8070
BRUMB!
LA-LA
KONC!
CONK!
HEJ, DEAD BOY! THINK FAST!!
HHH!
RAG
DOOF!
HEJ, PULLAPART BOY! RISE UND SHINE!
?
IT'S PRONOUNCED "HAY", AND I'VE BEEN UP SINCE DAWN!
YEH YEH...
THERE'S DONUTS IF YER HUNGRY..
BUH!
JUST LIKE TO LOOK...

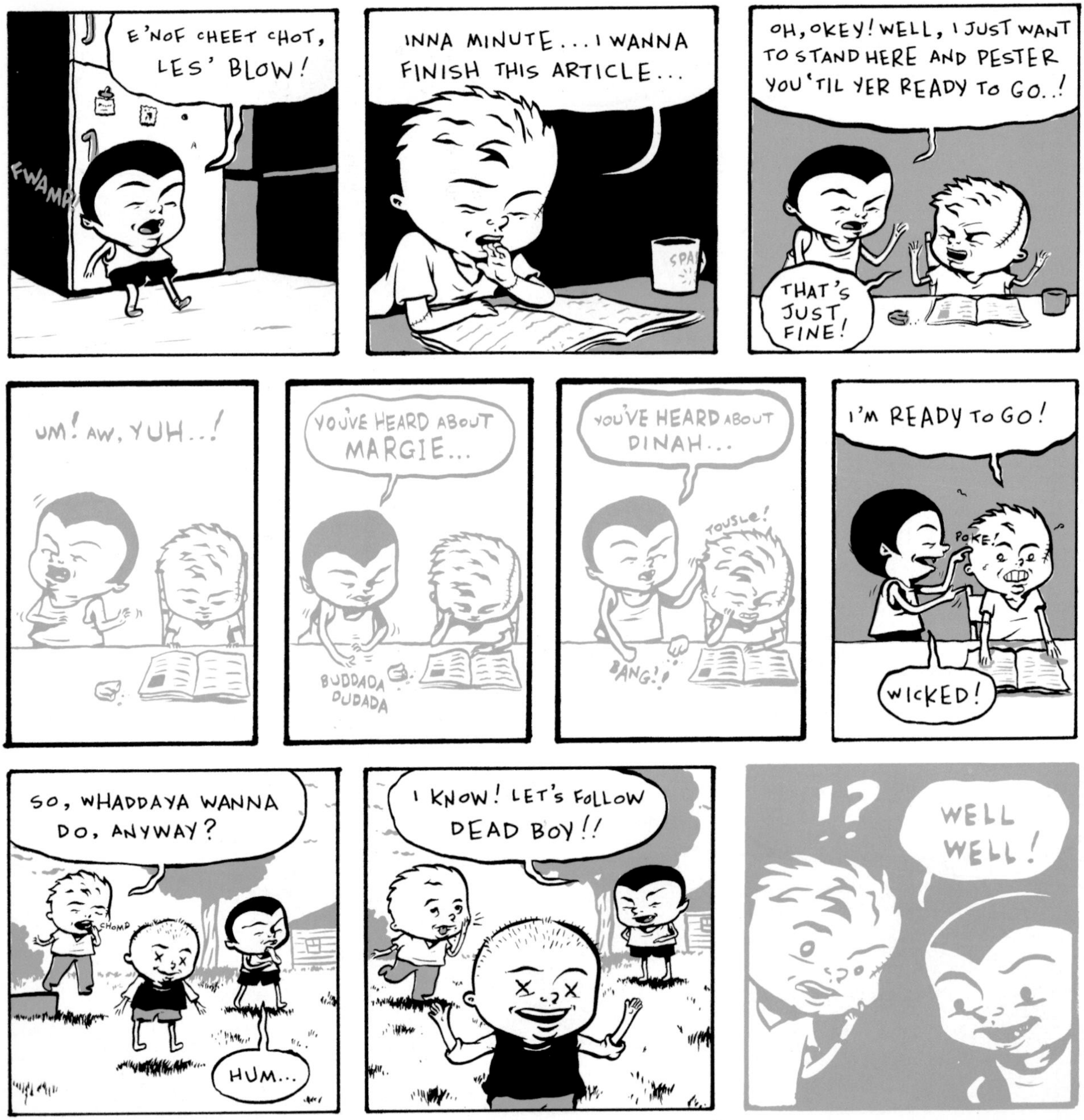
E'NOF CHEET CHOT, LES' BLOW!
FWAMP!
INNA MINUTE...I WANNA FINISH THIS ARTICLE...
OH, OKEY! WELL, I JUST WANT TO STAND HERE AND PESTER YOU 'TIL YER READY TO GO..!
THAT'S JUST FINE!
UM! AW, YUH...!
YOU'VE HEARD ABOUT MARGIE...
BUDDADA DUDADA
YOU'VE HEARD ABOUT DINAH...
TOUSLE!
BANG!
I'M READY TO GO!
POKE!
WICKED!
SO, WHADDAYA WANNA DO, ANYWAY?
CHOMP
HUM...
I KNOW! LET'S FOLLOW DEAD BOY!!
!?
WELL WELL!

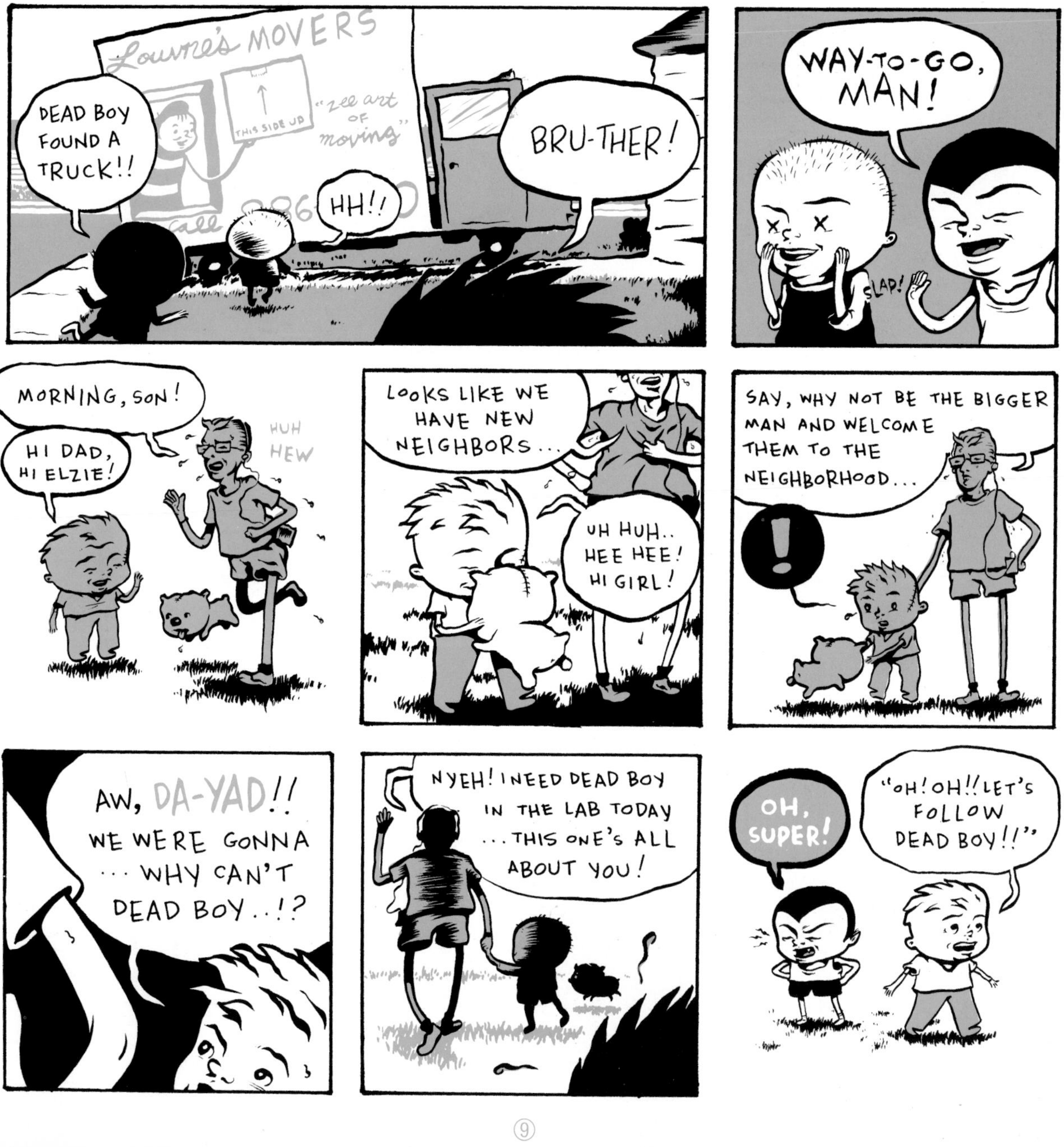
Lowne's MOVERS
THIS SIDE UP
"zee art of moving"
DEAD BOY FOUND A TRUCK!!
HH!!
BRU-THER!
WAY-TO-GO, MAN!
SLAP!
MORNING, SON!
HI DAD, HI ELZIE!
HUH HEW
LOOKS LIKE WE HAVE NEW NEIGHBORS...
UH HUH.. HEE HEE! HI GIRL!
SAY, WHY NOT BE THE BIGGER MAN AND WELCOME THEM TO THE NEIGHBORHOOD...
!
AW, DA-YAD!! WE WERE GONNA ... WHY CAN'T DEAD BOY..!?
NYEH! I NEED DEAD BOY IN THE LAB TODAY ... THIS ONE'S ALL ABOUT YOU!
OH, SUPER!
"OH! OH!! LET'S FOLLOW DEAD BOY!!"

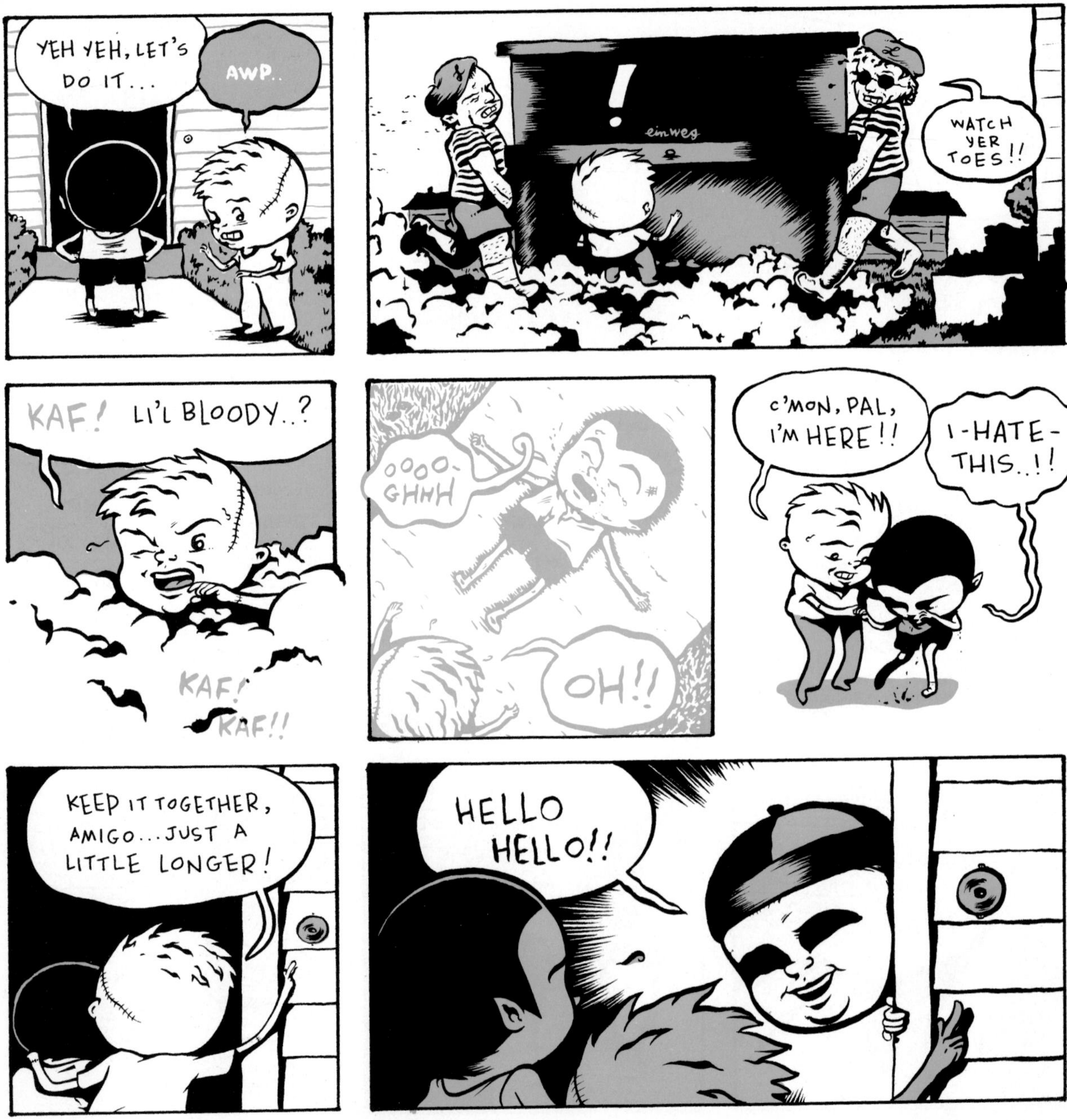
YEH YEH, LET'S DO IT...
AWP..
!
einweg
WATCH YER TOES!!
KAF! LI'L BLOODY..?
KAF! KAF!!
OOOO-GHHH
OH!!
C'MON, PAL, I'M HERE!!
I-HATE-THIS..!!
KEEP IT TOGETHER, AMIGO...JUST A LITTLE LONGER!
HELLO HELLO!!

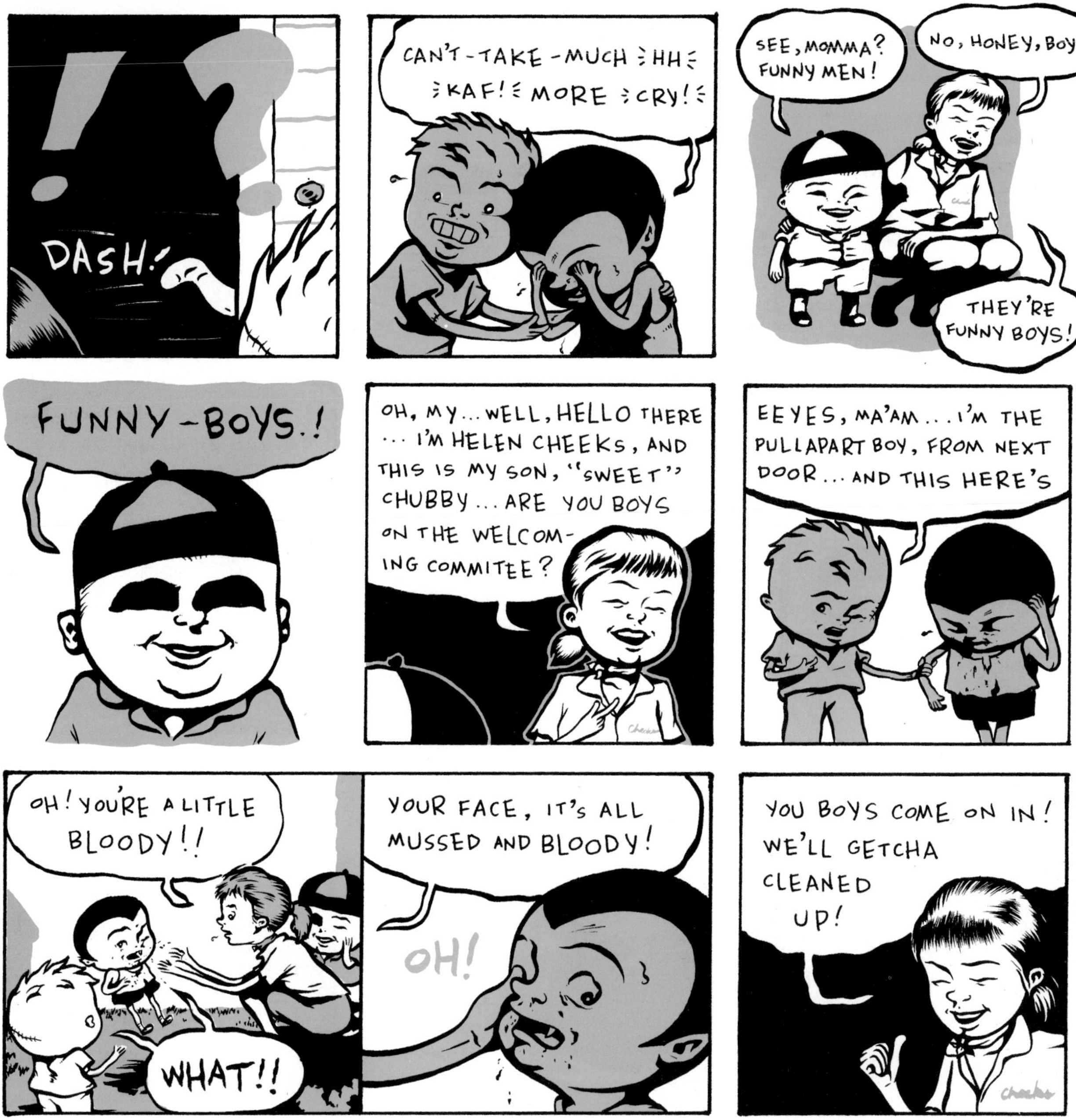
!
?
DASH!
CAN'T-TAKE-MUCH ≷HH≷ ≷KAF!≷ MORE ≷CRY!≷
SEE, MOMMA? FUNNY MEN!
NO, HONEY, BOYS!
THEY'RE FUNNY BOYS!
FUNNY-BOYS.!
OH, MY... WELL, HELLO THERE ... I'M HELEN CHEEKS, AND THIS IS MY SON, "SWEET" CHUBBY... ARE YOU BOYS ON THE WELCOM-ING COMMITEE?
EEYES, MA'AM... I'M THE PULLAPART BOY, FROM NEXT DOOR... AND THIS HERE'S
OH! YOU'RE A LITTLE BLOODY!!
WHAT!!
YOUR FACE, IT'S ALL MUSSED AND BLOODY!
OH!
YOU BOYS COME ON IN! WE'LL GETCHA CLEANED UP!

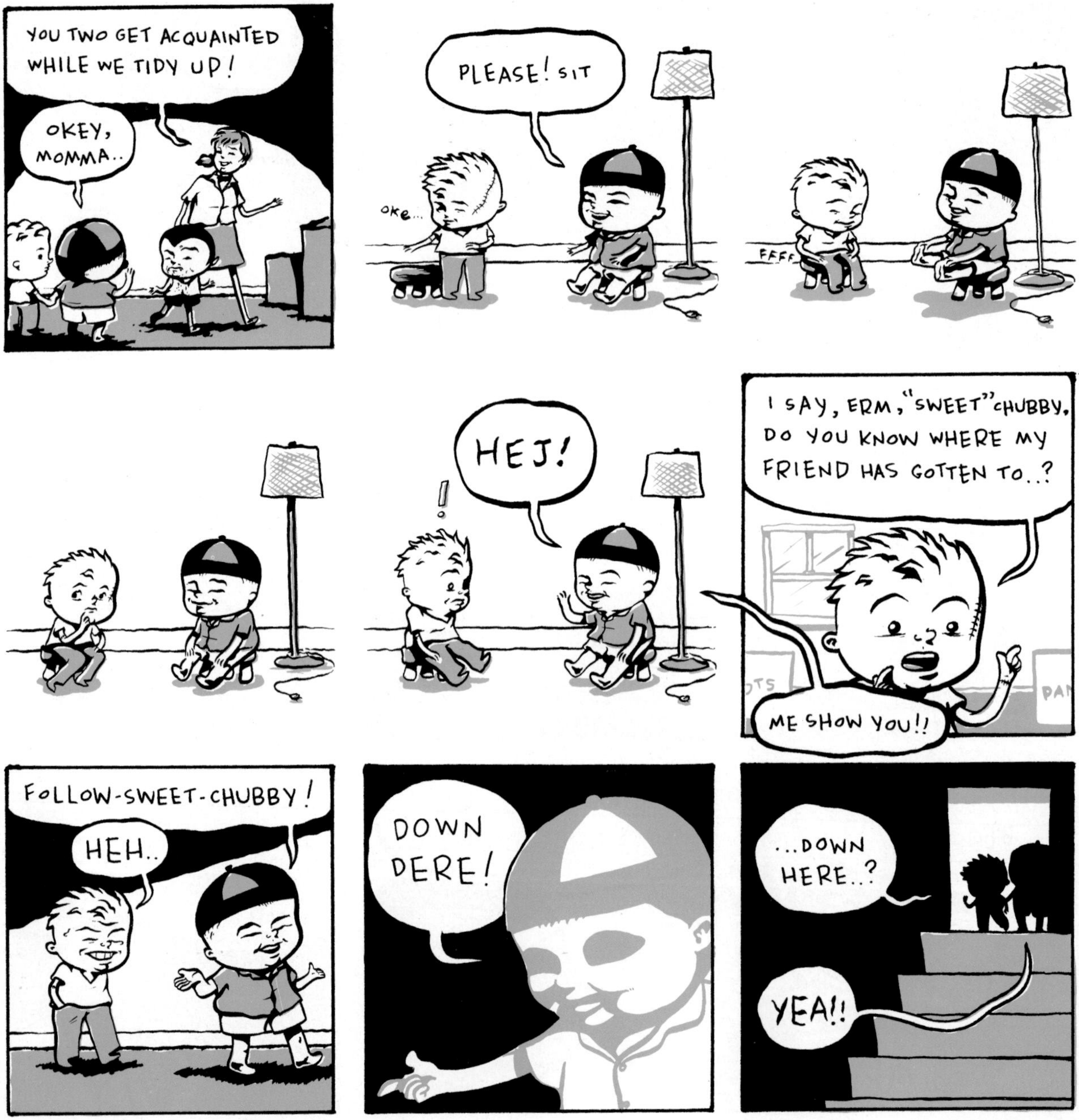
YOU TWO GET ACQUAINTED WHILE WE TIDY UP!
OKEY, MOMMA..
PLEASE! SIT
OKe...
FFFF
!
HEJ!
I SAY, ERM, "SWEET" CHUBBY, DO YOU KNOW WHERE MY FRIEND HAS GOTTEN TO..?
ME SHOW YOU!!
FOLLOW-SWEET-CHUBBY!
HEH..
DOWN DERE!
...DOWN HERE..?
YEA!!

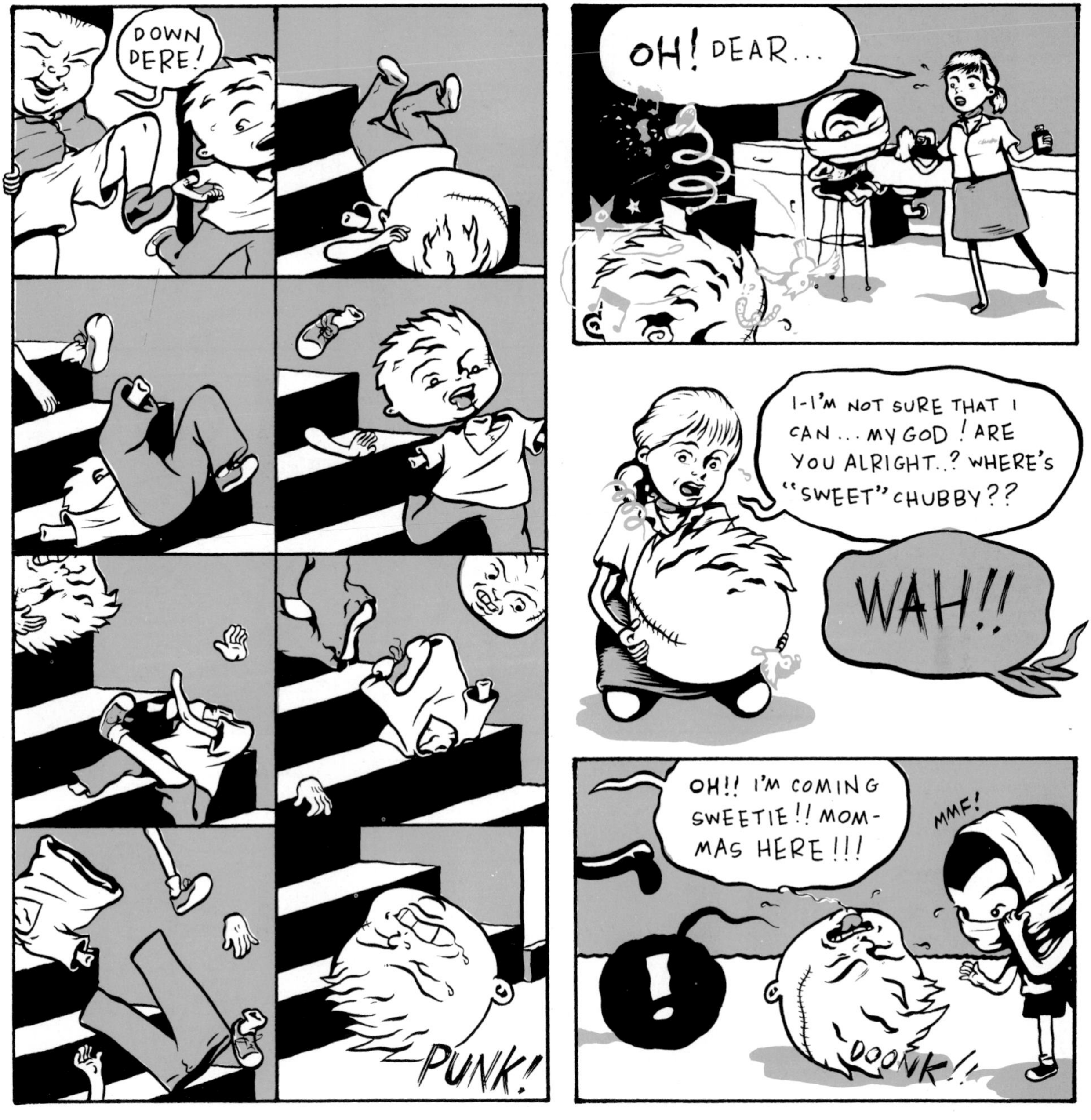
DOWN DERE!
PUNK!
OH! DEAR...
I-I'M NOT SURE THAT I CAN... MY GOD! ARE YOU ALRIGHT..? WHERE'S "SWEET" CHUBBY??
WAH!!
OH!! I'M COMING SWEETIE!! MOM-MAS HERE!!!
MMF!
DOONK!!

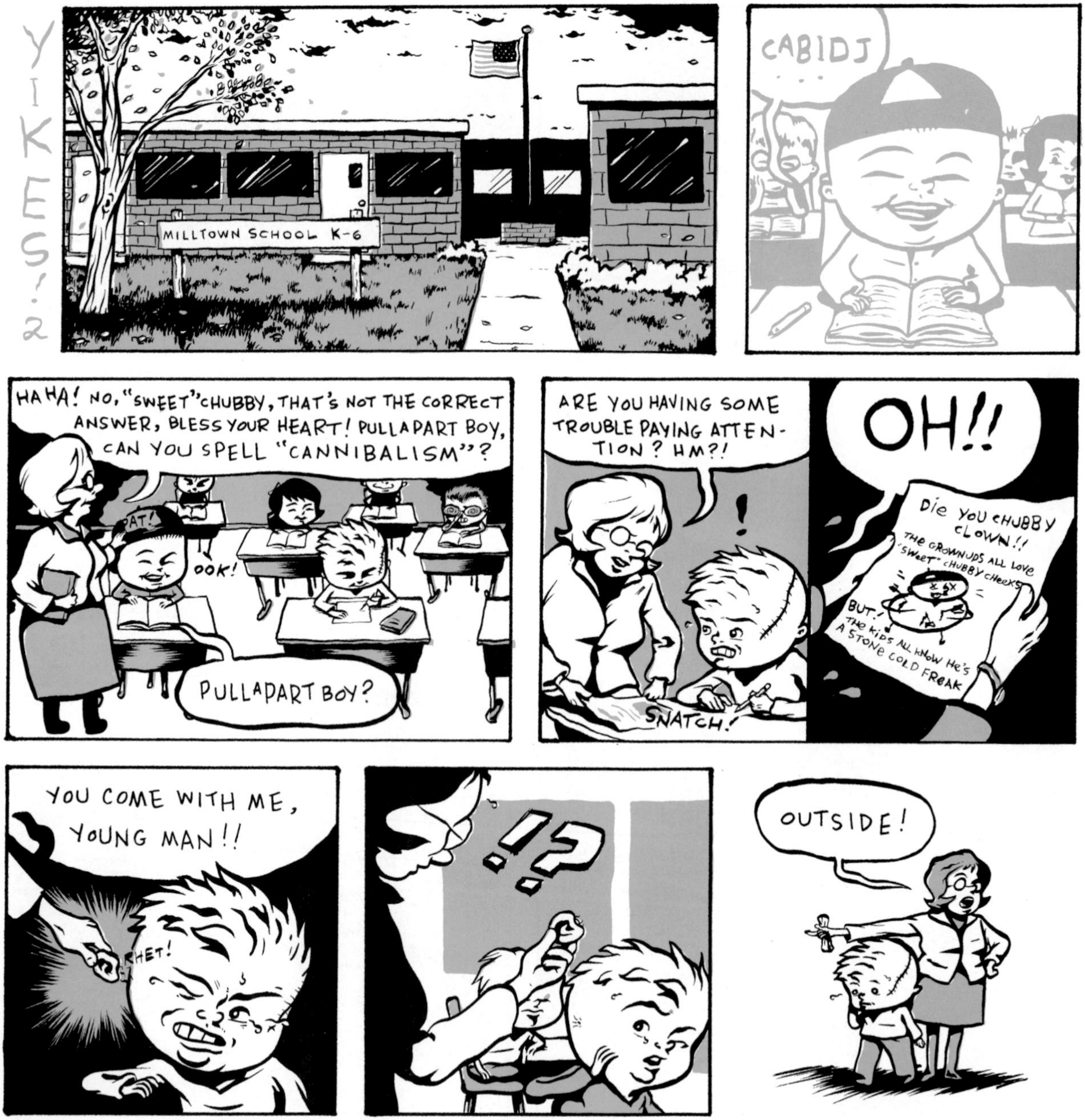
YIKES!2
MILLTOWN SCHOOL K-6
CABIDJ
HAHA! NO, "SWEET" CHUBBY, THAT'S NOT THE CORRECT ANSWER, BLESS YOUR HEART! PULLAPART BOY, CAN YOU SPELL "CANNIBALISM"?
PAT!
OOK!
PULLAPART BOY?
ARE YOU HAVING SOME TROUBLE PAYING ATTEN-TION? HM?!
!
SNATCH!
OH!!
DIE YOU CHUBBY CLOWN!!
THE GROWNUPS ALL LOVE "SWEET" CHUBBY CHEEKS
BUT! THE KIDS ALL KNOW HE'S A STONE COLD FREAK
YOU COME WITH ME, YOUNG MAN!!
RHET!
!?
OUTSIDE!

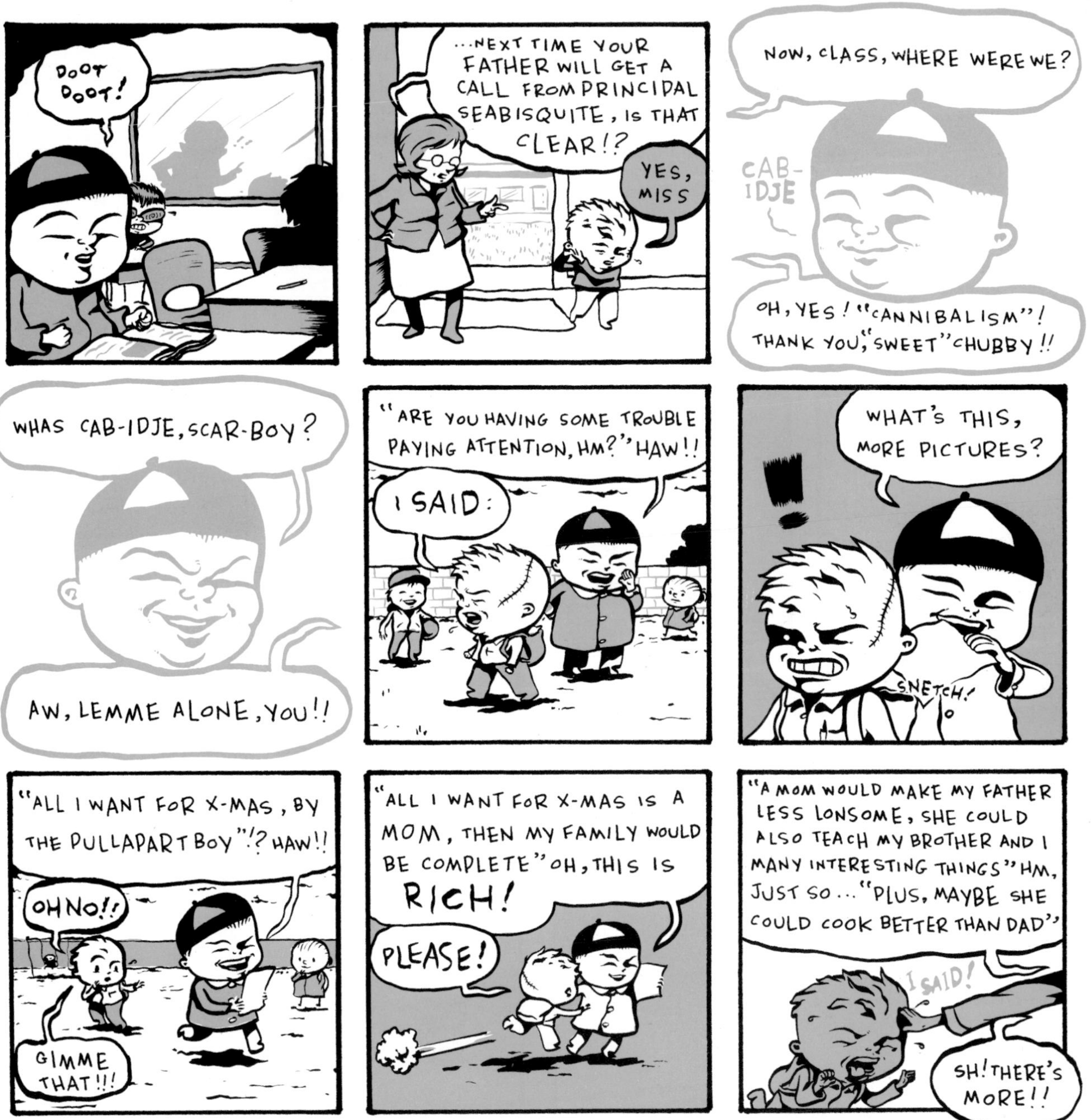
DOOT DOOT!
...NEXT TIME YOUR FATHER WILL GET A CALL FROM PRINCIPAL SEABISQUITE, IS THAT CLEAR!?
YES, MISS
NOW, CLASS, WHERE WERE WE?
CAB-IDJE
OH, YES! "CANNIBALISM"! THANK YOU, "SWEET" CHUBBY!!
WHAS CAB-IDJE, SCAR-BOY?
AW, LEMME ALONE, YOU!!
"ARE YOU HAVING SOME TROUBLE PAYING ATTENTION, HM?" HAW!!
I SAID:
WHAT'S THIS, MORE PICTURES?
SNETCH!
"ALL I WANT FOR X-MAS, BY THE PULLAPART BOY"!? HAW!!
OH NO!!
GIMME THAT!!!
"ALL I WANT FOR X-MAS IS A MOM, THEN MY FAMILY WOULD BE COMPLETE" OH, THIS IS RICH!
PLEASE!
"A MOM WOULD MAKE MY FATHER LESS LONSOME, SHE COULD ALSO TEACH MY BROTHER AND I MANY INTERESTING THINGS" HM, JUST SO... "PLUS, MAYBE SHE COULD COOK BETTER THAN DAD"
I SAID!
SH! THERE'S MORE!!

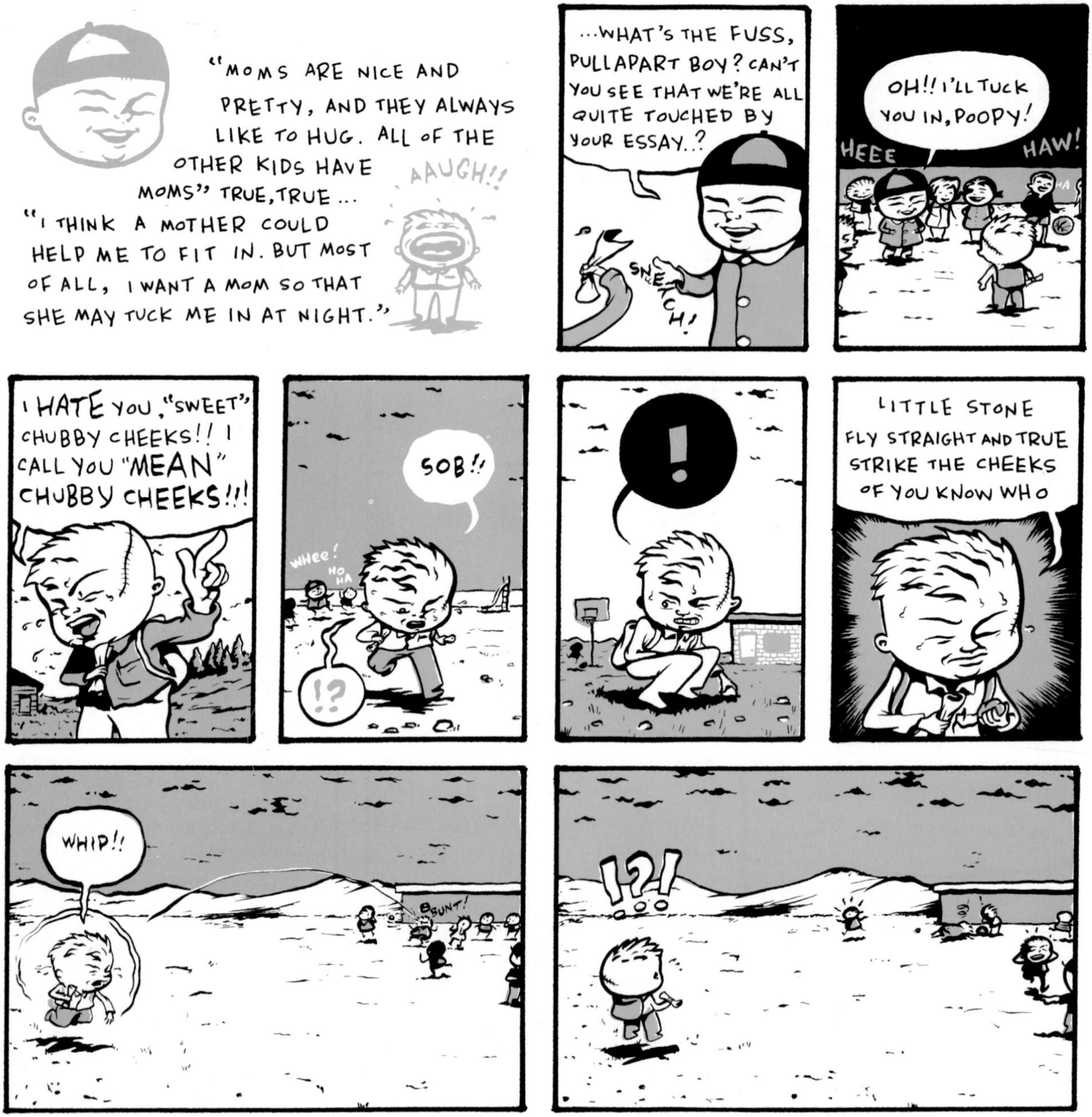
"MOMS ARE NICE AND PRETTY, AND THEY ALWAYS LIKE TO HUG. ALL OF THE OTHER KIDS HAVE MOMS" TRUE, TRUE...
AAUGH!!
"I THINK A MOTHER COULD HELP ME TO FIT IN. BUT MOST OF ALL, I WANT A MOM SO THAT SHE MAY TUCK ME IN AT NIGHT."
...WHAT'S THE FUSS, PULLAPART BOY? CAN'T YOU SEE THAT WE'RE ALL QUITE TOUCHED BY YOUR ESSAY..?
SNETCH!
OH!! I'LL TUCK YOU IN, POOPY!
HEEE
HAW!
HA
I HATE YOU, "SWEET" CHUBBY CHEEKS!! I CALL YOU "MEAN" CHUBBY CHEEKS!!!
SOB!!
WHee!
HO HA
!?
!
LITTLE STONE FLY STRAIGHT AND TRUE STRIKE THE CHEEKS OF YOU KNOW WHO
WHIP!!
BONT!
!?!

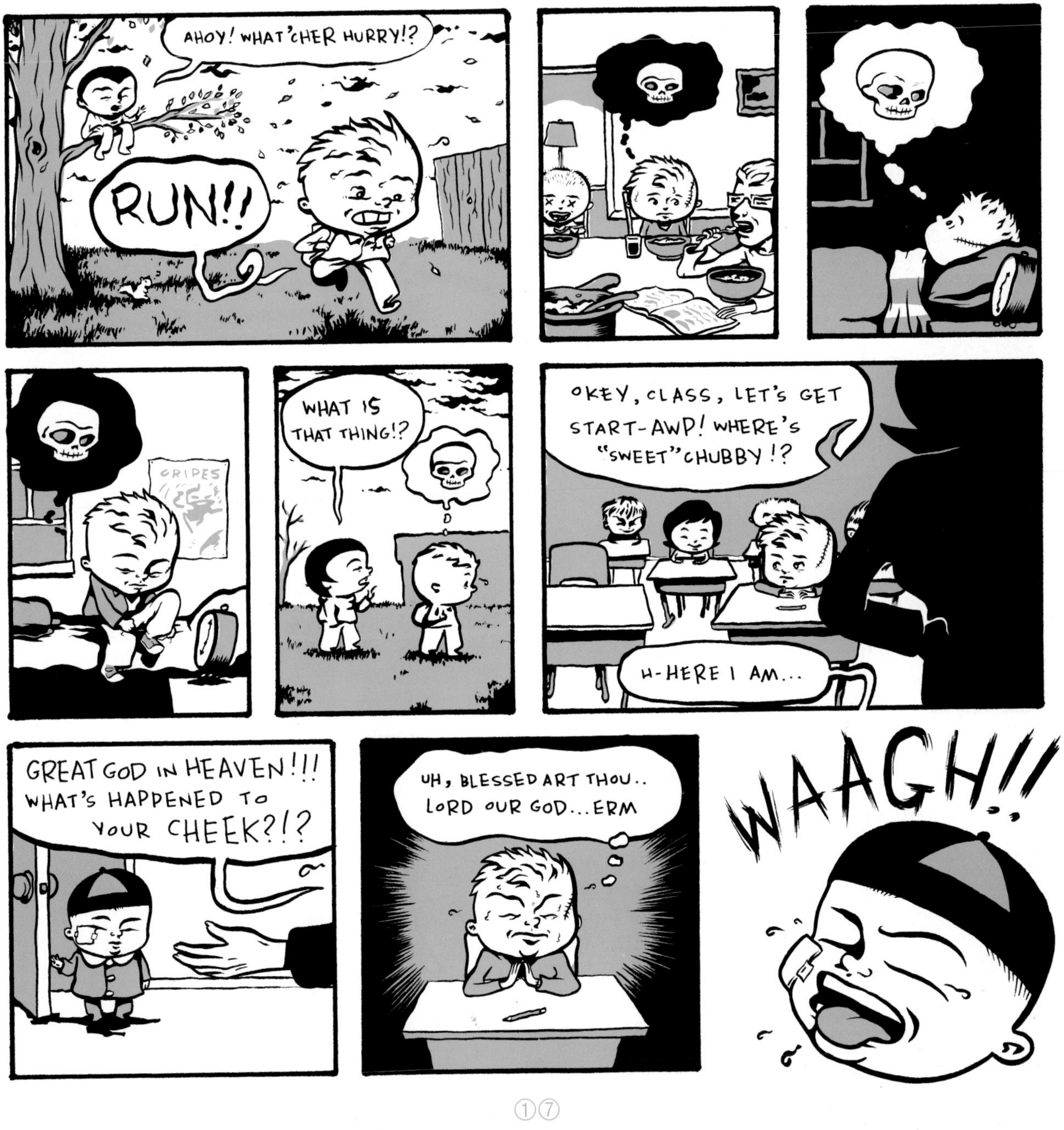
AHOY! WHAT'CHER HURRY!?
RUN!!
GRIPES
WHAT IS THAT THING!?
OKEY, CLASS, LET'S GET START-AWP! WHERE'S "SWEET" CHUBBY!?
H-HERE I AM...
GREAT GOD IN HEAVEN!!! WHAT'S HAPPENED TO YOUR CHEEK?!?
UH, BLESSED ART THOU.. LORD OUR GOD...ERM
WAAGH!!!

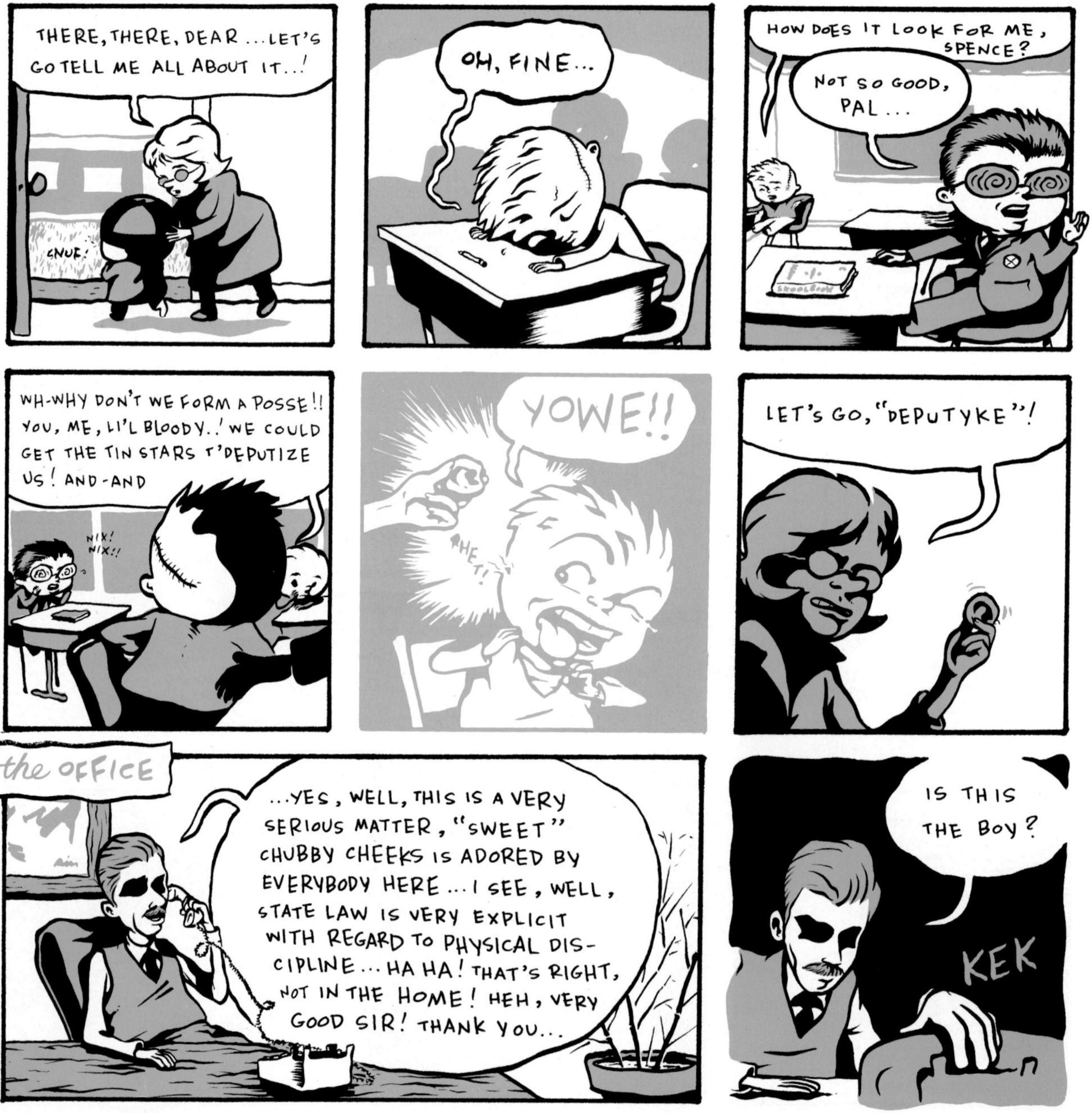
THERE, THERE, DEAR ... LET'S GO TELL ME ALL ABOUT IT..!
SNUF!
OH, FINE...
HOW DOES IT LOOK FOR ME, SPENCE?
NOT SO GOOD, PAL...
SKOOLBOOK
WH-WHY DON'T WE FORM A POSSE!! YOU, ME, LI'L BLOODY..! WE COULD GET THE TIN STARS T'DEPUTIZE US! AND-AND
NIX! NIX!!
YOWE!!
LET'S GO, "DEPUTYKE"!
the OFFICE
...YES, WELL, THIS IS A VERY SERIOUS MATTER, "SWEET" CHUBBY CHEEKS IS ADORED BY EVERYBODY HERE ... I SEE, WELL, STATE LAW IS VERY EXPLICIT WITH REGARD TO PHYSICAL DIS-CIPLINE ... HA HA! THAT'S RIGHT, NOT IN THE HOME! HEH, VERY GOOD SIR! THANK YOU...
IS THIS THE BOY?
KEK

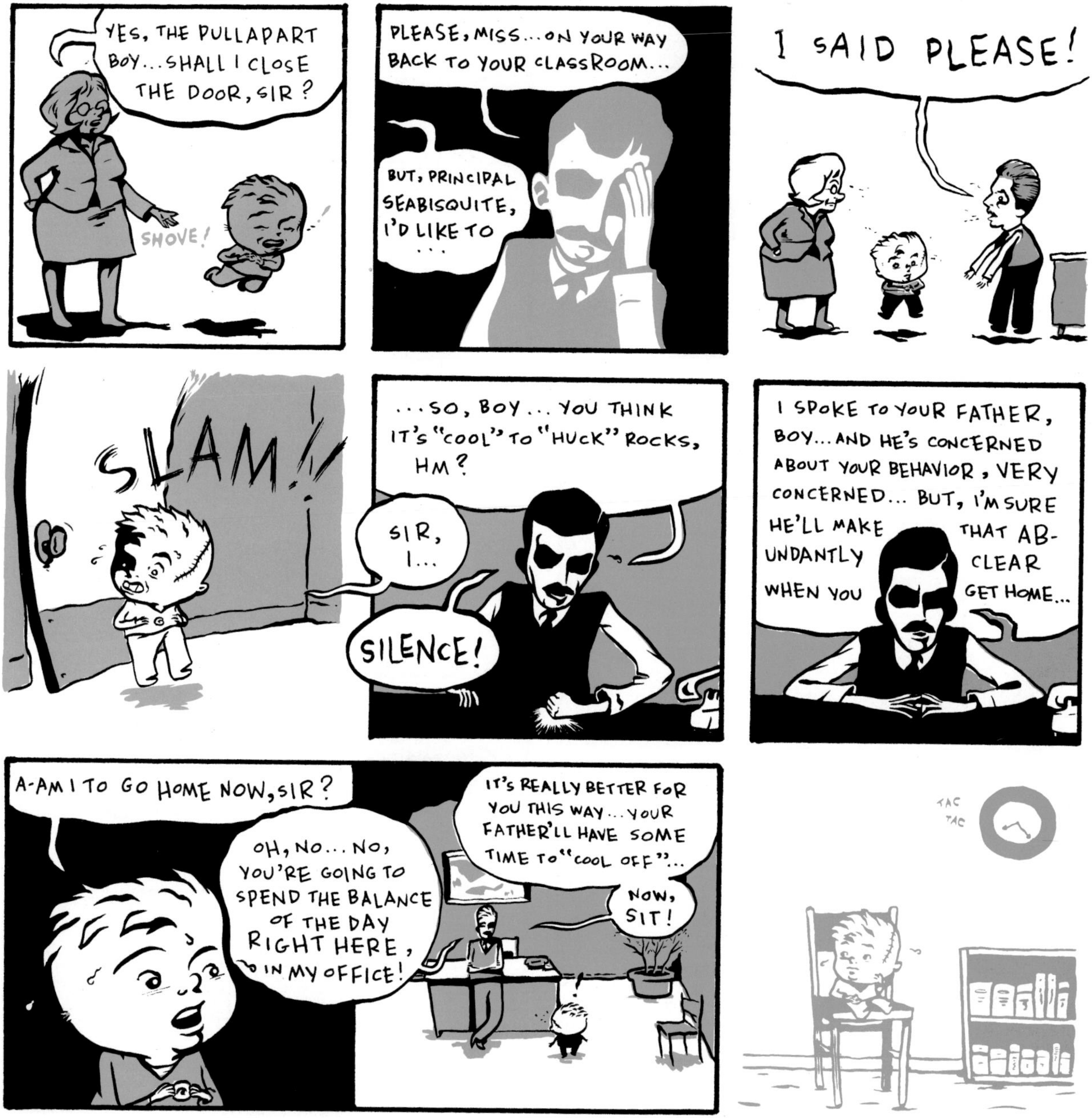
YES, THE PULLAPART BOY... SHALL I CLOSE THE DOOR, SIR?
SHOVE!
PLEASE, MISS... ON YOUR WAY BACK TO YOUR CLASSROOM...
BUT, PRINCIPAL SEABISQUITE, I'D LIKE TO . . .
I SAID PLEASE!
SLAM!!
...SO, BOY... YOU THINK IT'S "COOL" TO "HUCK" ROCKS, HM?
SIR, I...
SILENCE!
I SPOKE TO YOUR FATHER, BOY... AND HE'S CONCERNED ABOUT YOUR BEHAVIOR, VERY CONCERNED... BUT, I'M SURE HE'LL MAKE THAT AB- UNDANTLY CLEAR WHEN YOU GET HOME...
A-AM I TO GO HOME NOW, SIR?
OH, NO... NO, YOU'RE GOING TO SPEND THE BALANCE OF THE DAY RIGHT HERE, IN MY OFFICE!
IT'S REALLY BETTER FOR YOU THIS WAY... YOUR FATHER'LL HAVE SOME TIME TO "COOL OFF"...
NOW, SIT!
TAC
TAC

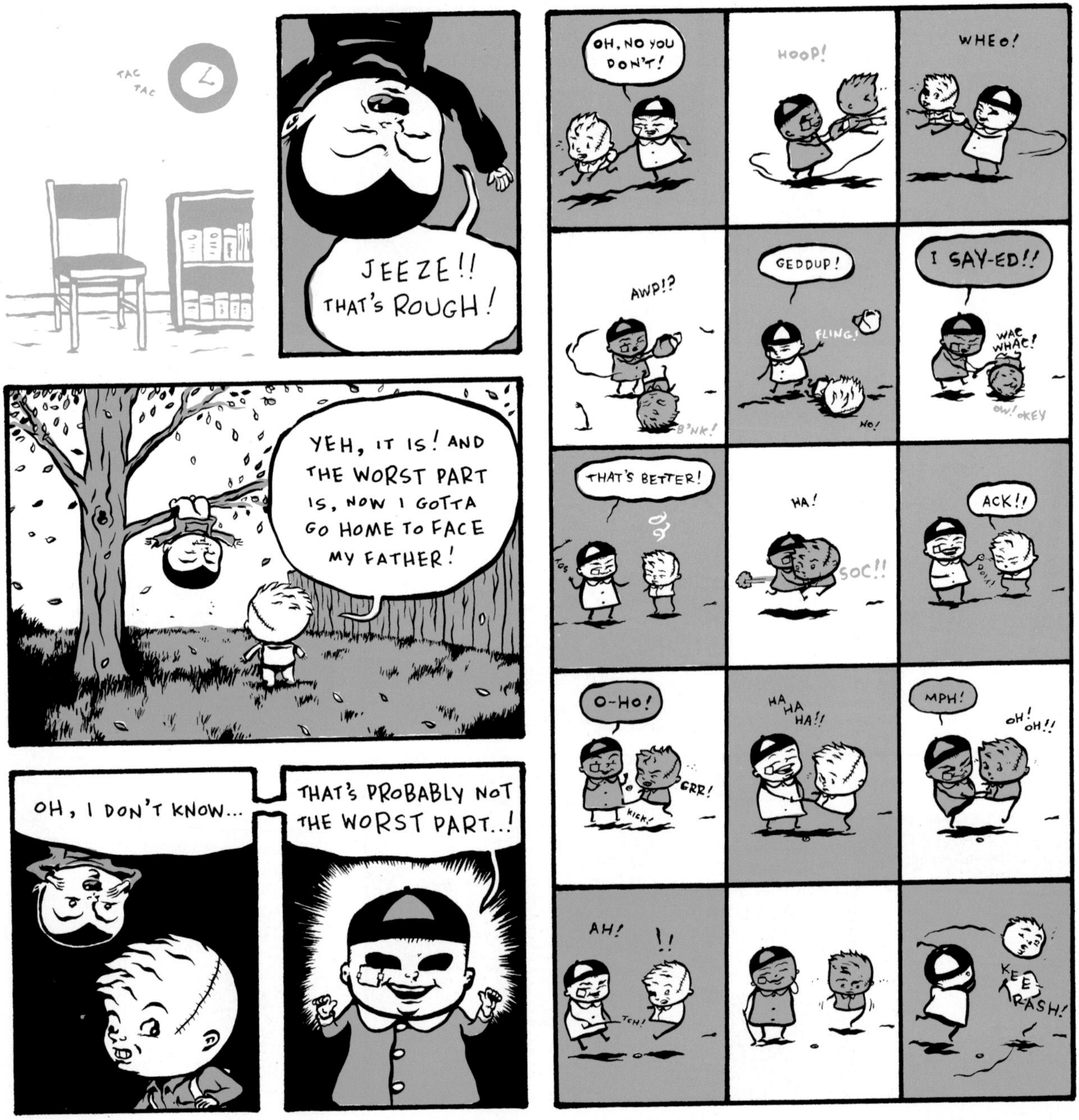

TAC
TAC
JEEZE!! THAT'S ROUGH!
YEH, IT IS! AND THE WORST PART IS, NOW I GOTTA GO HOME TO FACE MY FATHER!
OH, I DON'T KNOW...
THAT'S PROBABLY NOT THE WORST PART...!
OH, NO YOU DON'T!
HOOP!
WHEO!
AWP!?
B'NK!
GEDDUP!
FLING!
NO!
I SAY-ED!!
WAC WHAC!
OW! OKEY
THAT'S BETTER!
HA!
SOC!!
ACK!!
O-HO!
KICK!
GRR!
HA HA HA!!
MPH!
OH! OH!!
AH!
!!
TCH!
KEE RASH!

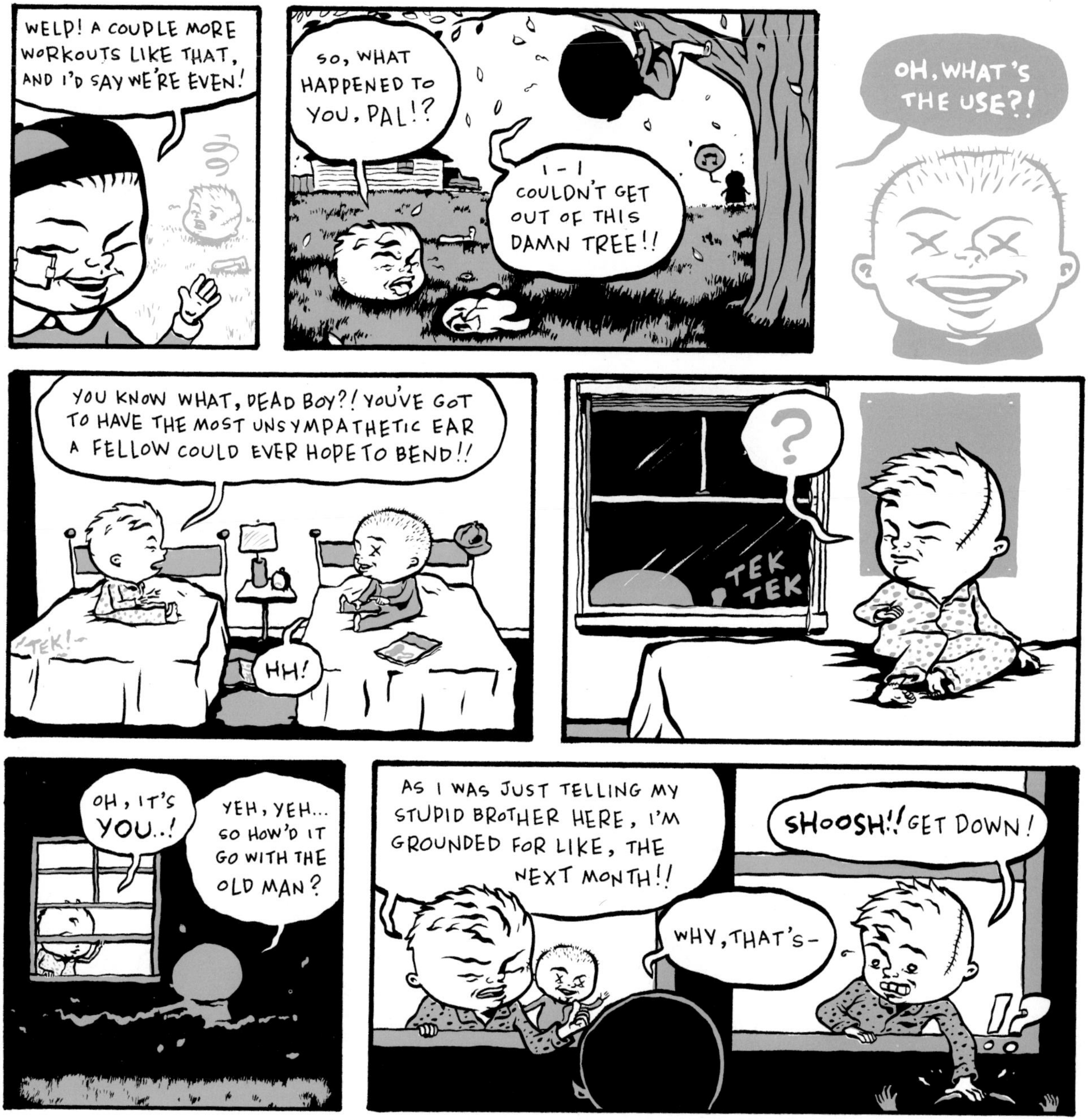
WELP! A COUPLE MORE WORKOUTS LIKE THAT, AND I'D SAY WE'RE EVEN!
SO, WHAT HAPPENED TO YOU, PAL!?
I - I COULDN'T GET OUT OF THIS DAMN TREE!!
OH, WHAT'S THE USE?!
YOU KNOW WHAT, DEAD BOY?! YOU'VE GOT TO HAVE THE MOST UNSYMPATHETIC EAR A FELLOW COULD EVER HOPE TO BEND!!
TEK!
HH!
?
TEK TEK
OH, IT'S YOU..!
YEH, YEH... SO HOW'D IT GO WITH THE OLD MAN?
AS I WAS JUST TELLING MY STUPID BROTHER HERE, I'M GROUNDED FOR LIKE, THE NEXT MONTH!!
WHY, THAT'S-
SHOOSH!! GET DOWN!

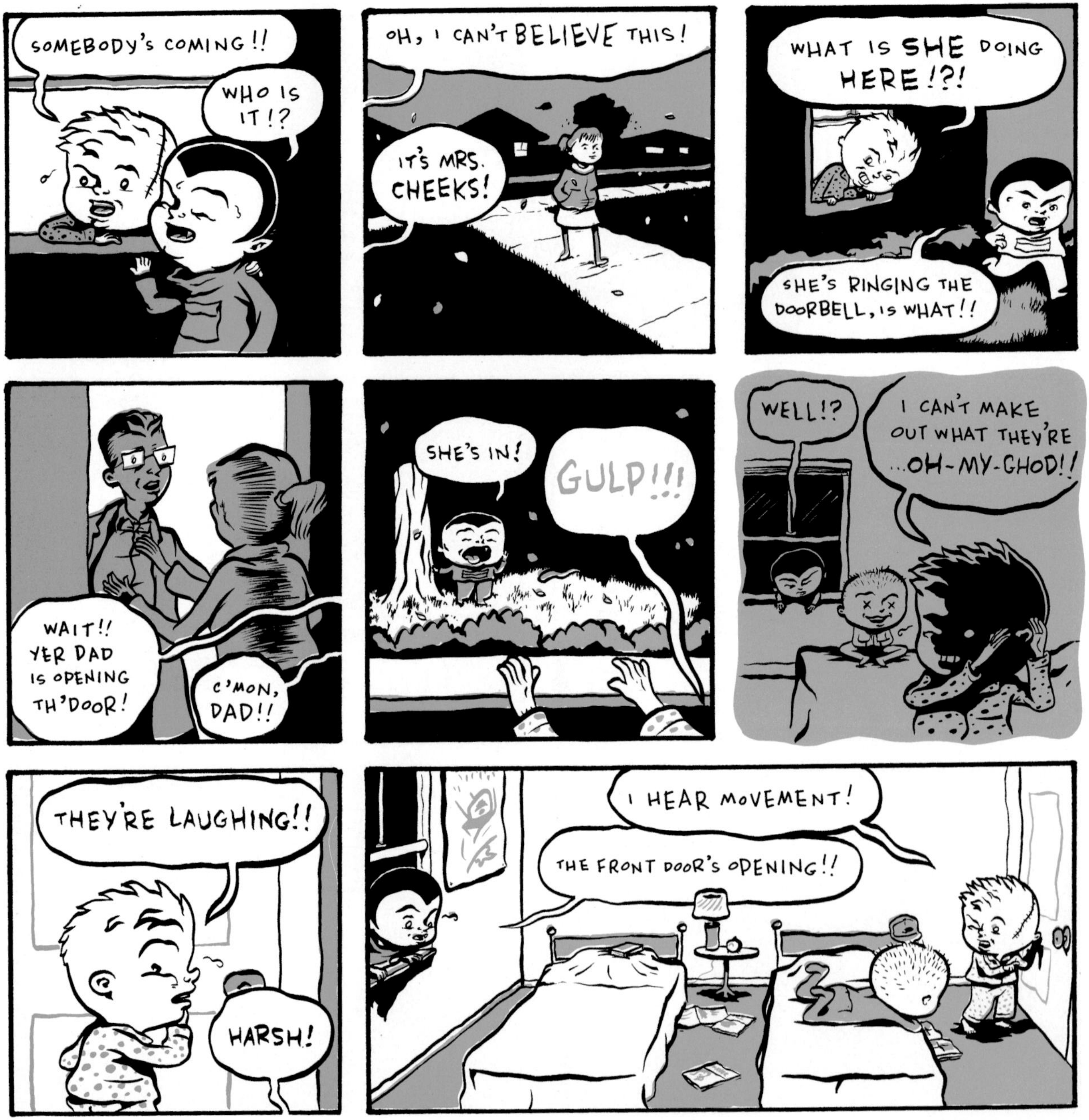
SOMEBODY'S COMING!!
WHO IS IT!?
OH, I CAN'T BELIEVE THIS!
IT'S MRS. CHEEKS!
WHAT IS SHE DOING HERE!?!
SHE'S RINGING THE DOORBELL, IS WHAT!!
WAIT!! YER DAD IS OPENING TH'DOOR!
C'MON, DAD!!
SHE'S IN!
GULP!!!
WELL!?
I CAN'T MAKE OUT WHAT THEY'RE ...OH-MY-GHOD!!
THEY'RE LAUGHING!!
HARSH!
I HEAR MOVEMENT!
THE FRONT DOOR'S OPENING!!

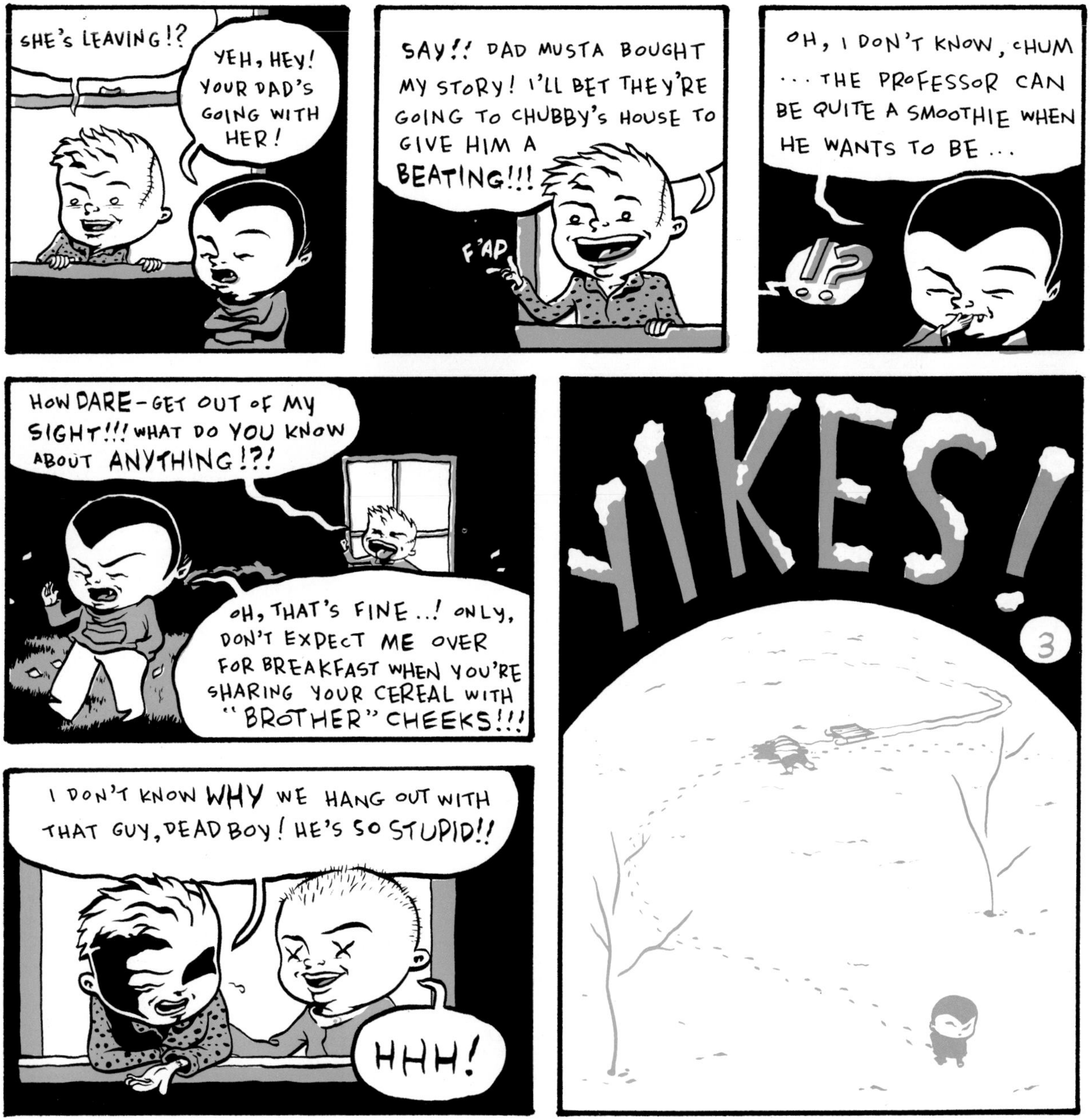
SHE'S LEAVING!?
YEH, HEY! YOUR DAD'S GOING WITH HER!
SAY!! DAD MUSTA BOUGHT MY STORY! I'LL BET THEY'RE GOING TO CHUBBY'S HOUSE TO GIVE HIM A BEATING!!!
F'AP
OH, I DON'T KNOW, CHUM ... THE PROFESSOR CAN BE QUITE A SMOOTHIE WHEN HE WANTS TO BE ...
!?
HOW DARE-GET OUT OF MY SIGHT!!! WHAT DO YOU KNOW ABOUT ANYTHING!?!
OH, THAT'S FINE ..! ONLY, DON'T EXPECT ME OVER FOR BREAKFAST WHEN YOU'RE SHARING YOUR CEREAL WITH "BROTHER" CHEEKS!!!
YIKES!
3
I DON'T KNOW WHY WE HANG OUT WITH THAT GUY, DEAD BOY! HE'S SO STUPID!!
HHH!

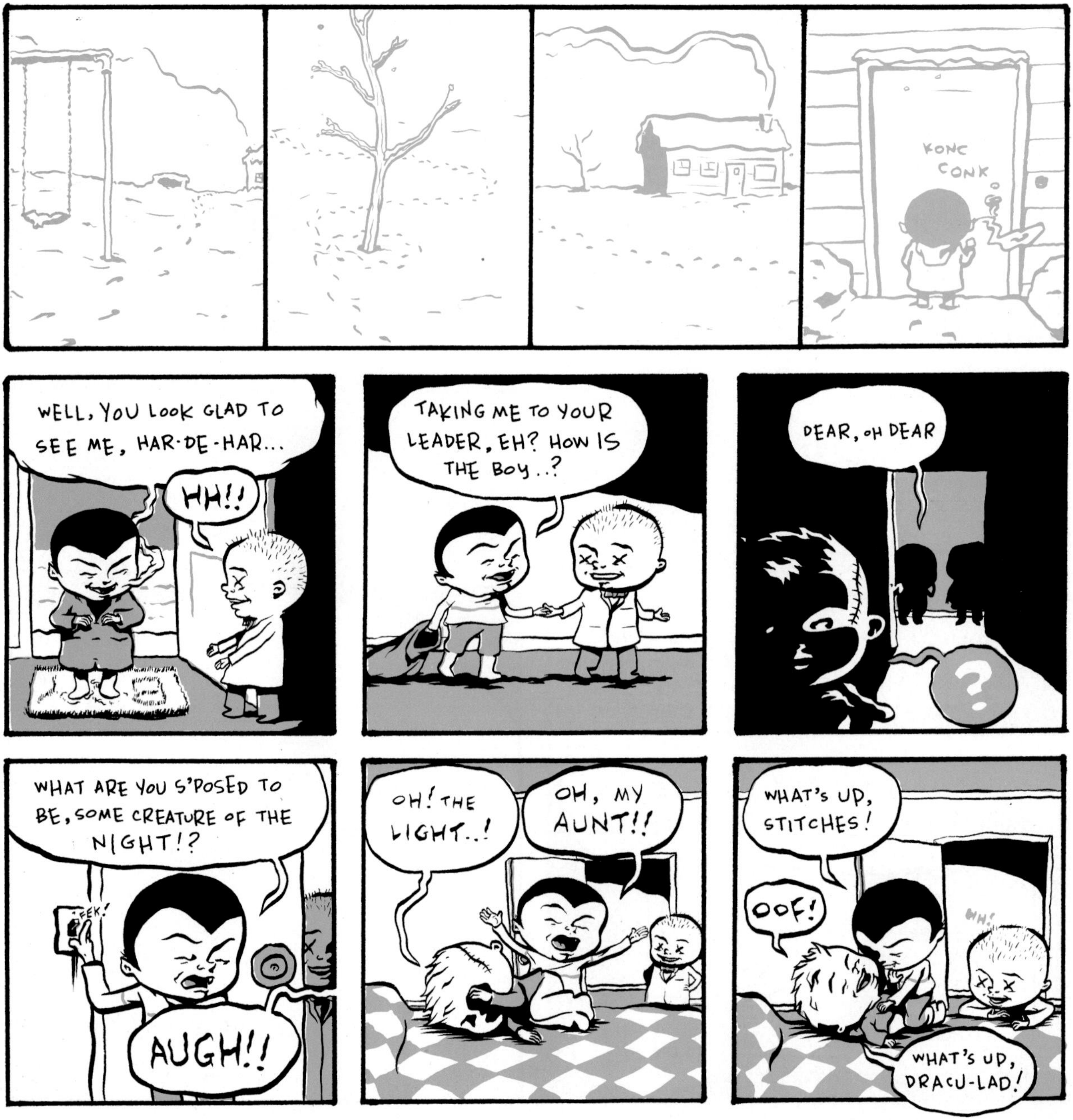
KONC
CONK
WELL, YOU LOOK GLAD TO SEE ME, HAR-DE-HAR...
HH!!
TAKING ME TO YOUR LEADER, EH? HOW IS THE BOY..?
DEAR, OH DEAR
?
WHAT ARE YOU S'POSED TO BE, SOME CREATURE OF THE NIGHT!?
FEK!
AUGH!!
OH! THE LIGHT..!
OH, MY AUNT!!
WHAT'S UP, STITCHES!
OOF!
WHAT'S UP, DRACU-LAD!

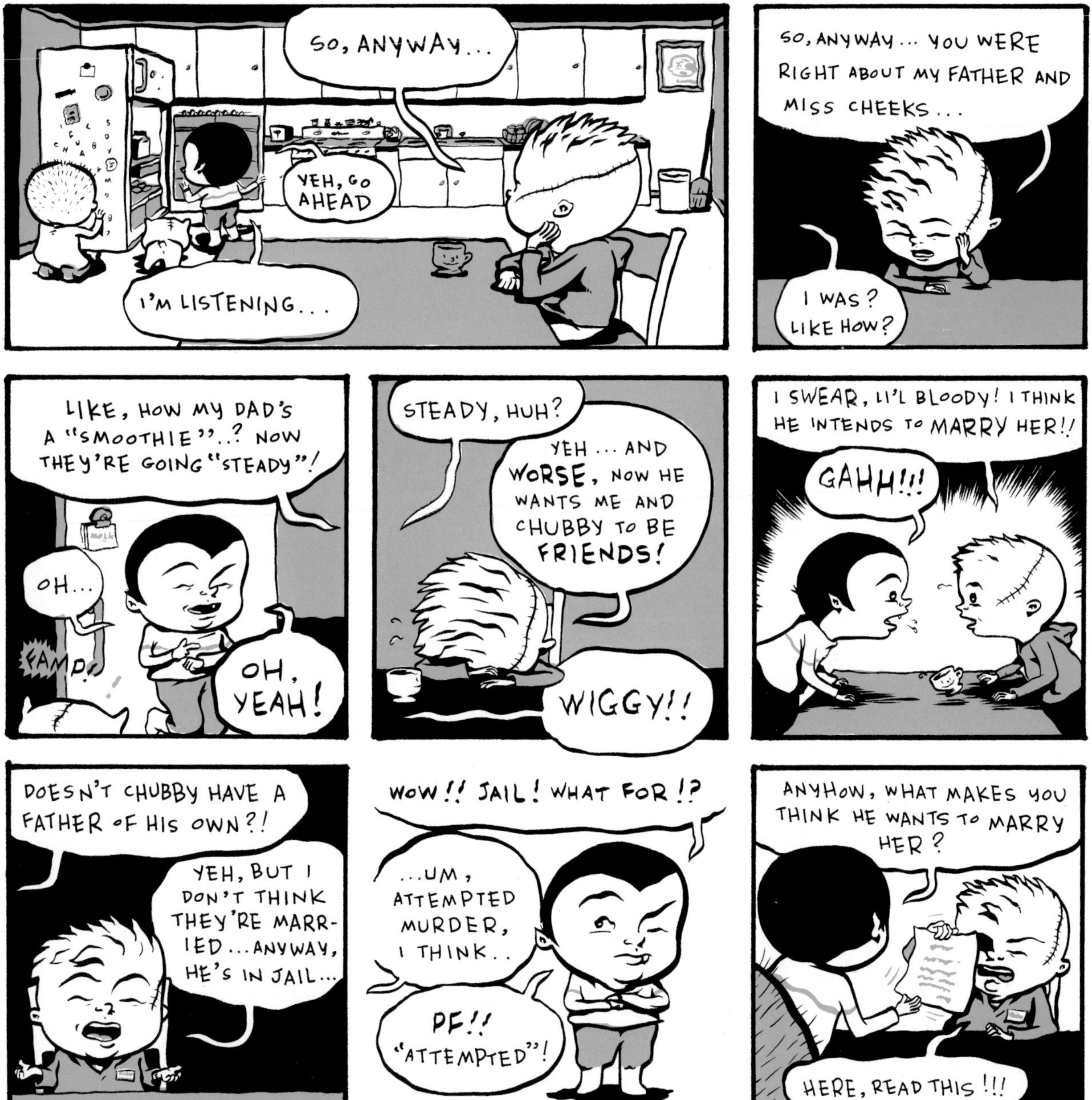
SO, ANYWAY...
YEH, GO AHEAD
I'M LISTENING...
SO, ANYWAY... YOU WERE RIGHT ABOUT MY FATHER AND MISS CHEEKS...
I WAS? LIKE HOW?
LIKE, HOW MY DAD'S A "SMOOTHIE"..? NOW THEY'RE GOING "STEADY"!
OH...
FAMP!
OH, YEAH!
STEADY, HUH?
YEH... AND WORSE, NOW HE WANTS ME AND CHUBBY TO BE FRIENDS!
WIGGY!!
I SWEAR, LI'L BLOODY! I THINK HE INTENDS TO MARRY HER!!
GAHH!!!
DOESN'T CHUBBY HAVE A FATHER OF HIS OWN?!
YEH, BUT I DON'T THINK THEY'RE MARR-IED... ANYWAY, HE'S IN JAIL...
WOW!! JAIL! WHAT FOR!?
...UM, ATTEMPTED MURDER, I THINK..
PF!! "ATTEMPTED"!
ANYHOW, WHAT MAKES YOU THINK HE WANTS TO MARRY HER?
HERE, READ THIS!!!

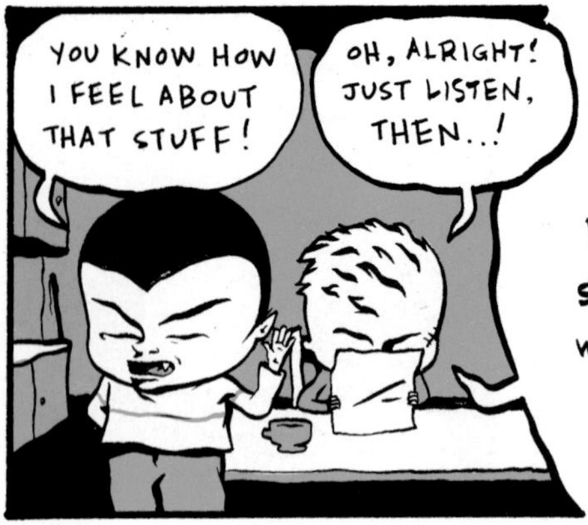
YOU KNOW HOW I FEEL ABOUT THAT STUFF!
OH, ALRIGHT! JUST LISTEN, THEN..!

MISS HELEN CHEEKS

MISS HELEN CHEEKS IS QUITE THE FEMALE
BUT IT'S TOUGH RAISING KIDS WHEN THE FATHER'S IN JAIL
SHE HAS A LITTLE BAKE SHOP, ON MARKET STREET
WHERE I ORDER WEDDING CAKES - THE TWO OF US EAT!

XOXO PROF. BOY

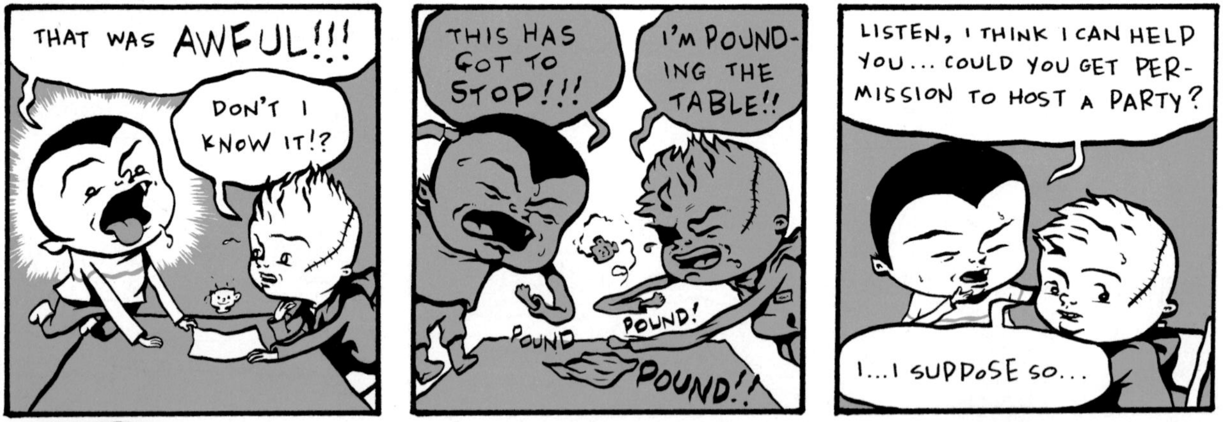
THAT WAS AWFUL!!!
DON'T I KNOW IT!?
THIS HAS GOT TO STOP!!!
I'M POUNDING THE TABLE!!
POUND
POUND!
POUND!!
LISTEN, I THINK I CAN HELP YOU... COULD YOU GET PERMISSION TO HOST A PARTY?
I...I SUPPOSE SO...

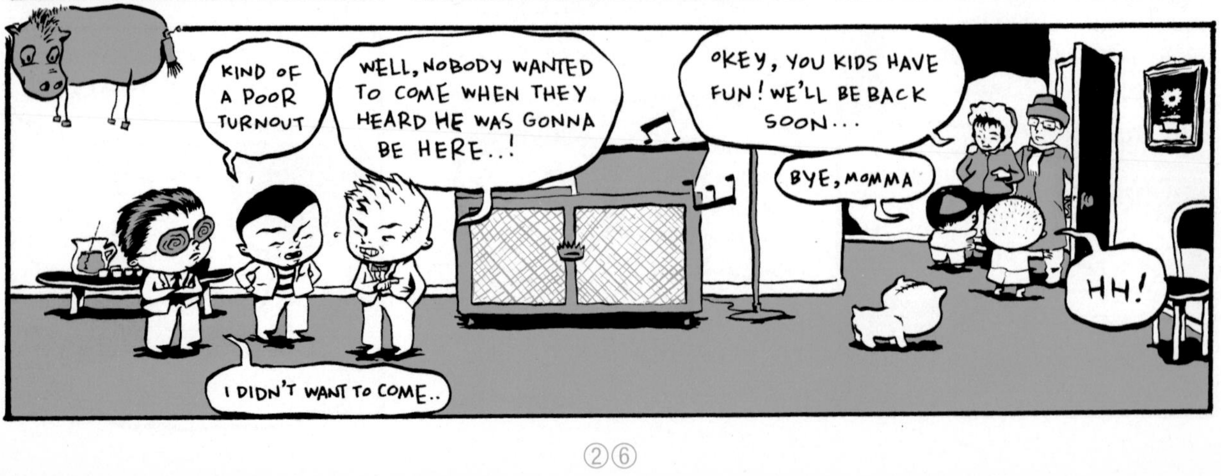
KIND OF A POOR TURNOUT
WELL, NOBODY WANTED TO COME WHEN THEY HEARD HE WAS GONNA BE HERE..!
OKEY, YOU KIDS HAVE FUN! WE'LL BE BACK SOON...
BYE, MOMMA
HH!
I DIDN'T WANT TO COME..

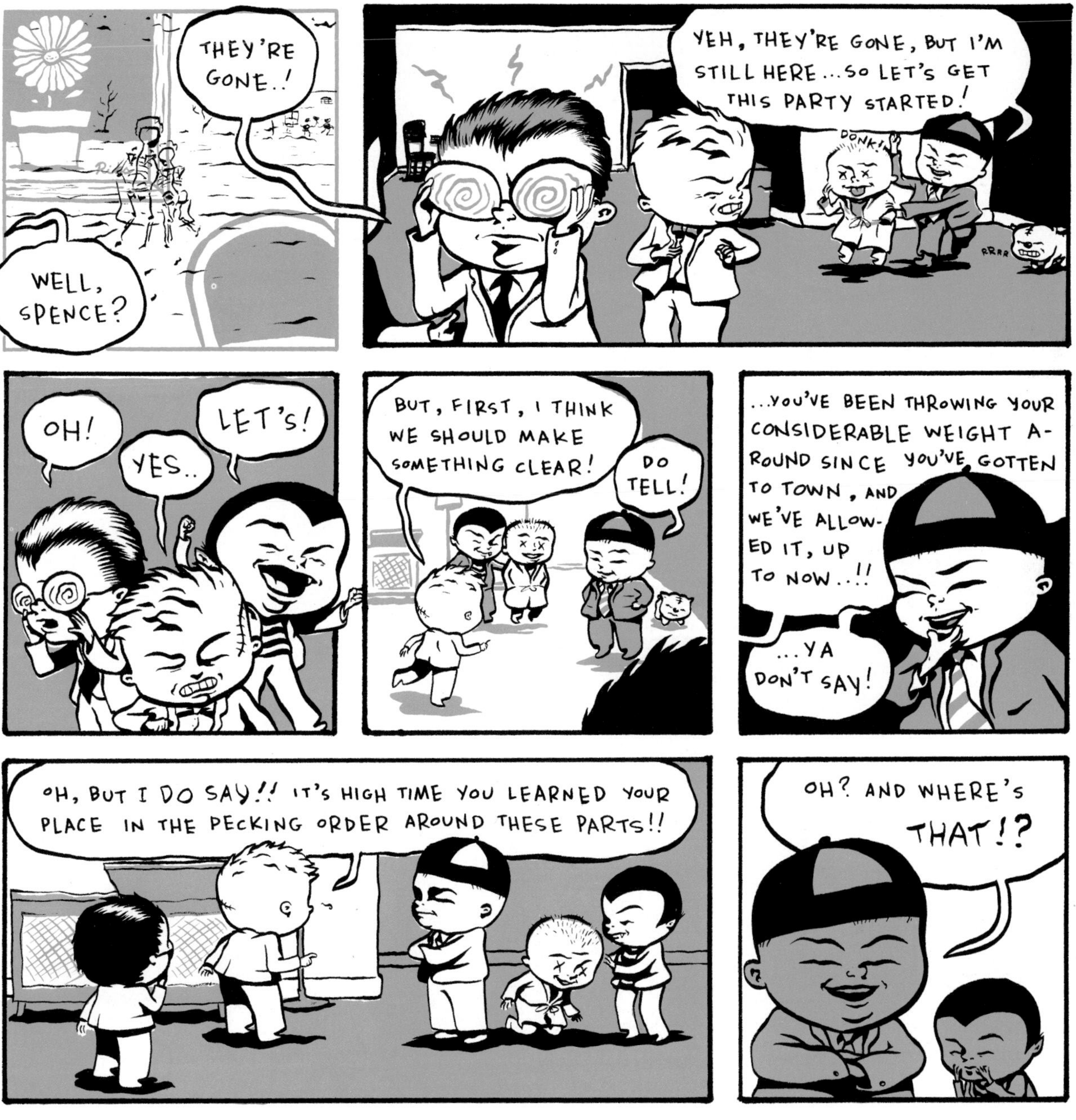
THEY'RE GONE..!
WELL, SPENCE?
YEH, THEY'RE GONE, BUT I'M STILL HERE... SO LET'S GET THIS PARTY STARTED!
DONK!
RRRR
OH!
YES..
LET'S!
BUT, FIRST, I THINK WE SHOULD MAKE SOMETHING CLEAR!
DO TELL!
...YOU'VE BEEN THROWING YOUR CONSIDERABLE WEIGHT A-ROUND SINCE YOU'VE GOTTEN TO TOWN, AND WE'VE ALLOW-ED IT, UP TO NOW...!!
...YA DON'T SAY!
OH, BUT I DO SAY!! IT'S HIGH TIME YOU LEARNED YOUR PLACE IN THE PECKING ORDER AROUND THESE PARTS!!
OH? AND WHERE'S THAT!?

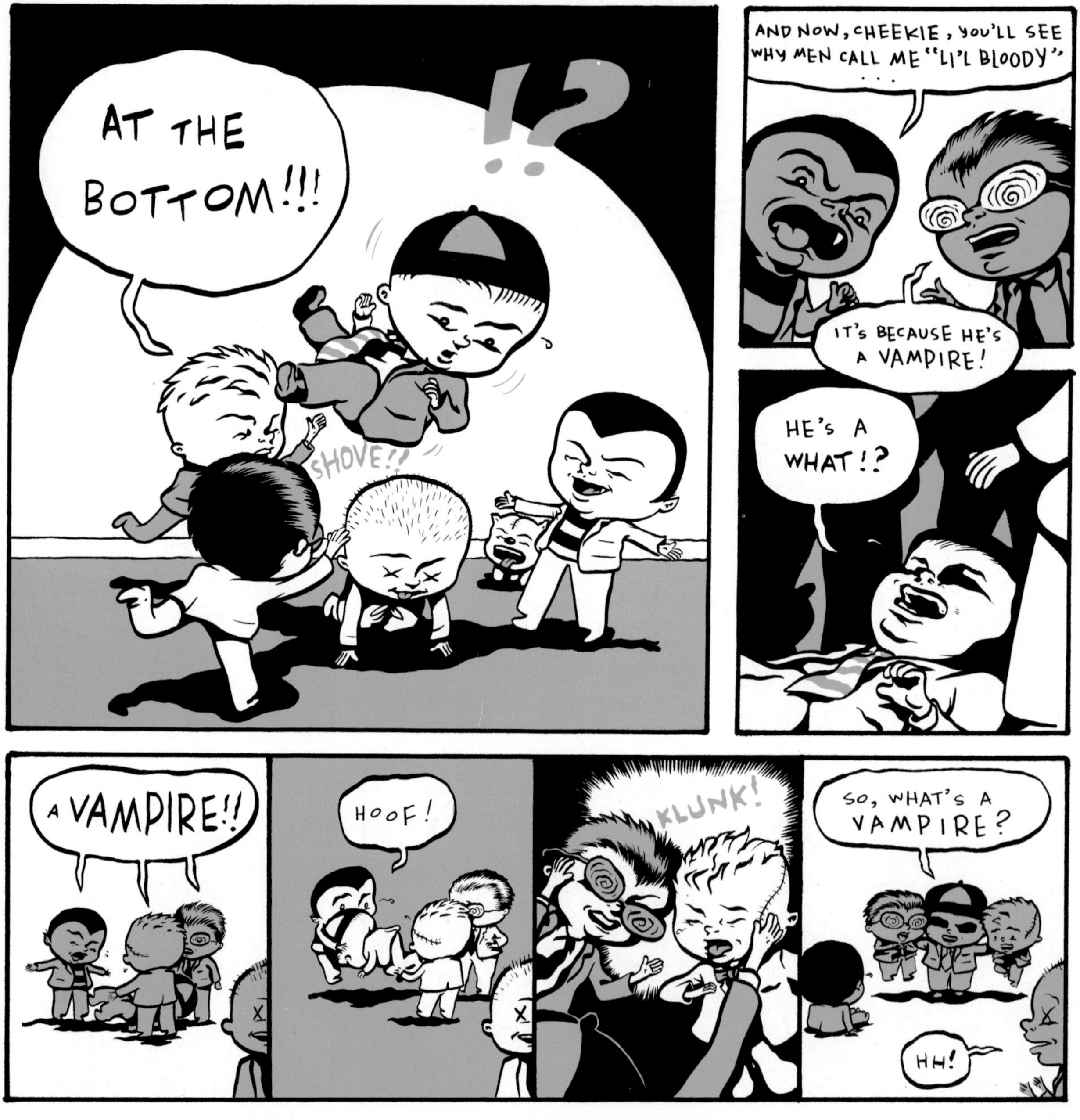
AT THE BOTTOM!!!
!?
SHOVE!!
AND NOW, CHEEKIE, YOU'LL SEE WHY MEN CALL ME "LI'L BLOODY" . . .
IT'S BECAUSE HE'S A VAMPIRE!
HE'S A WHAT!?
A VAMPIRE!!
HOOF!
KLUNK!
SO, WHAT'S A VAMPIRE?
HH!

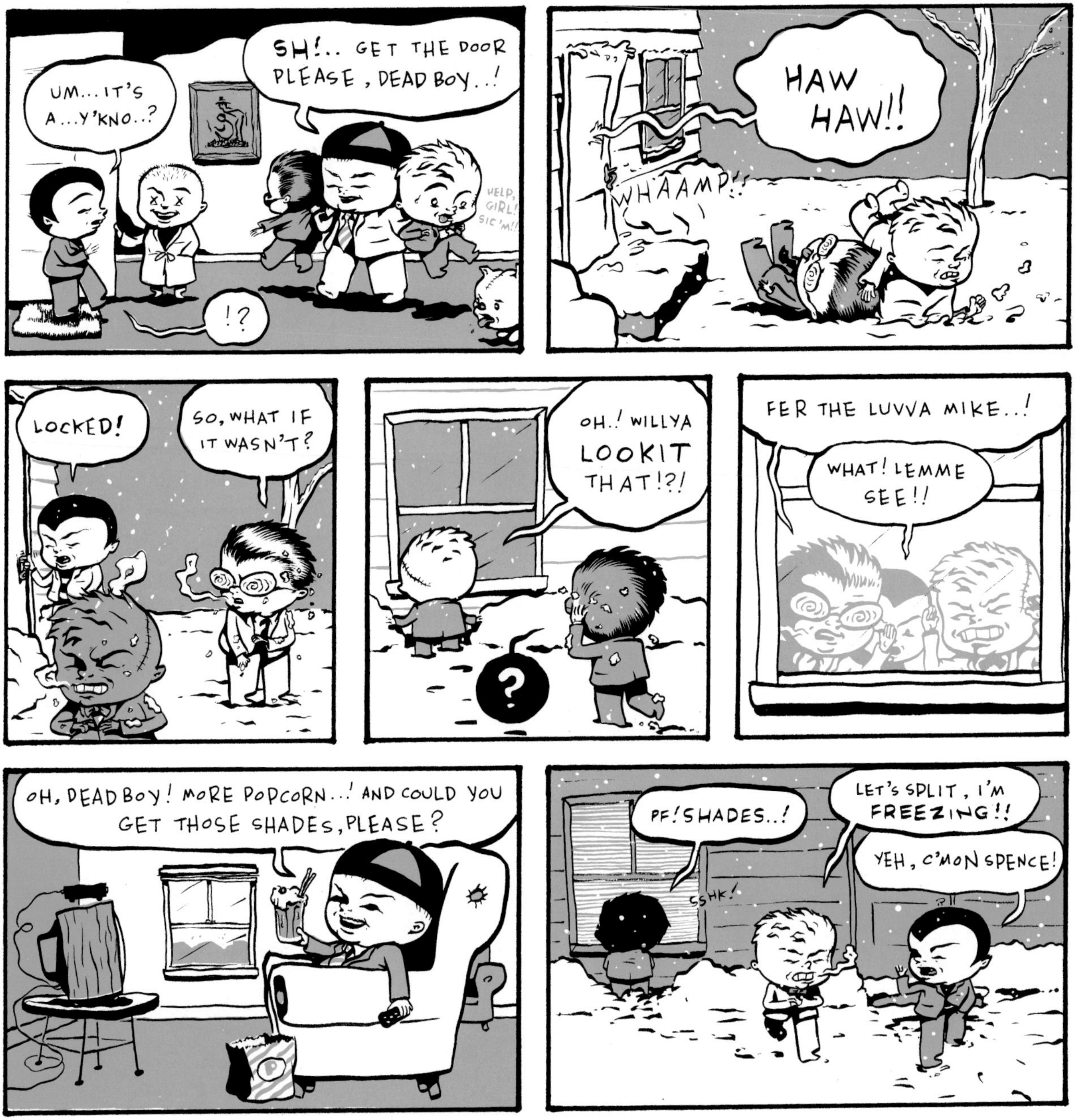
UM... IT'S A...Y'KNO..?
SH!.. GET THE DOOR PLEASE, DEAD BOY..!
HELP, GIRL! SIC 'M!!
!?
HAW HAW!!
WHAAMP!!
LOCKED!
SO, WHAT IF IT WASN'T?
OH..! WILLYA LOOKIT THAT!?!
FER THE LUVVA MIKE..!
WHAT! LEMME SEE!!
OH, DEAD BOY! MORE POPCORN..! AND COULD YOU GET THOSE SHADES, PLEASE?
PF! SHADES..!
SSHK!
LET'S SPLIT, I'M FREEZING!!
YEH, C'MON SPENCE!

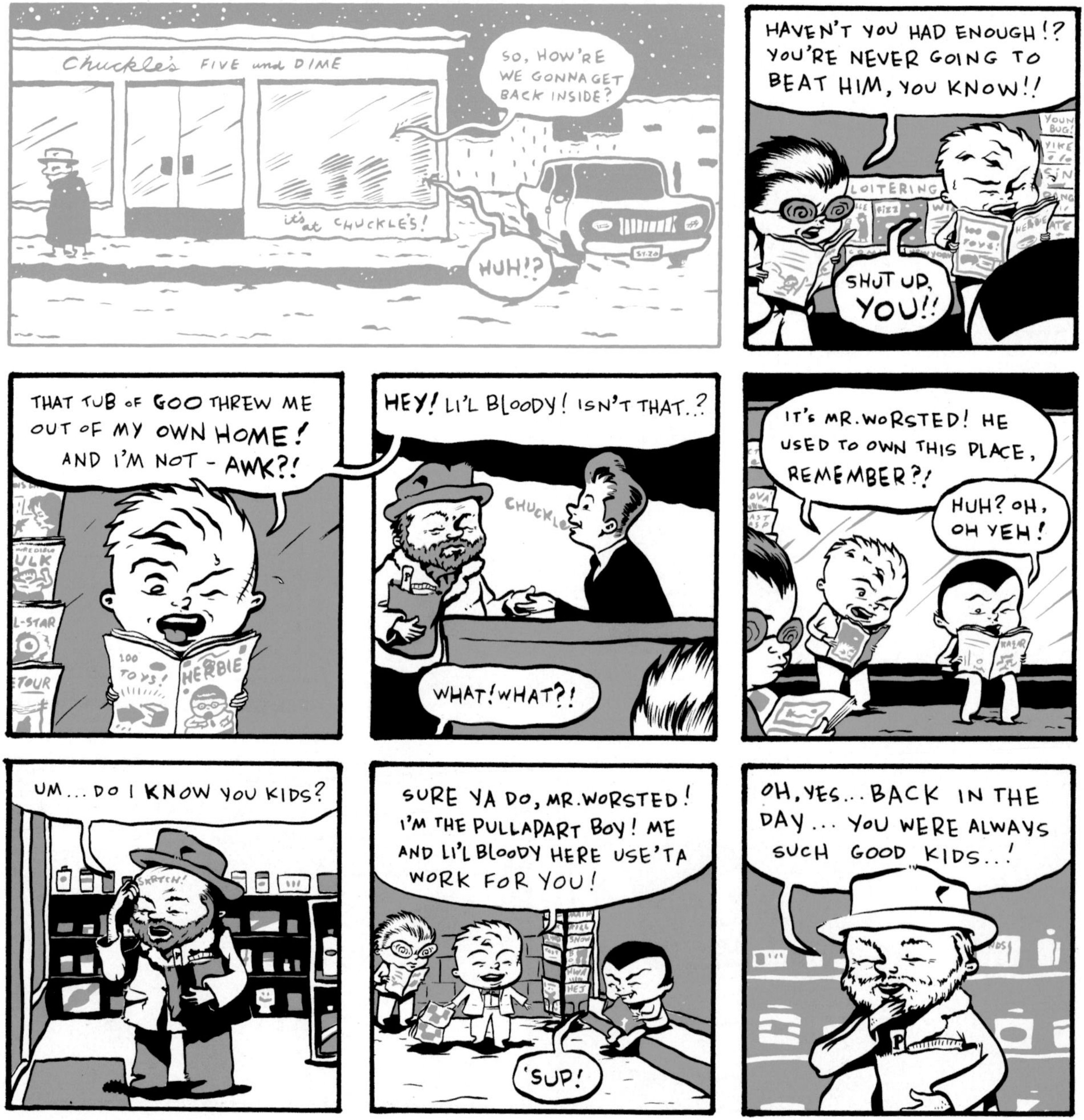
Chuckle's FIVE and DIME
SO, HOW'RE WE GONNA GET BACK INSIDE?
it's at CHUCKLE'S!
HUH!?
HAVEN'T YOU HAD ENOUGH!? YOU'RE NEVER GOING TO BEAT HIM, YOU KNOW!!
LOITERING
SHUT UP, YOU!!
THAT TUB OF GOO THREW ME OUT OF MY OWN HOME! AND I'M NOT - AWK?!
100 TOYS! HERBIE
HEY! LI'L BLOODY! ISN'T THAT..?
CHUCKLE
WHAT! WHAT?!
IT'S MR. WORSTED! HE USED TO OWN THIS PLACE, REMEMBER?!
HUH? OH, OH YEH!
UM... DO I KNOW YOU KIDS?
SKRTCH!
SURE YA DO, MR. WORSTED! I'M THE PULLAPART BOY! ME AND LI'L BLOODY HERE USE'TA WORK FOR YOU!
'SUP!
OH, YES... BACK IN THE DAY... YOU WERE ALWAYS SUCH GOOD KIDS...!

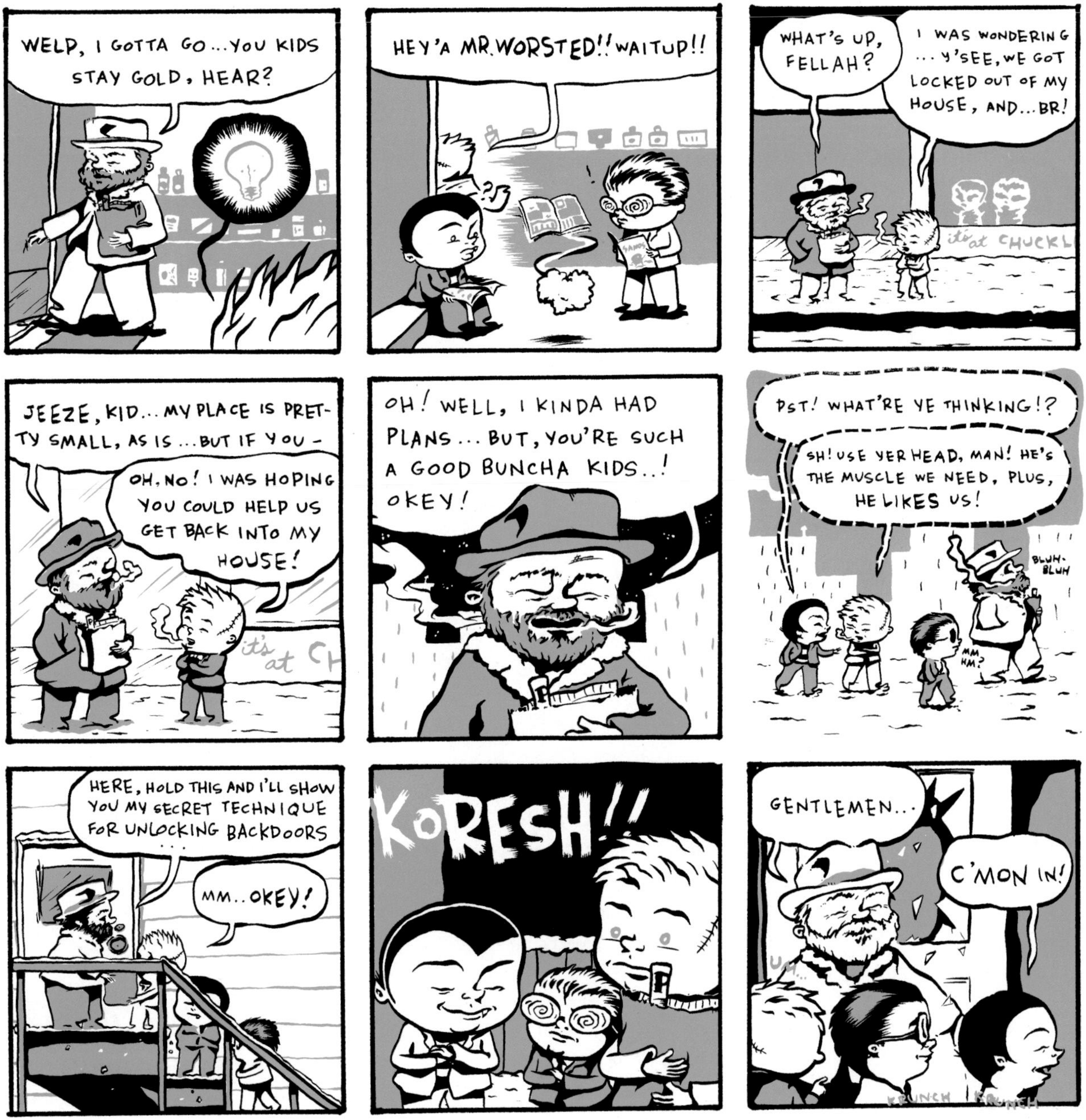
WELP, I GOTTA GO... YOU KIDS STAY GOLD, HEAR?
HEY'A MR. WORSTED!! WAIT UP!!
WHAT'S UP, FELLAH?
I WAS WONDERING ... Y'SEE, WE GOT LOCKED OUT OF MY HOUSE, AND... BR!
it's at CHUCKL
JEEZE, KID... MY PLACE IS PRETTY SMALL, AS IS... BUT IF YOU -
OH, NO! I WAS HOPING YOU COULD HELP US GET BACK INTO MY HOUSE!
OH! WELL, I KINDA HAD PLANS... BUT, YOU'RE SUCH A GOOD BUNCHA KIDS..! OKEY!
PST! WHAT'RE YE THINKING!?
SH! USE YER HEAD, MAN! HE'S THE MUSCLE WE NEED, PLUS, HE LIKES US!
BLUH-BLUH
MM HM?
HERE, HOLD THIS AND I'LL SHOW YOU MY SECRET TECHNIQUE FOR UNLOCKING BACKDOORS...
MM.. OKEY!
KORESH!!
GENTLEMEN...
C'MON IN!
UH...
KRUNCH KRUNCH

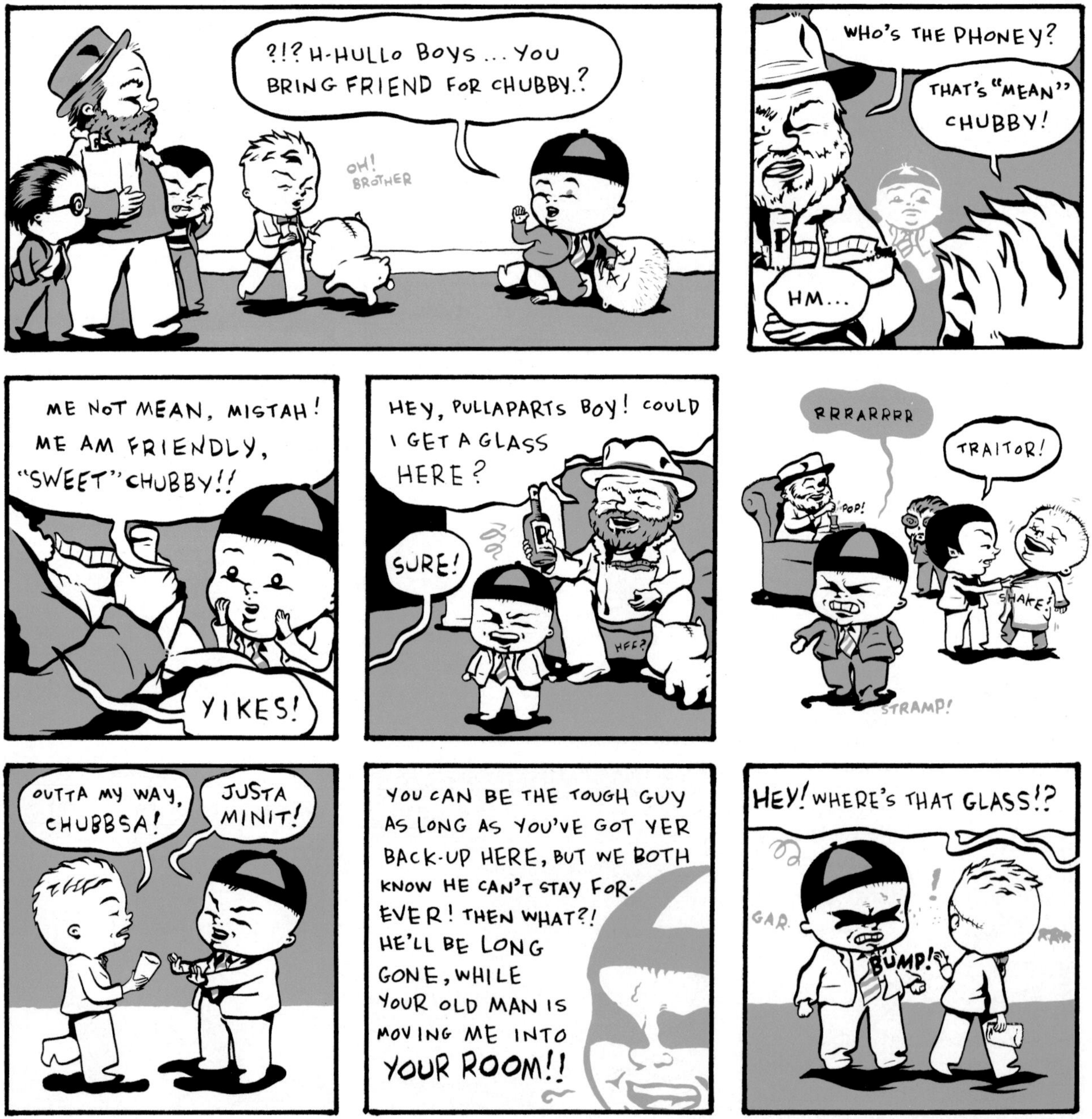

?!? H-HULLO BOYS... YOU BRING FRIEND FOR CHUBBY.?
OH! BROTHER
WHO'S THE PHONEY?
THAT'S "MEAN" CHUBBY!
HM...
ME NOT MEAN, MISTAH! ME AM FRIENDLY, "SWEET" CHUBBY!!
YIKES!
HEY, PULLAPARTS BOY! COULD I GET A GLASS HERE?
SURE!
HFF?
RRRARRRR
TRAITOR!
POP!
SHAKE!
STRAMP!
OUTTA MY WAY, CHUBBSA!
JUSTA MINIT!
YOU CAN BE THE TOUGH GUY AS LONG AS YOU'VE GOT YER BACK-UP HERE, BUT WE BOTH KNOW HE CAN'T STAY FOR-EVER! THEN WHAT?! HE'LL BE LONG GONE, WHILE YOUR OLD MAN IS MOVING ME INTO YOUR ROOM!!
HEY! WHERE'S THAT GLASS!?
GAR.
BUMP!

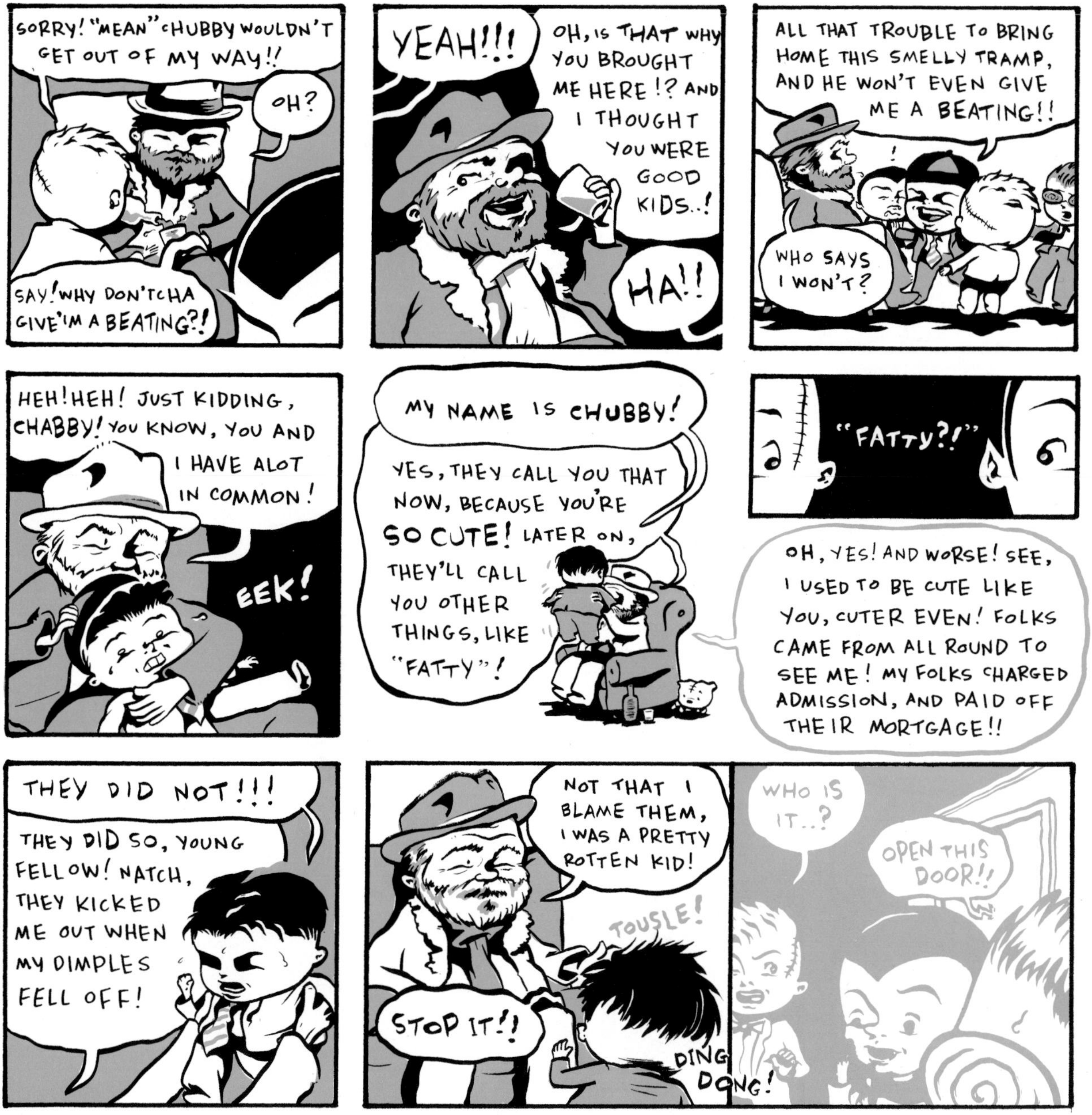
SORRY! "MEAN" CHUBBY WOULDN'T GET OUT OF MY WAY!!
OH?
SAY! WHY DON'TCHA GIVE'IM A BEATING?!
YEAH!!!
OH, IS THAT WHY YOU BROUGHT ME HERE!? AND I THOUGHT YOU WERE GOOD KIDS..!
HA!!
ALL THAT TROUBLE TO BRING HOME THIS SMELLY TRAMP, AND HE WON'T EVEN GIVE ME A BEATING!!
!
WHO SAYS I WON'T?
HEH! HEH! JUST KIDDING, CHABBY! YOU KNOW, YOU AND I HAVE ALOT IN COMMON!
EEK!
MY NAME IS CHUBBY!
YES, THEY CALL YOU THAT NOW, BECAUSE YOU'RE SO CUTE! LATER ON, THEY'LL CALL YOU OTHER THINGS, LIKE "FATTY"!
"FATTY?!"
OH, YES! AND WORSE! SEE, I USED TO BE CUTE LIKE YOU, CUTER EVEN! FOLKS CAME FROM ALL ROUND TO SEE ME! MY FOLKS CHARGED ADMISSION, AND PAID OFF THEIR MORTGAGE!!
THEY DID NOT!!!
THEY DID SO, YOUNG FELLOW! NATCH, THEY KICKED ME OUT WHEN MY DIMPLES FELL OFF!
NOT THAT I BLAME THEM, I WAS A PRETTY ROTTEN KID!
TOUSLE!
STOP IT!!
DING DONG!
WHO IS IT..?
OPEN THIS DOOR!!

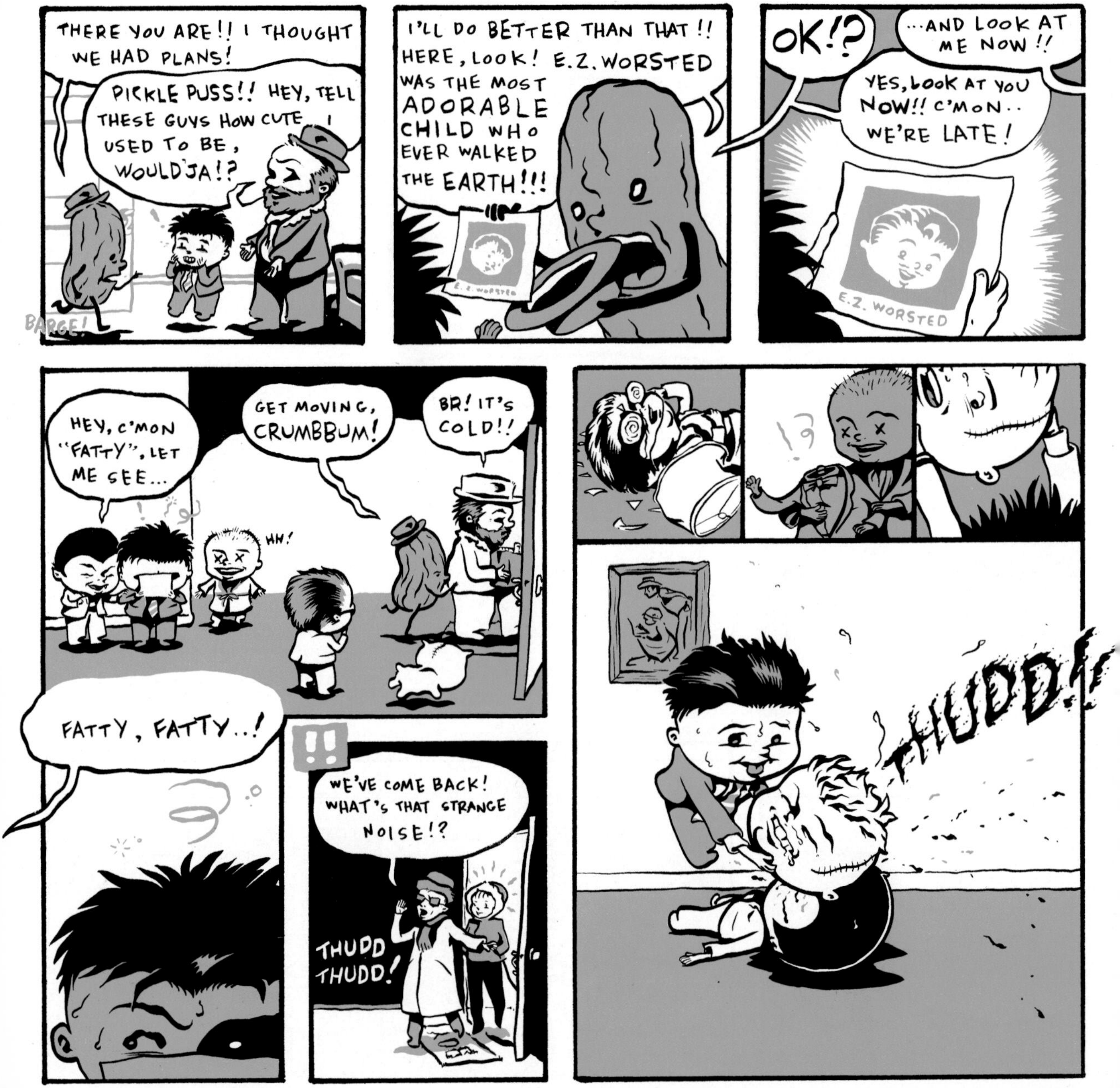
THERE YOU ARE!! I THOUGHT WE HAD PLANS!
PICKLE PUSS!! HEY, TELL THESE GUYS HOW CUTE I USED TO BE, WOULD'JA!?
BARGE!
I'LL DO BETTER THAN THAT!! HERE, LOOK! E.Z. WORSTED WAS THE MOST ADORABLE CHILD WHO EVER WALKED THE EARTH!!!
OK!?
...AND LOOK AT ME NOW!!
YES, LOOK AT YOU NOW!! C'MON.. WE'RE LATE!
E.Z. WORSTED
HEY, C'MON "FATTY", LET ME SEE...
GET MOVING, CRUMBBUM!
BR! IT'S COLD!!
HH!
FATTY, FATTY..!
!!
WE'VE COME BACK! WHAT'S THAT STRANGE NOISE!?
THUDD THUDD!
THUDD!!

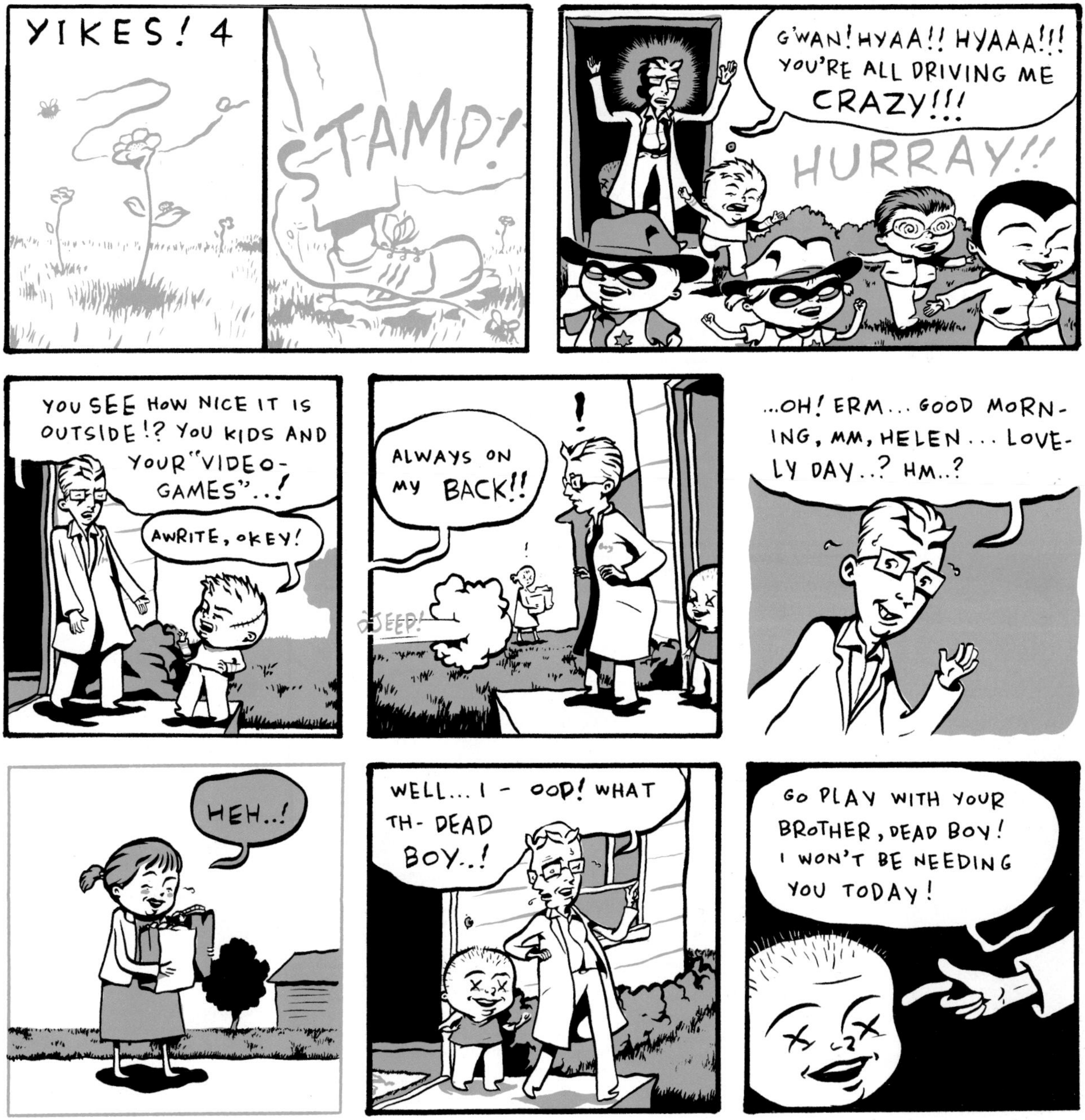
YIKES! 4
STAMP!
G'WAN! HYAA!! HYAAA!!! YOU'RE ALL DRIVING ME CRAZY!!!
HURRAY!!
YOU SEE HOW NICE IT IS OUTSIDE!? YOU KIDS AND YOUR "VIDEO-GAMES"..!
AWRITE, OKEY!
!
ALWAYS ON MY BACK!!
JEEP!
...OH! ERM... GOOD MORNING, MM, HELEN... LOVELY DAY..? HM..?
HEH..!
WELL... I - OOP! WHAT TH- DEAD BOY..!
GO PLAY WITH YOUR BROTHER, DEAD BOY! I WON'T BE NEEDING YOU TODAY!

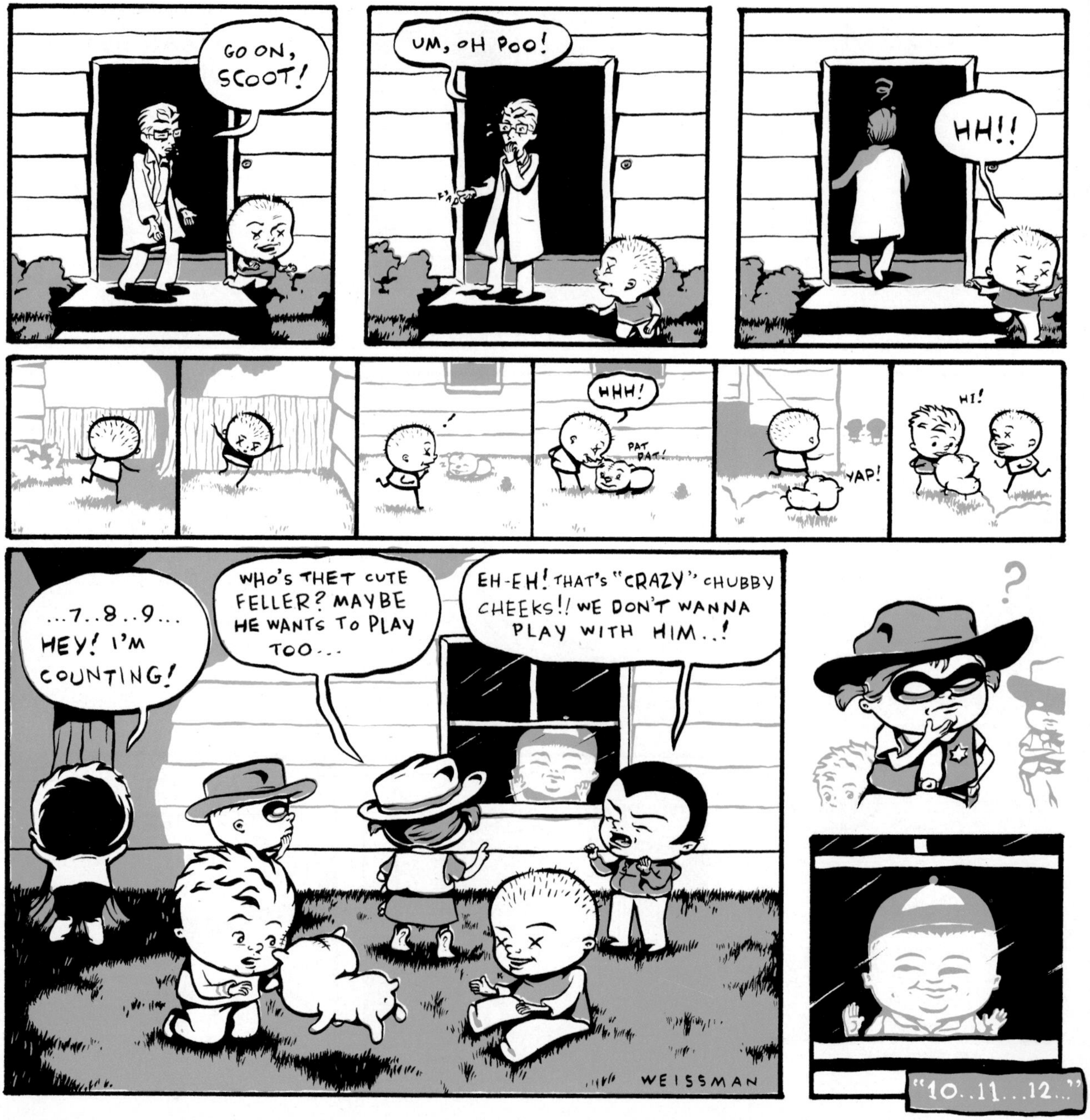
GO ON, SCOOT!
UM, OH POO!
HH!!
HHH!
PAT PAT!
YAP!
HI!
...7..8..9... HEY! I'M COUNTING!
WHO'S THET CUTE FELLER? MAYBE HE WANTS TO PLAY TOO...
EH-EH! THAT'S "CRAZY" CHUBBY CHEEKS!! WE DON'T WANNA PLAY WITH HIM..!
WEISSMAN
?
"10..11...12.."

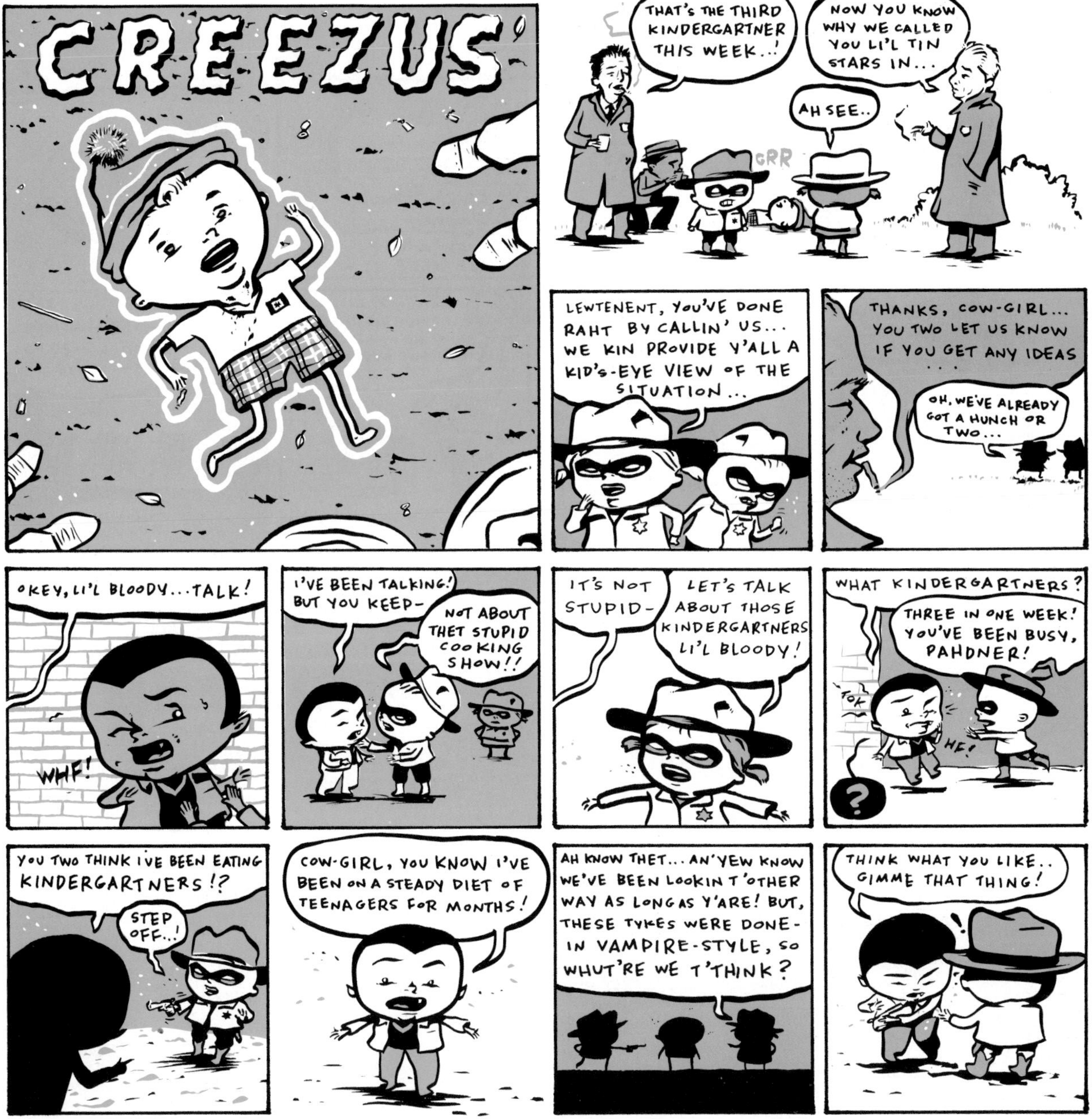
CREEZUS'
THAT'S THE THIRD KINDERGARTNER THIS WEEK..!
NOW YOU KNOW WHY WE CALLED YOU LI'L TIN STARS IN...
AH SEE..
GRR
LEWTENENT, YOU'VE DONE RAHT BY CALLIN' US... WE KIN PROVIDE Y'ALL A KID'S-EYE VIEW OF THE SITUATION...
THANKS, COW-GIRL... YOU TWO LET US KNOW IF YOU GET ANY IDEAS...
OH, WE'VE ALREADY GOT A HUNCH OR TWO...
OKEY, LI'L BLOODY... TALK!
WHF!
I'VE BEEN TALKING! BUT YOU KEEP-
NOT ABOUT THET STUPID COOKING SHOW!!
IT'S NOT STUPID-
LET'S TALK ABOUT THOSE KINDERGARTNERS LI'L BLOODY!
WHAT KINDERGARTNERS?
THREE IN ONE WEEK! YOU'VE BEEN BUSY, PAHDNER!
TOK
HE!
?
YOU TWO THINK I'VE BEEN EATING KINDERGARTNERS!?
STEP OFF..!
COW-GIRL, YOU KNOW I'VE BEEN ON A STEADY DIET OF TEENAGERS FOR MONTHS!
AH KNOW THET... AN'YEW KNOW WE'VE BEEN LOOKIN T'OTHER WAY AS LONG AS Y'ARE! BUT, THESE TYKES WERE DONE-IN VAMPIRE-STYLE, SO WHUT'RE WE T'THINK?
THINK WHAT YOU LIKE.. GIMME THAT THING!
!

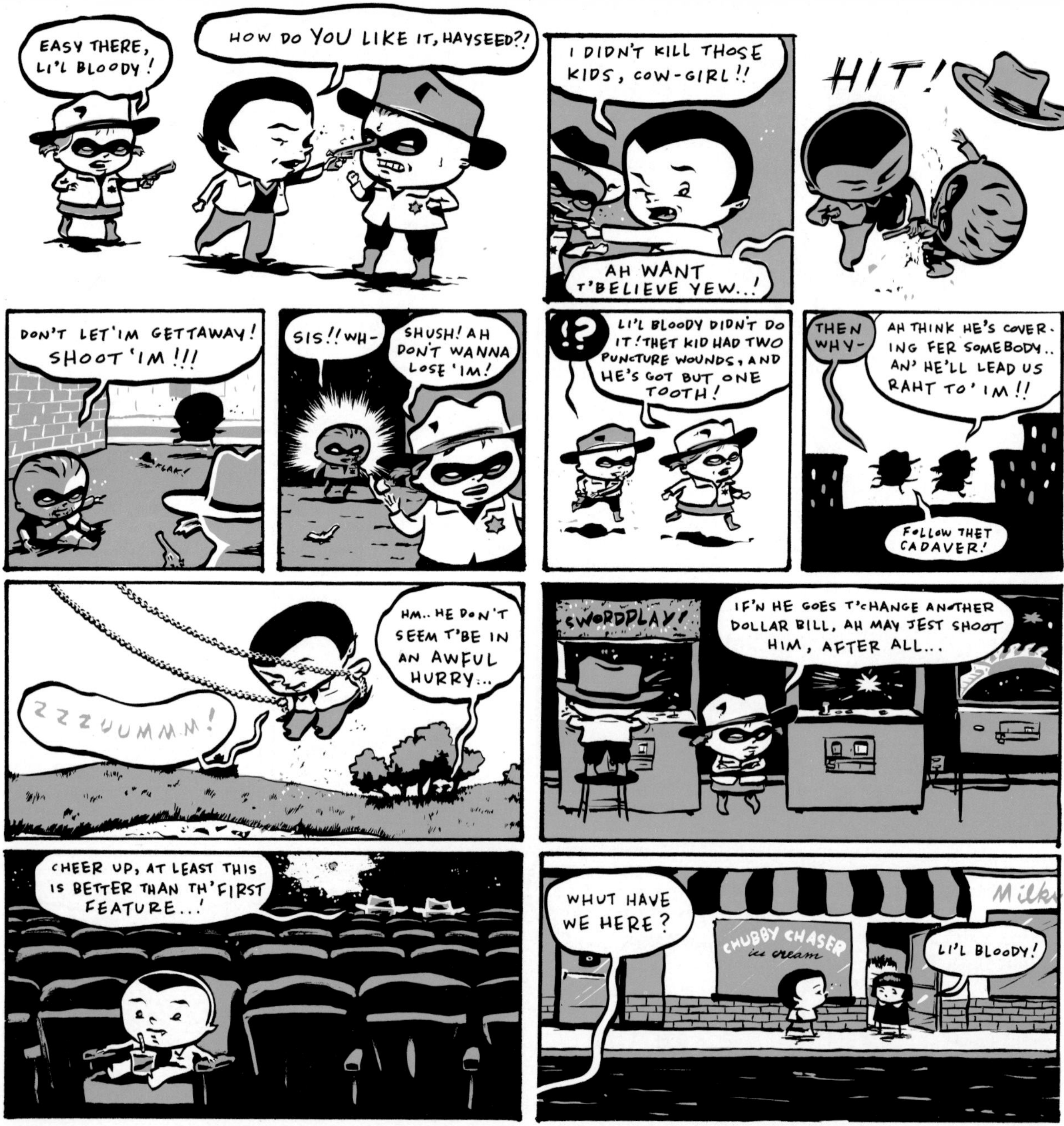
EASY THERE, LI'L BLOODY!
HOW DO YOU LIKE IT, HAYSEED?!
I DIDN'T KILL THOSE KIDS, COW-GIRL!!
AH WANT T'BELIEVE YEW...!
HIT!
DON'T LET'IM GETTAWAY! SHOOT'IM!!!
SIS!! WH-
SHUSH! AH DON'T WANNA LOSE 'IM!
!?
LI'L BLOODY DIDN'T DO IT! THET KID HAD TWO PUNCTURE WOUNDS, AND HE'S GOT BUT ONE TOOTH!
THEN WHY-
AH THINK HE'S COVERING FER SOMEBODY.. AN' HE'LL LEAD US RAHT TO'IM!!
FOLLOW THET CADAVER!
ZZZUUMMM!
HM.. HE DON'T SEEM T'BE IN AN AWFUL HURRY...
SWORDPLAY!
IF'N HE GOES T'CHANGE ANOTHER DOLLAR BILL, AH MAY JEST SHOOT HIM, AFTER ALL...
CHEER UP, AT LEAST THIS IS BETTER THAN TH' FIRST FEATURE..!
WHUT HAVE WE HERE?
Milk
CHUBBY CHASER ice cream
LI'L BLOODY!

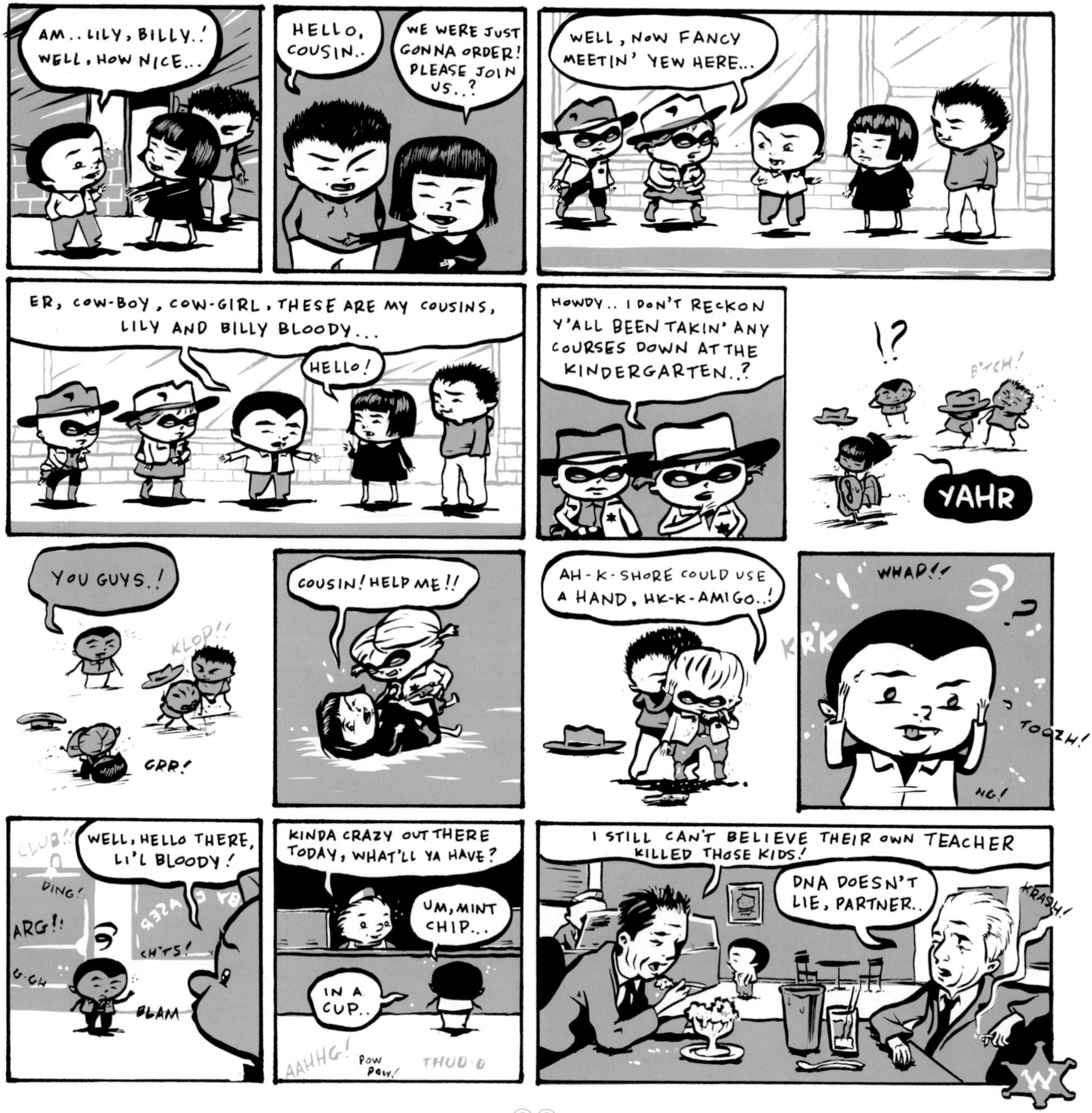
AM.. LILY, BILLY..! WELL, HOW NICE...
HELLO, COUSIN..
WE WERE JUST GONNA ORDER! PLEASE JOIN US..?
WELL, NOW FANCY MEETIN' YEW HERE...
ER, COW-BOY, COW-GIRL, THESE ARE MY COUSINS, LILY AND BILLY BLOODY...
HELLO!
HOWDY.. I DON'T RECKON Y'ALL BEEN TAKIN' ANY COURSES DOWN AT THE KINDERGARTEN..?
!?
YAHR
YOU GUYS..!
KLOP!!
GRR!
COUSIN! HELP ME!!
AH-K-SHORE COULD USE A HAND, HK-K-AMIGO..!
KRK
WHAP!!
TOOZH!
NG!
CLUB!!
WELL, HELLO THERE, LI'L BLOODY!
DING!
ARG!!
CH'TS!
U-GH
BLAM
KINDA CRAZY OUT THERE TODAY, WHAT'LL YA HAVE?
UM, MINT CHIP...
IN A CUP..
AAHHG!
POW POW!
THUD-O
I STILL CAN'T BELIEVE THEIR OWN TEACHER KILLED THOSE KIDS!
DNA DOESN'T LIE, PARTNER..
KRASH!

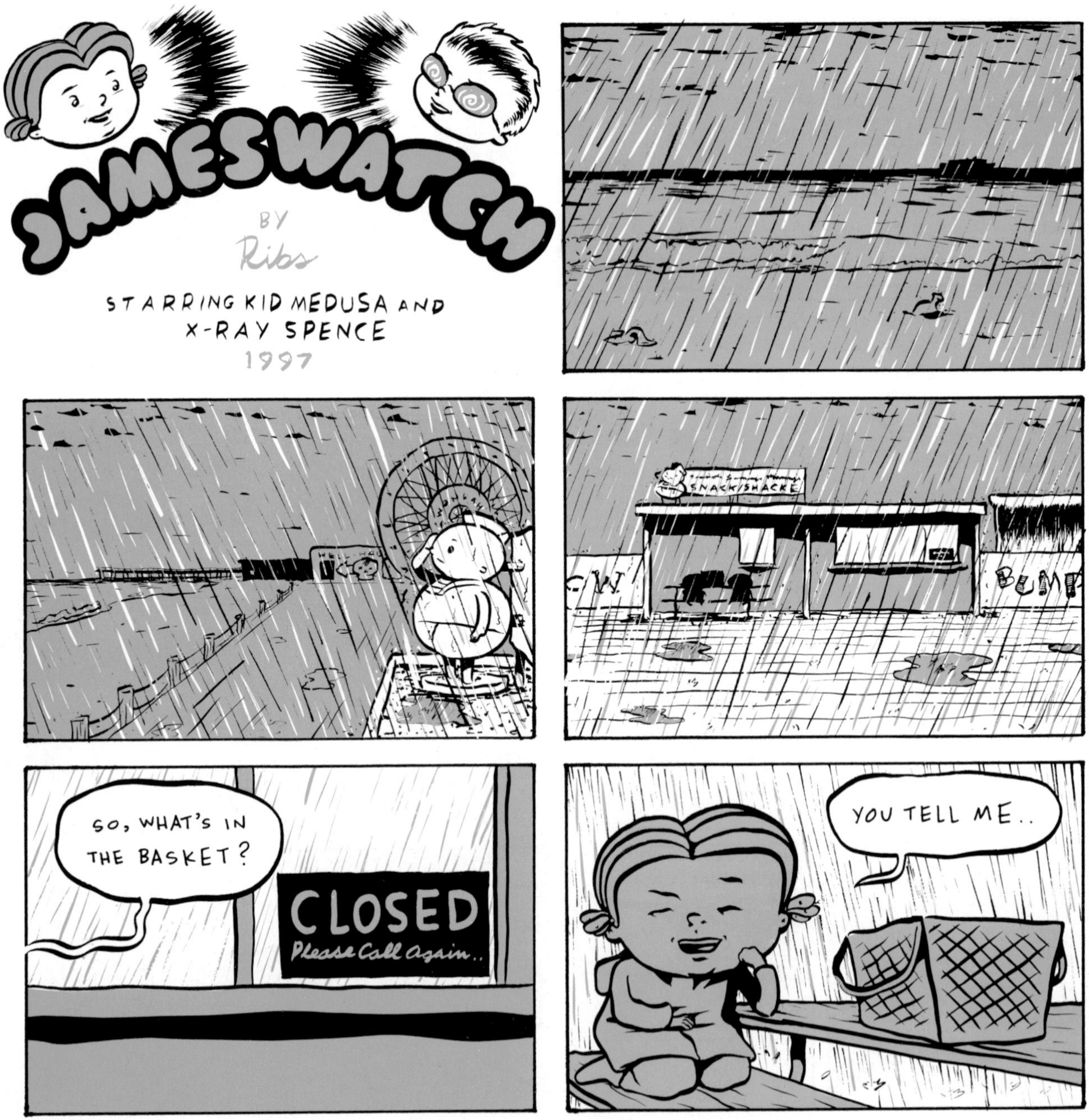
JAMESWATCH
BY
Ribs
STARRING KID MEDUSA AND
X-RAY SPENCE
1997
SNACK/SHACKE
SO, WHAT'S IN THE BASKET?
CLOSED
Please Call Again..
YOU TELL ME..

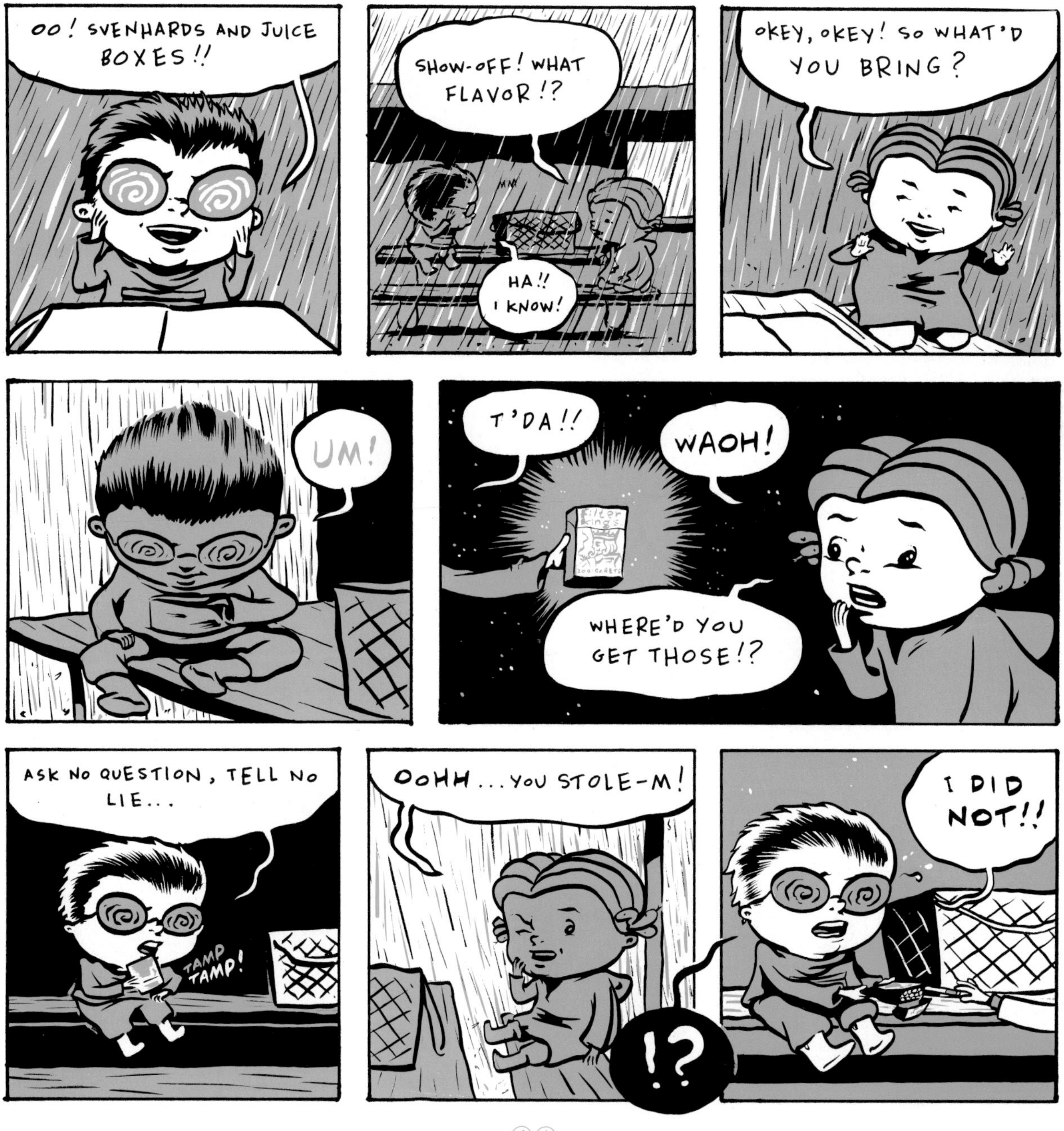
OO! SVENHARDS AND JUICE BOXES!!
SHOW-OFF! WHAT FLAVOR!?
HA!! I KNOW!
OKEY, OKEY! SO WHAT'D YOU BRING?
UM!
T'DA!!
WAOH!
WHERE'D YOU GET THOSE!?
ASK NO QUESTION, TELL NO LIE...
TAMP TAMP!
OOHH...YOU STOLE-M!
!?
I DID NOT!!

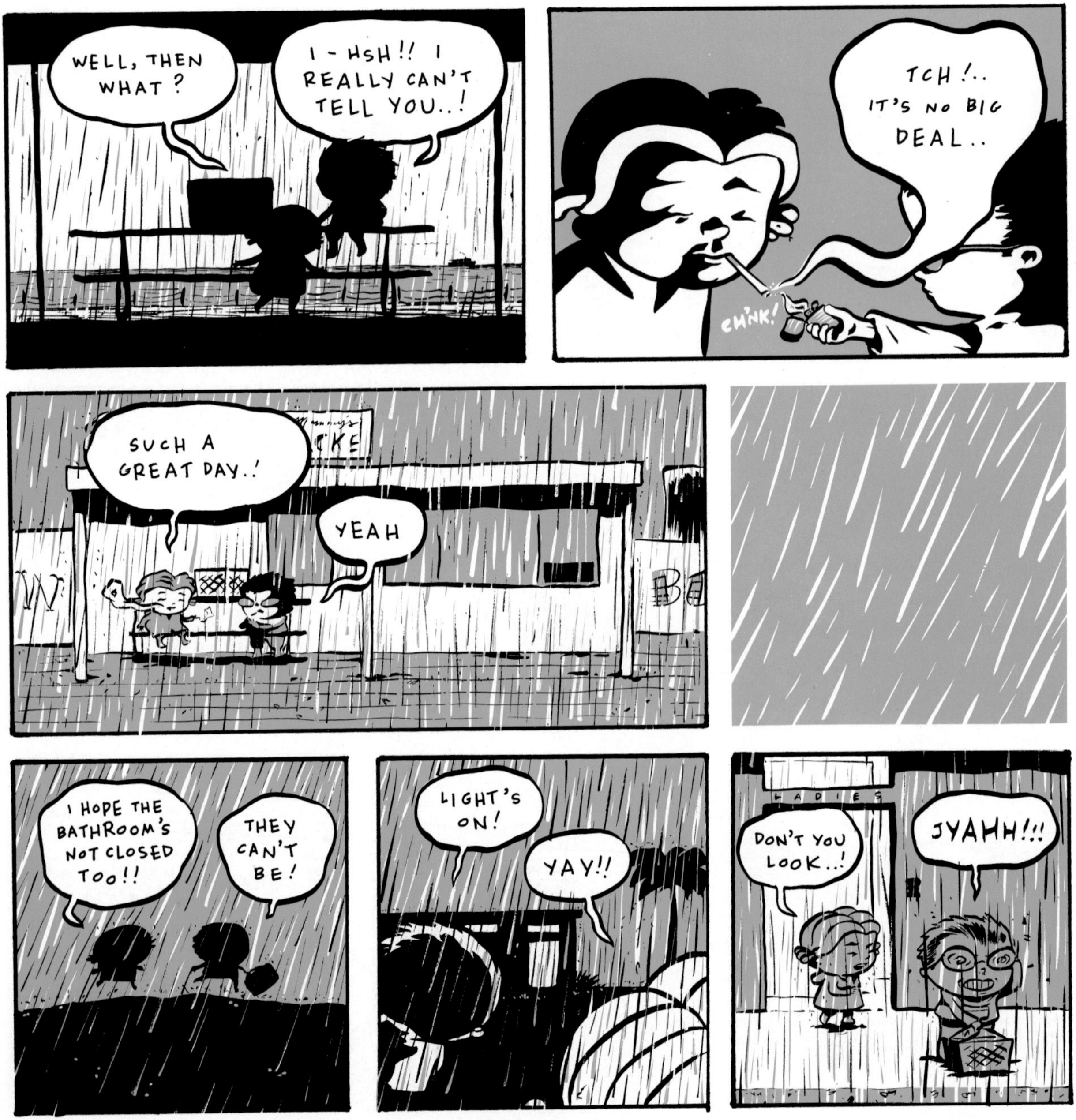
WELL, THEN WHAT?
I-HSH!! I REALLY CAN'T TELL YOU..!
TCH!.. IT'S NO BIG DEAL..
CHINK!
SUCH A GREAT DAY..!
YEAH
I HOPE THE BATHROOM'S NOT CLOSED TOO!!
THEY CAN'T BE!
LIGHT'S ON!
YAY!!
LADIES
DON'T YOU LOOK..!
JYAHH!!!

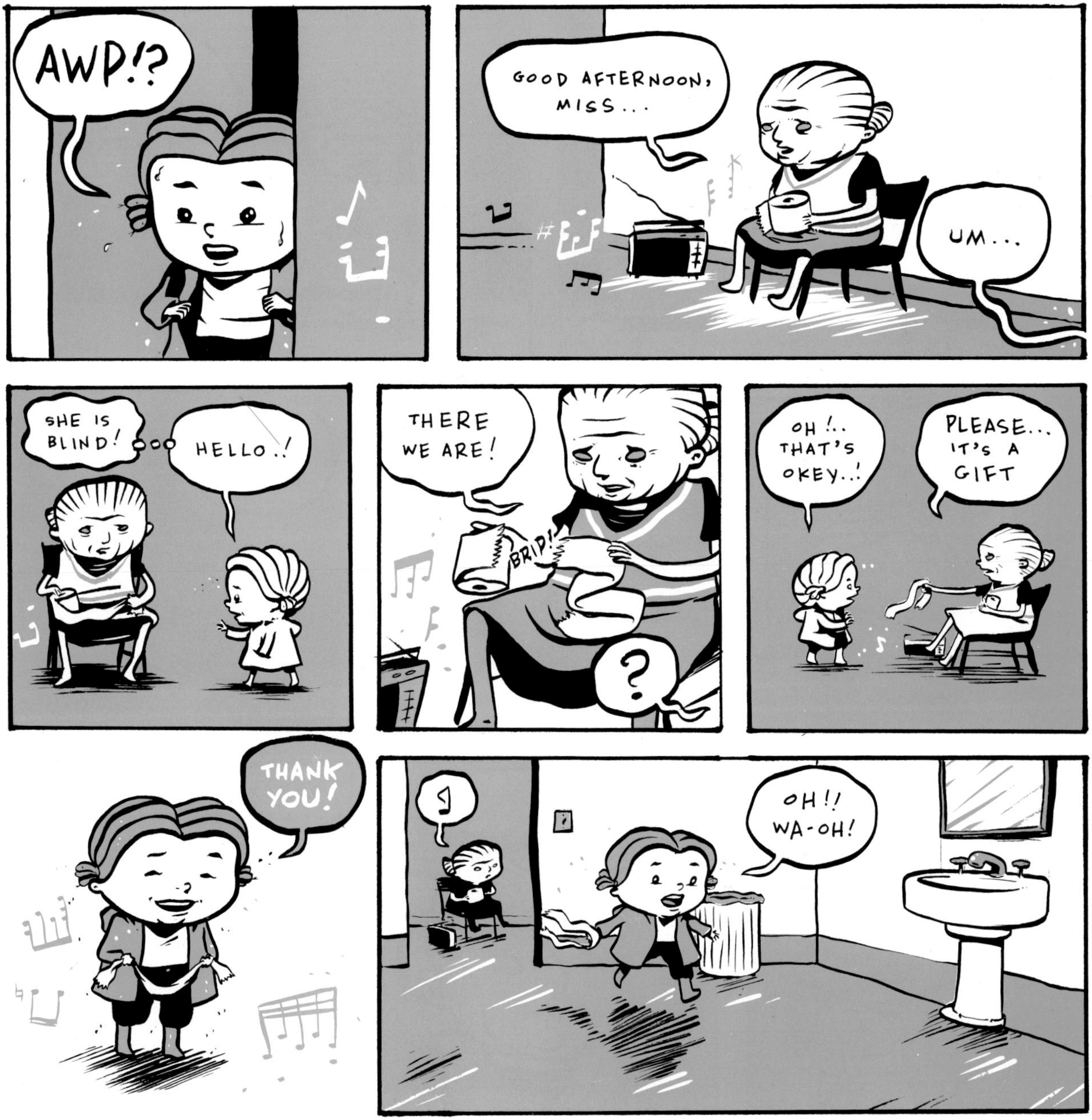
AWP!?
GOOD AFTERNOON, MISS...
UM...
SHE IS BLIND!
HELLO..!
THERE WE ARE!
BRIP!
?
OH!.. THAT'S OKEY..!
PLEASE... IT'S A GIFT
THANK YOU!
OH!! WA-OH!

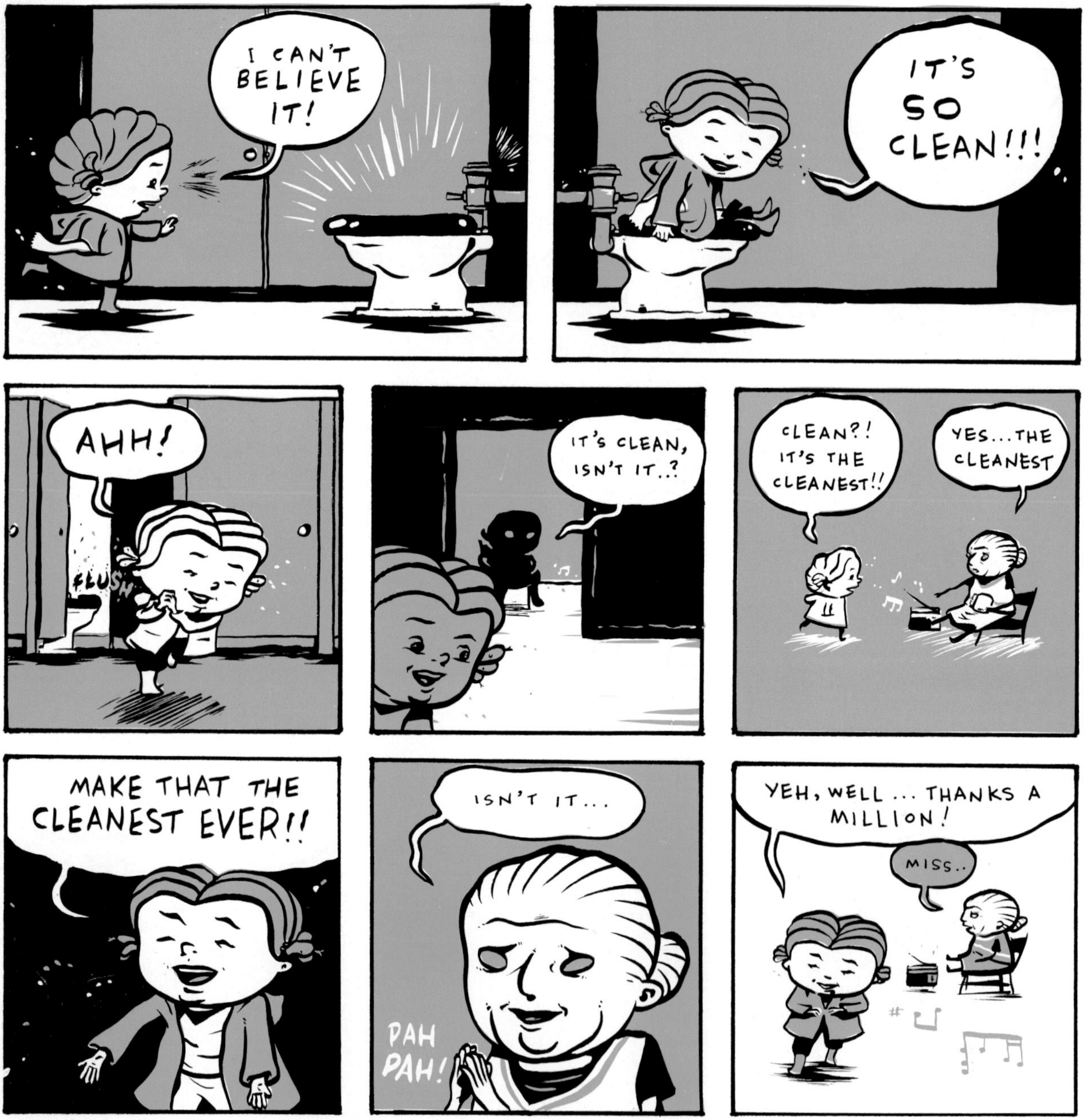
I CAN'T BELIEVE IT!
IT'S SO CLEAN!!!
AHH!
FLUSH
IT'S CLEAN, ISN'T IT..?
CLEAN?! IT'S THE CLEANEST!!
YES...THE CLEANEST
MAKE THAT THE CLEANEST EVER!!
ISN'T IT...
DAH DAH!
YEH, WELL... THANKS A MILLION!
MISS..

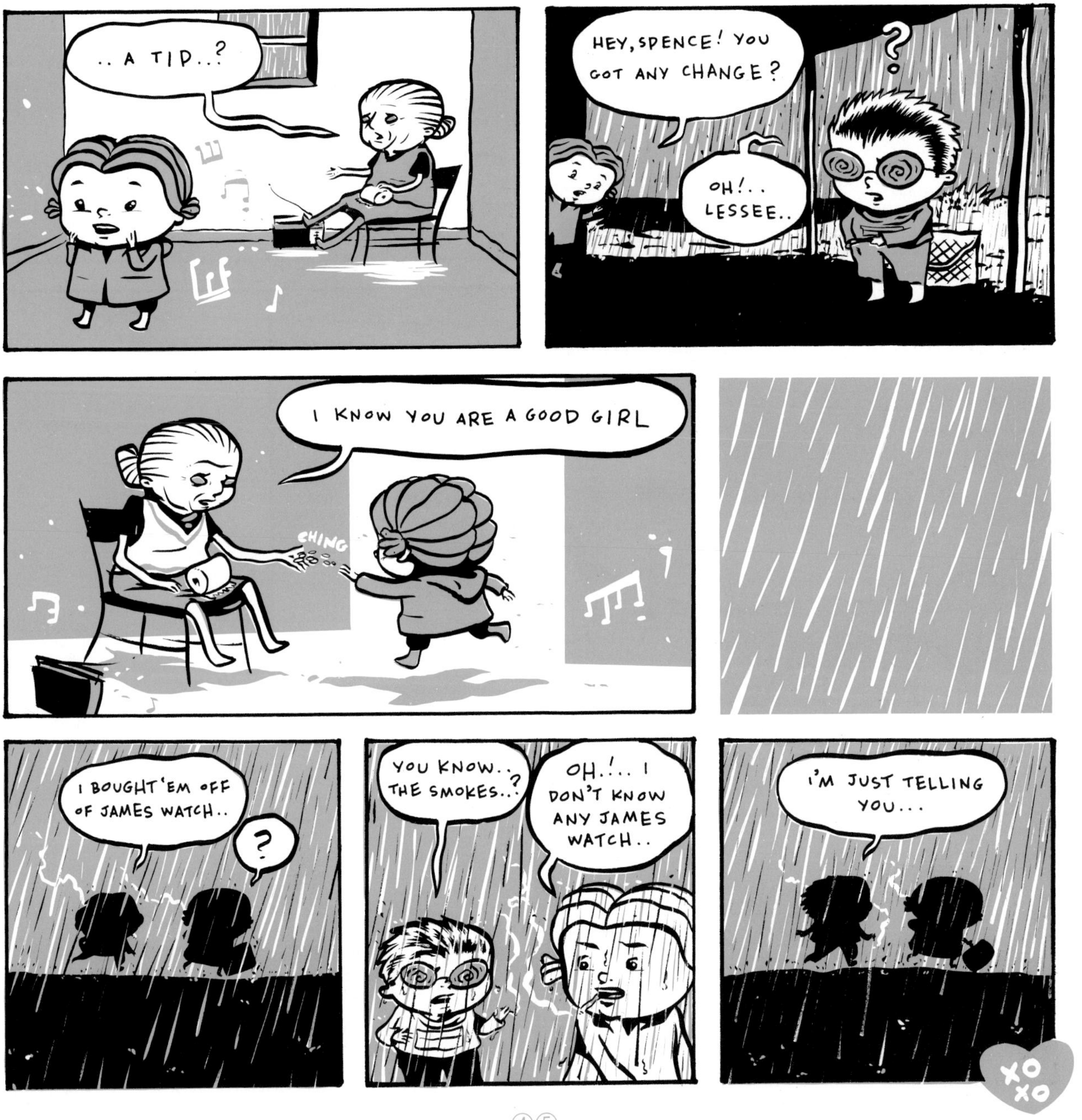
.. A TIP..?
HEY, SPENCE! YOU GOT ANY CHANGE?
?
OH!.. LESSEE..
I KNOW YOU ARE A GOOD GIRL
CHING
I BOUGHT 'EM OFF OF JAMES WATCH..
?
YOU KNOW.. THE SMOKES..?
OH..!.. I DON'T KNOW ANY JAMES WATCH..
I'M JUST TELLING YOU...
XO XO

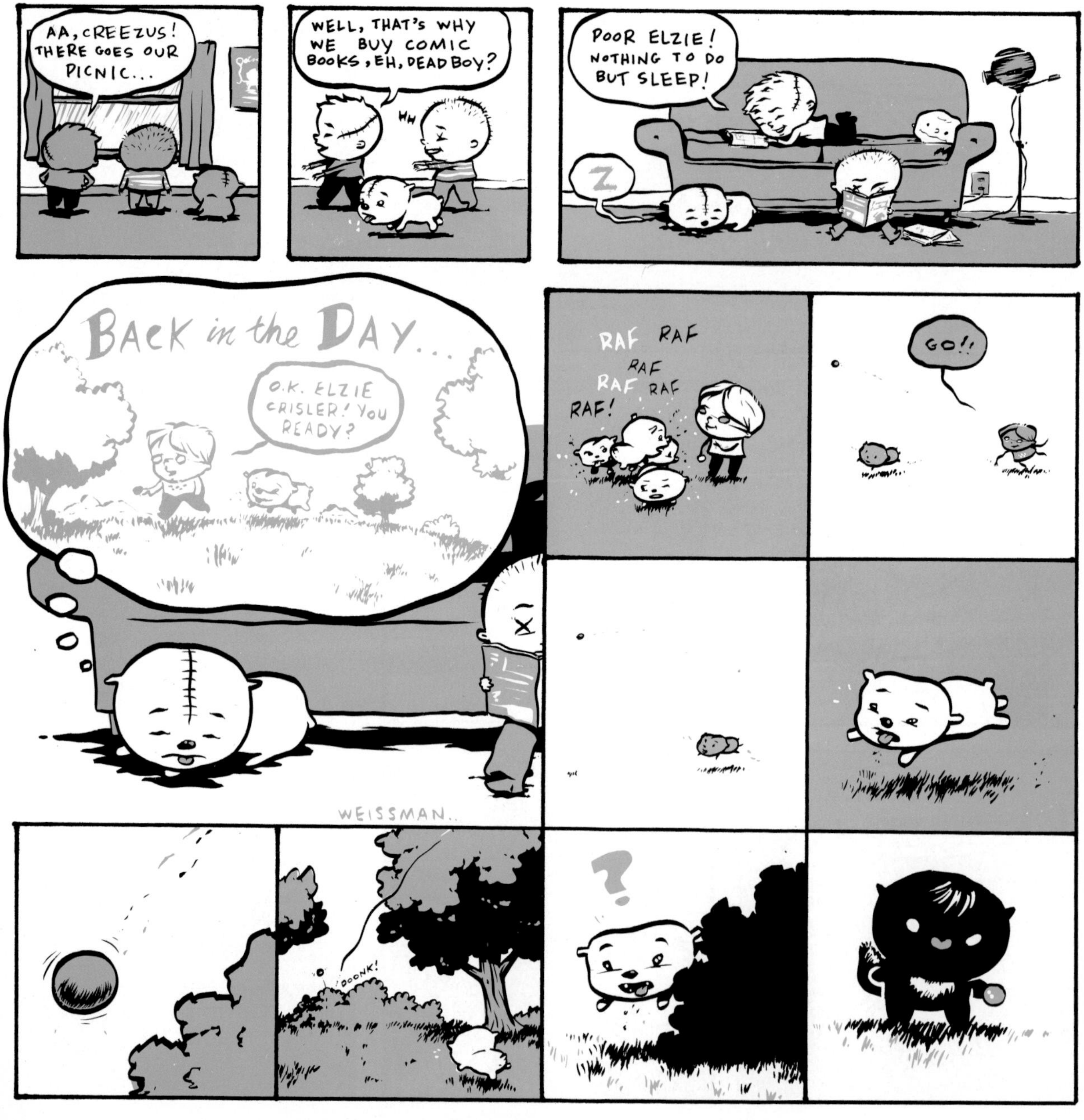
AA, CREEZUS! THERE GOES OUR PICNIC...
WELL, THAT'S WHY WE BUY COMIC BOOKS, EH, DEAD BOY?
HH
POOR ELZIE! NOTHING TO DO BUT SLEEP!
Z
BACK in the DAY...
O.K. ELZIE CRISLER! YOU READY?
RAF RAF RAF RAF RAF RAF!
GO!!
WEISSMAN..
DOONK!
?

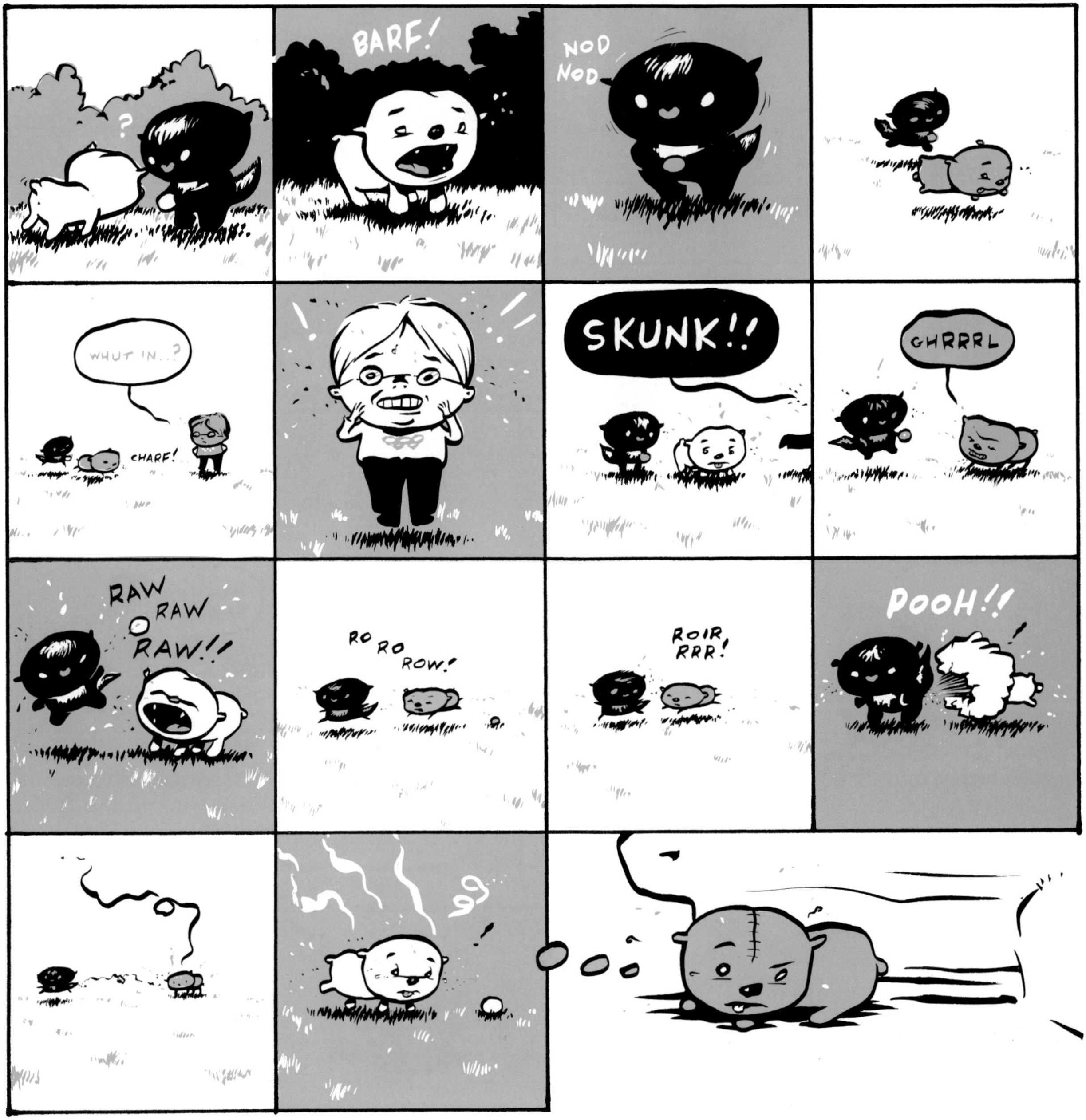
?
BARF!
NOD
NOD
WHUT IN...?
CHARF!
SKUNK!!
GHRRRL
RAW
RAW
RAW!!
RO
RO
ROW!
ROIR,
RRR!
POOH!!

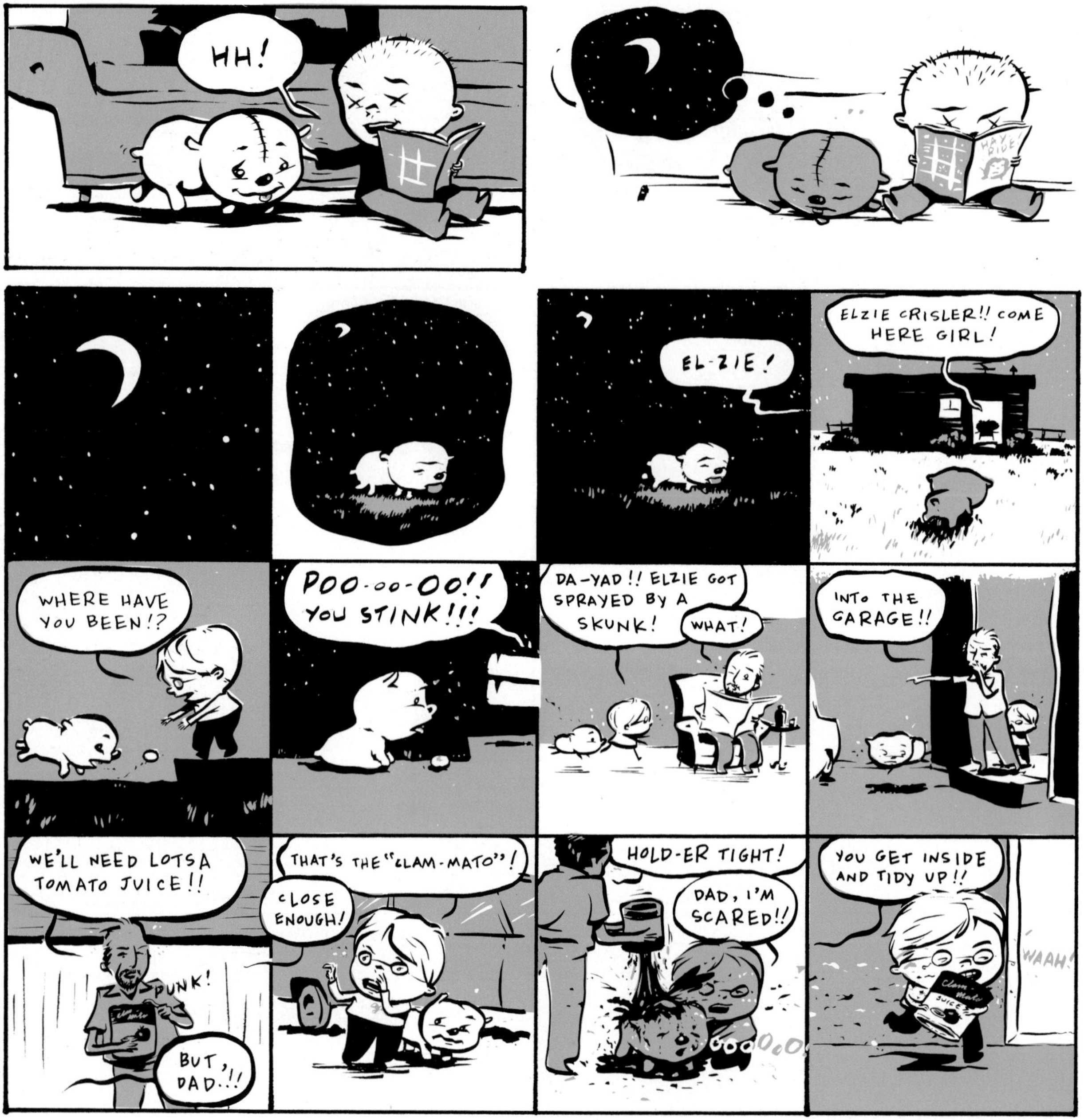
HH!
EL-ZIE!
ELZIE CRISLER!! COME HERE GIRL!
WHERE HAVE YOU BEEN!?
POO-oo-OO!! YOU STINK!!!
DA-YAD!! ELZIE GOT SPRAYED BY A SKUNK!
WHAT!
INTO THE GARAGE!!
WE'LL NEED LOTSA TOMATO JUICE!!
PUNK!
BUT, DAD..!!
THAT'S THE "CLAM-MATO"!
CLOSE ENOUGH!
HOLD-ER TIGHT!
DAD, I'M SCARED!!
YOU GET INSIDE AND TIDY UP!!
WAAH!

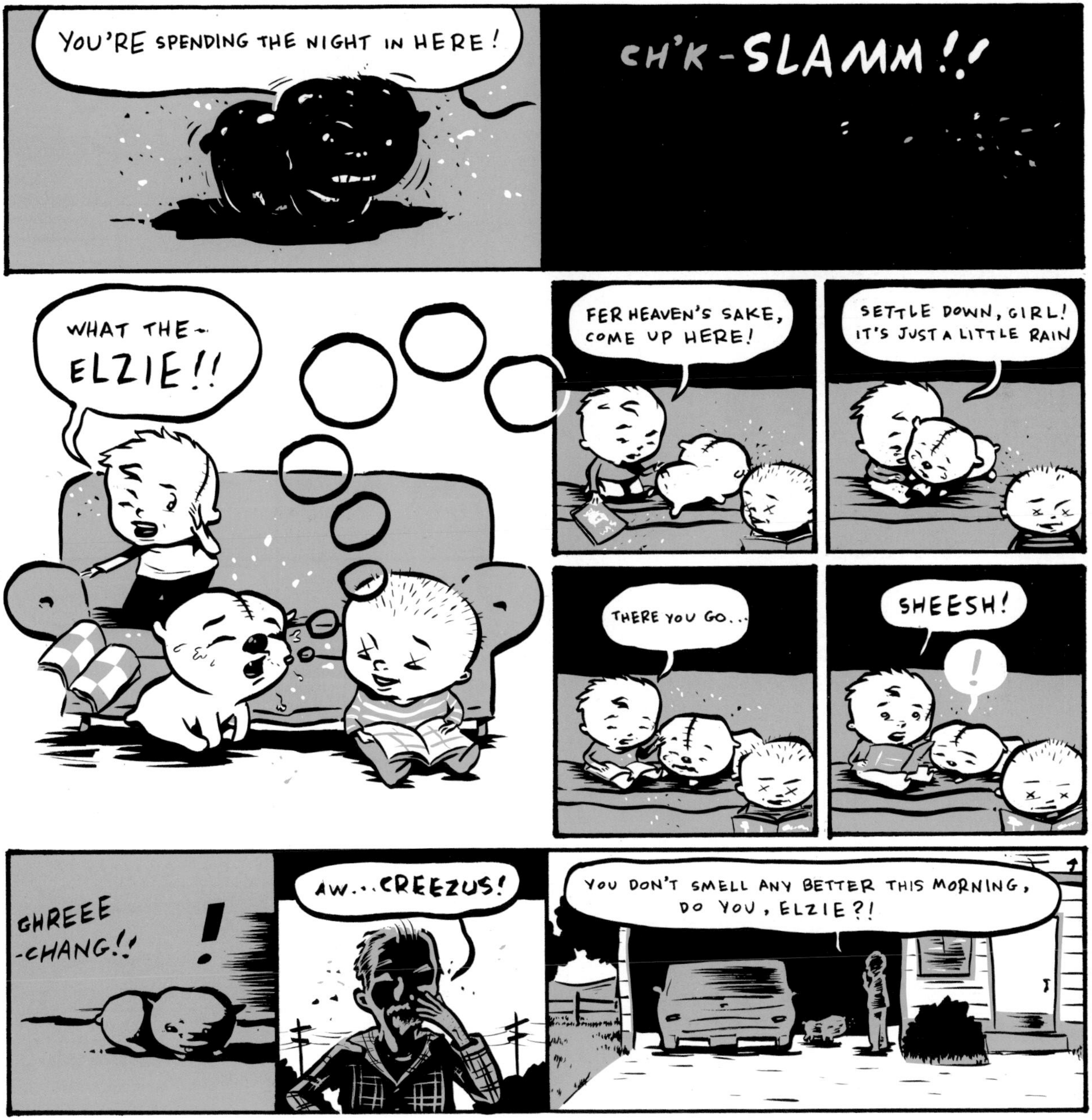
YOU'RE SPENDING THE NIGHT IN HERE!
CH'K-SLAMM!!
WHAT THE-
ELZIE!!
FER HEAVEN'S SAKE, COME UP HERE!
SETTLE DOWN, GIRL! IT'S JUST A LITTLE RAIN
THERE YOU GO...
SHEESH!
!
GHREEE -CHANG!!
!
AW...CREEZUS!
YOU DON'T SMELL ANY BETTER THIS MORNING, DO YOU, ELZIE?!

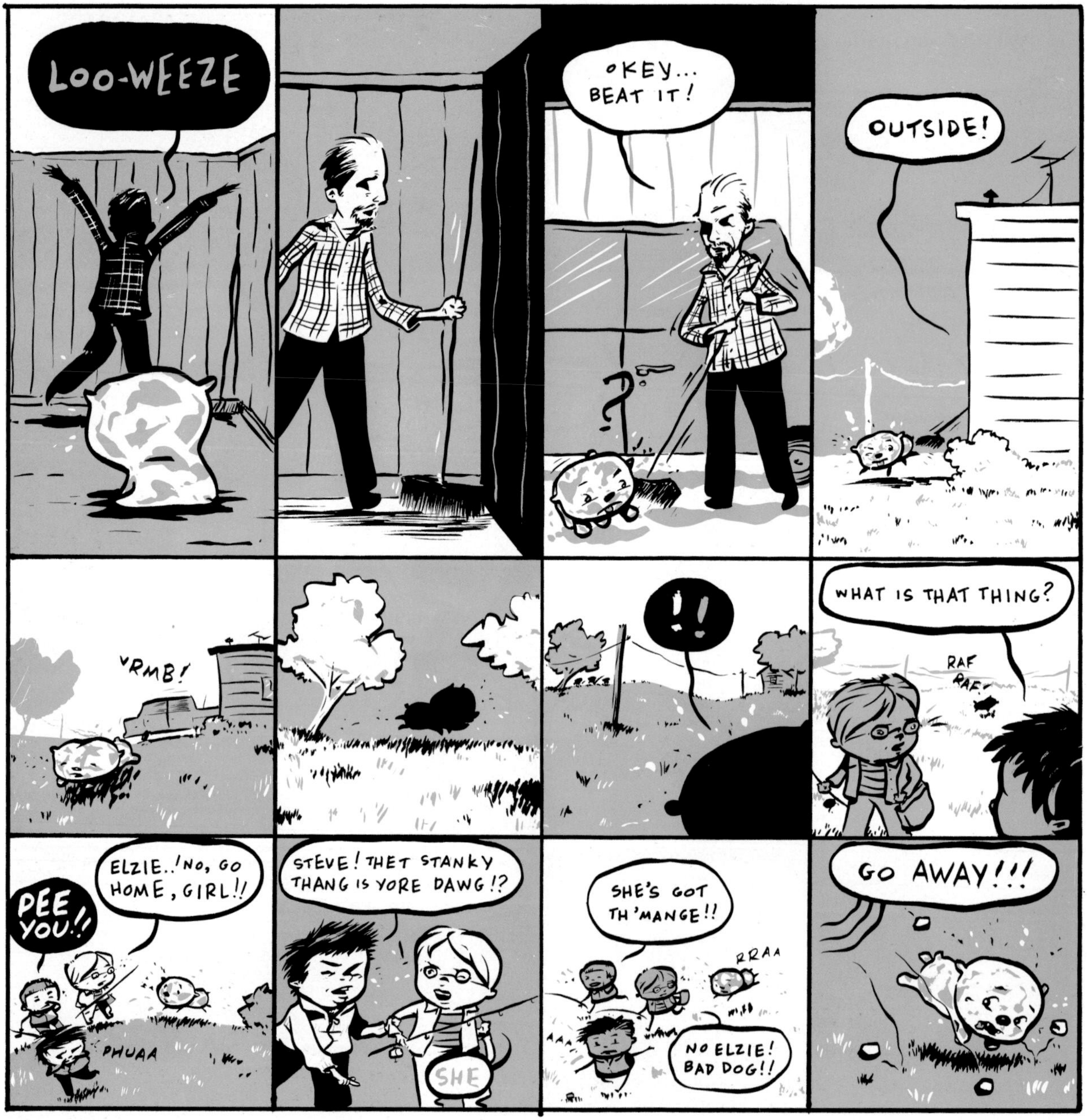
LOO-WEEZE
OKEY... BEAT IT!
?
OUTSIDE!
VRMB!
!!
WHAT IS THAT THING?
RAF RAF
PEE YOU!!
ELZIE..! NO, GO HOME, GIRL!!
PHUAA
STEVE! THET STANKY THANG IS YORE DAWG!?
SHE
SHE'S GOT TH'MANGE!!
RRAA
NO ELZIE! BAD DOG!!
GO AWAY!!!

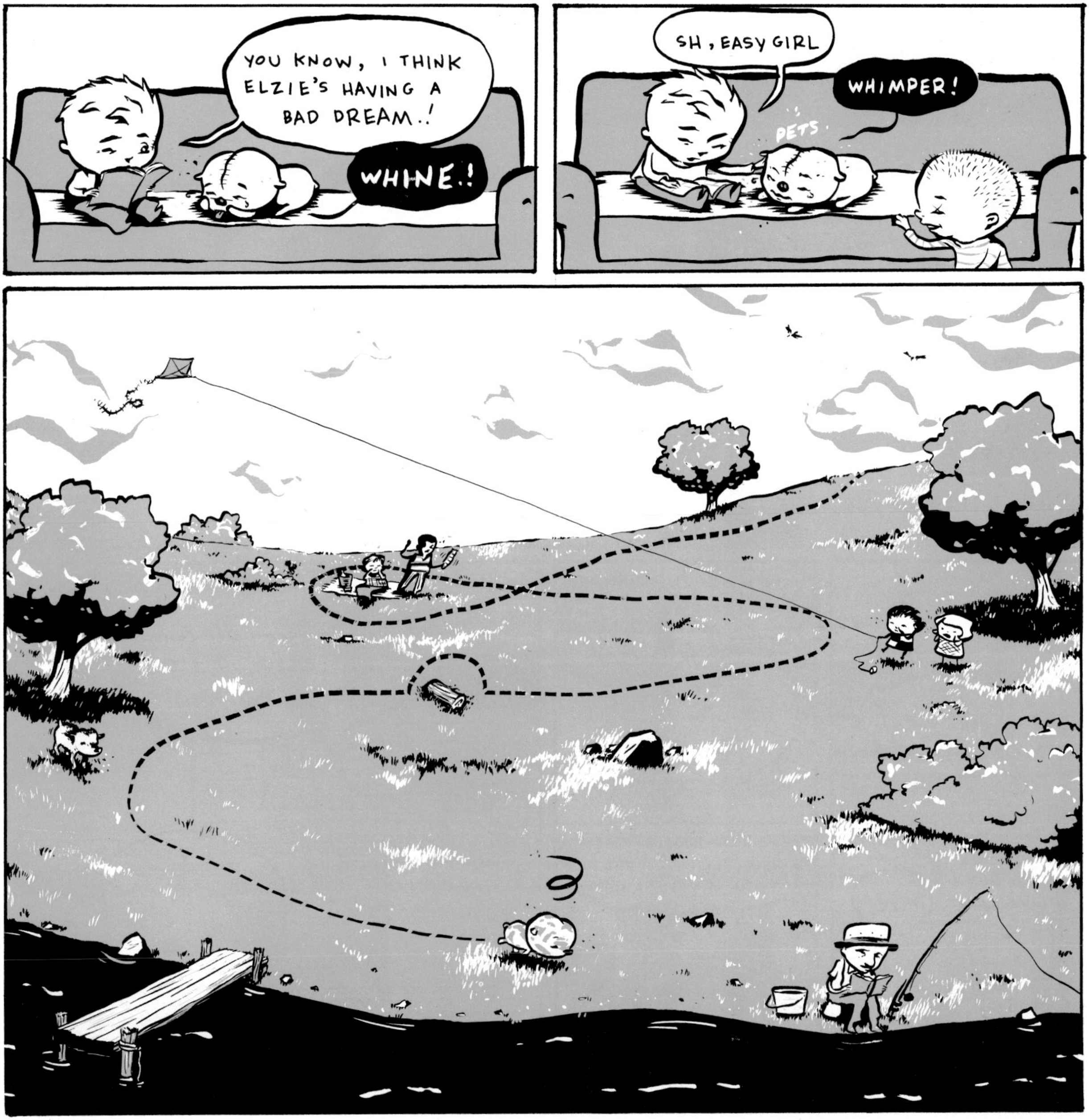
YOU KNOW, I THINK ELZIE'S HAVING A BAD DREAM.!
WHINE.!
SH, EASY GIRL
PETS
WHIMPER!

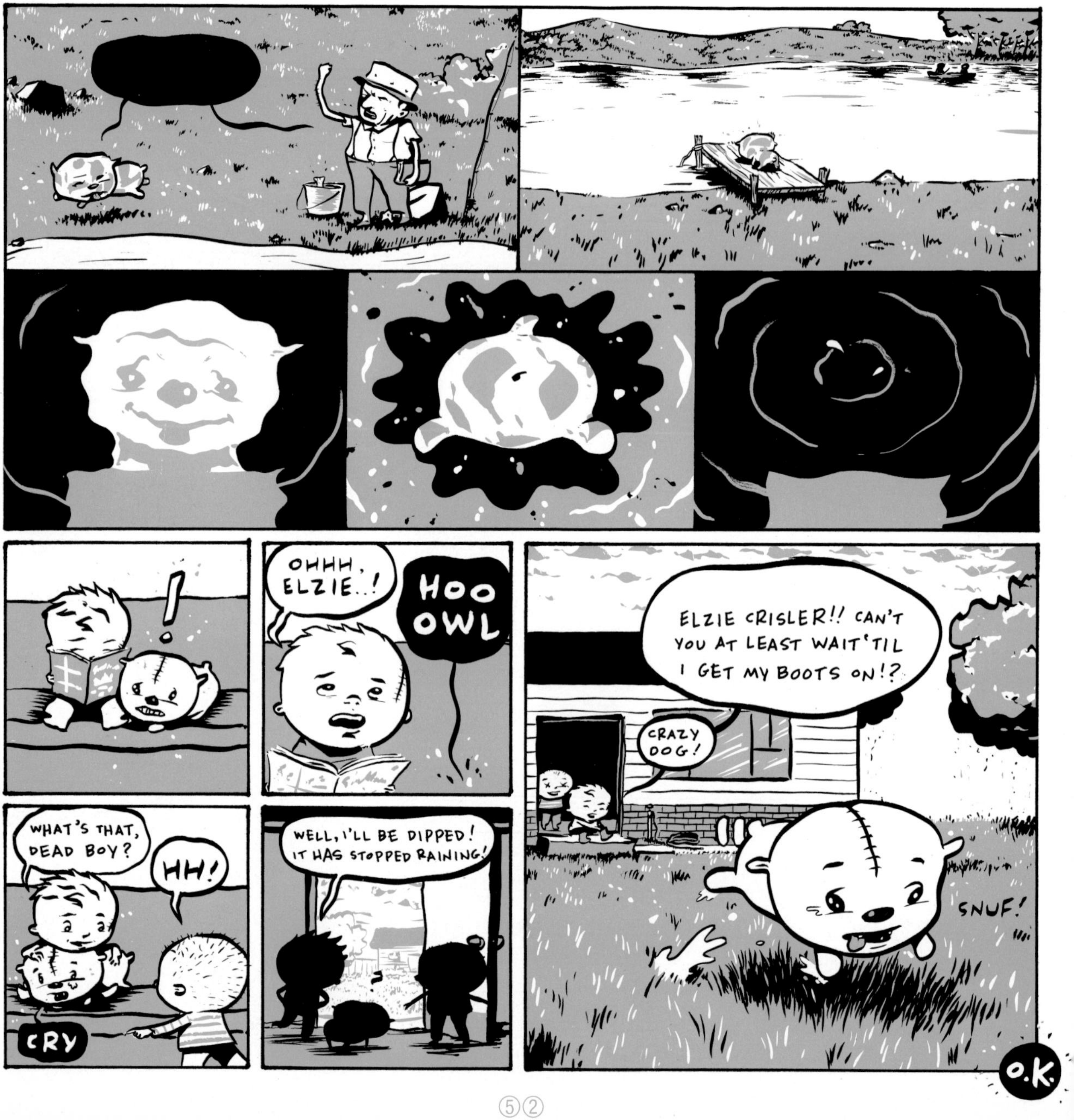
OHHH, ELZIE..!
HOO OWL
WHAT'S THAT, DEAD BOY?
HH!
CRY
WELL, I'LL BE DIPPED! IT HAS STOPPED RAINING!
ELZIE CRISLER!! CAN'T YOU AT LEAST WAIT'TIL I GET MY BOOTS ON!?
CRAZY DOG!
SNUF!
O.K.

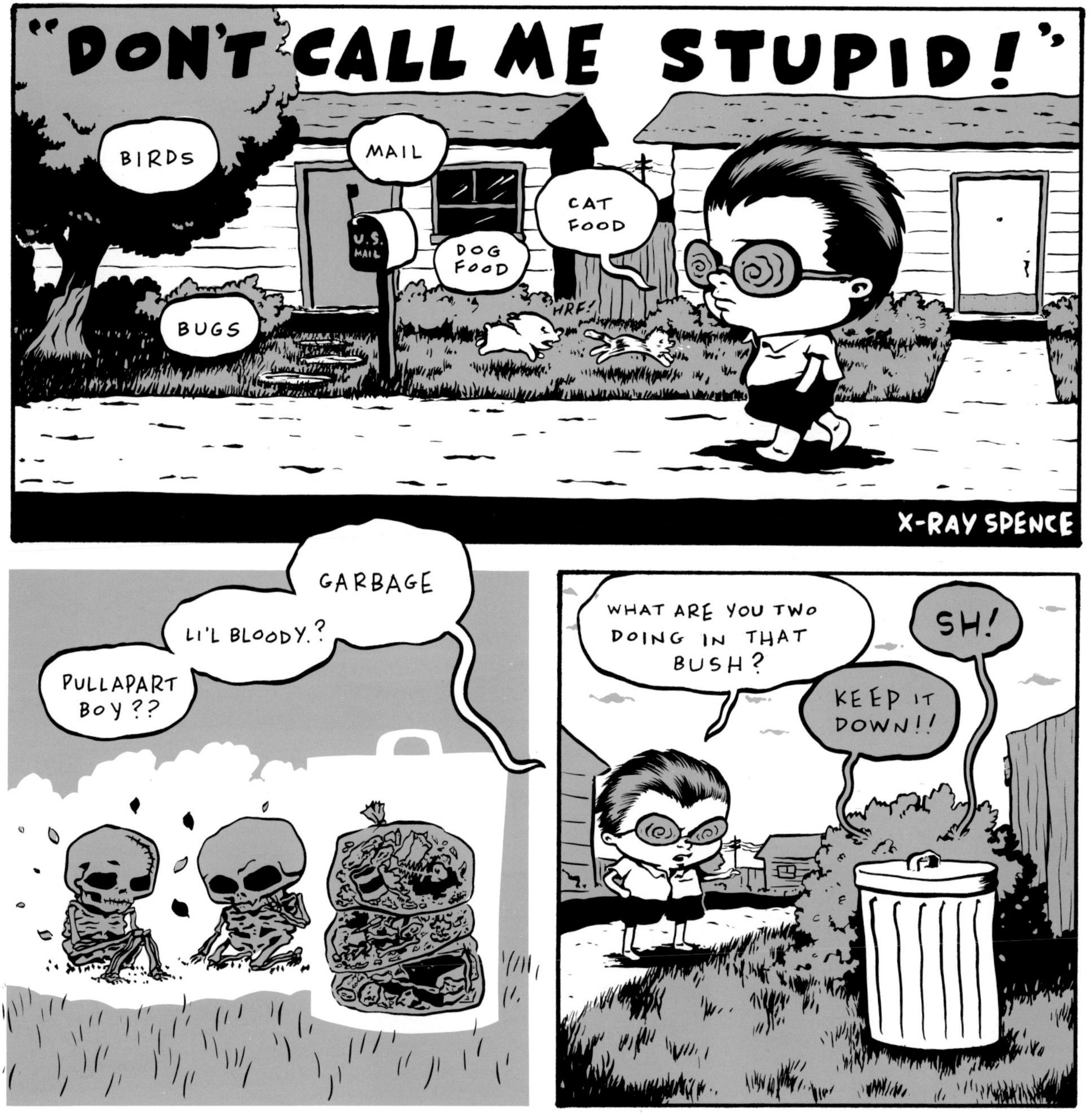
"DON'T CALL ME STUPID!"
BIRDS
MAIL
CAT FOOD
U.S. MAIL
DOG FOOD
BUGS
HRF!
X-RAY SPENCE
GARBAGE
LI'L BLOODY.?
PULLAPART BOY??
WHAT ARE YOU TWO DOING IN THAT BUSH?
SH!
KEEP IT DOWN!!

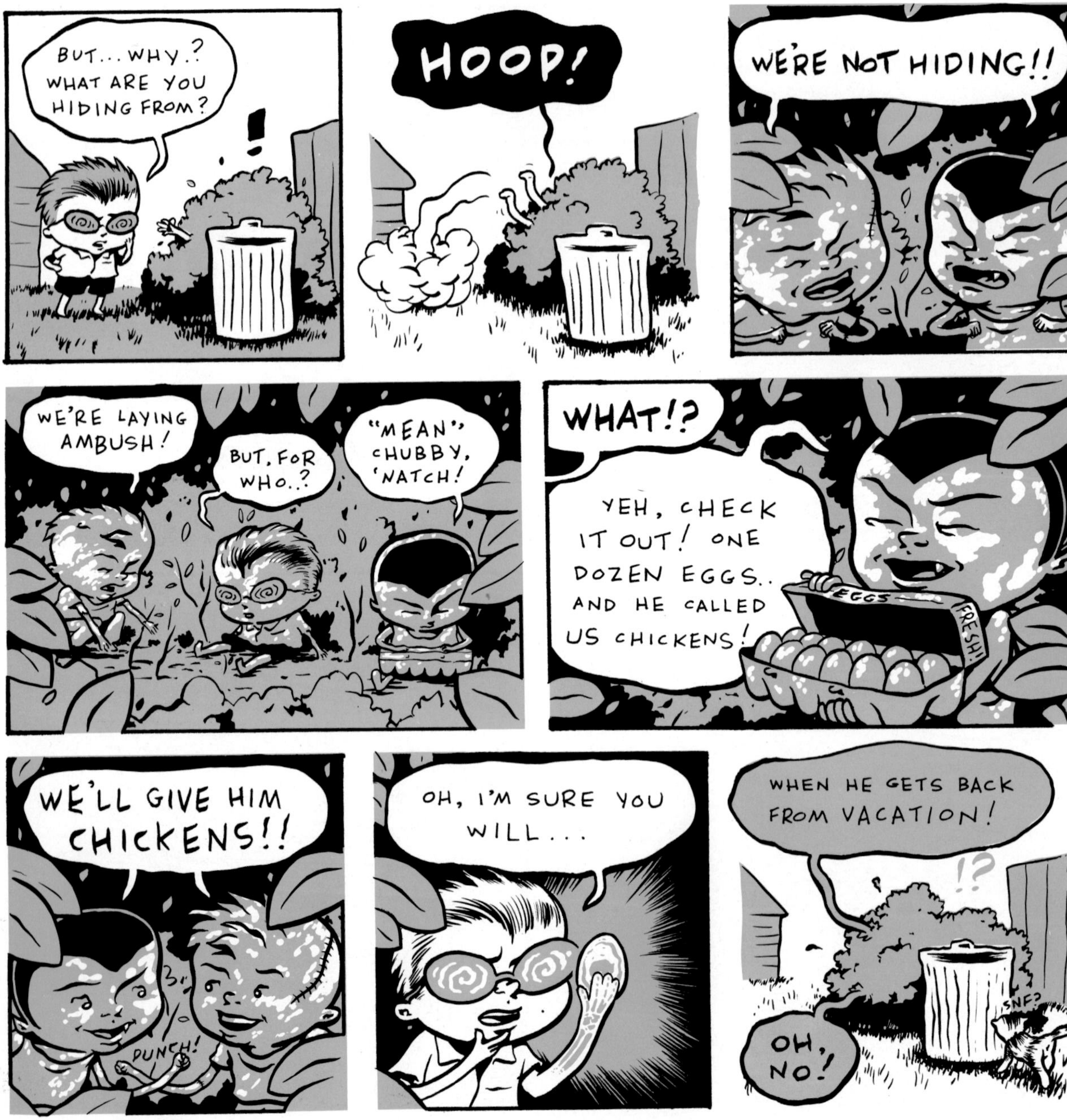
BUT... WHY..? WHAT ARE YOU HIDING FROM?
!
HOOP!
WE'RE NOT HIDING!!
WE'RE LAYING AMBUSH!
BUT, FOR WHO..?
"MEAN" CHUBBY, 'NATCH!
WHAT!?
YEH, CHECK IT OUT! ONE DOZEN EGGS.. AND HE CALLED US CHICKENS!
EGGS
FRESH!
WE'LL GIVE HIM CHICKENS!!
PUNCH!
OH, I'M SURE YOU WILL...
WHEN HE GETS BACK FROM VACATION!
!?
SNF?
OH, NO!

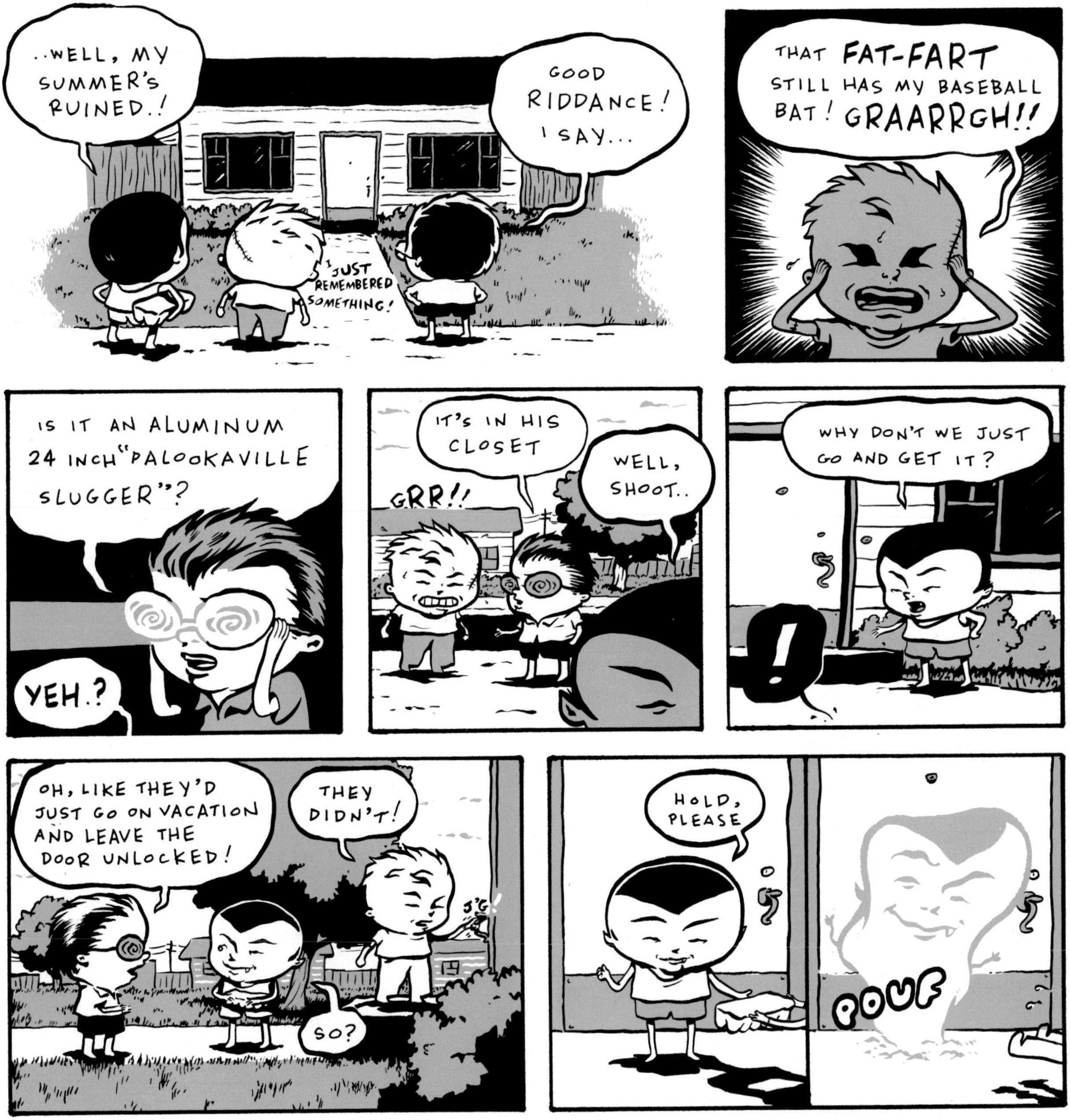

..WELL, MY SUMMER'S RUINED..!
GOOD RIDDANCE! I SAY...
I JUST REMEMBERED SOMETHING!
THAT FAT-FART STILL HAS MY BASEBALL BAT! GRAARRGH!!
IS IT AN ALUMINUM 24 INCH "PALOOKAVILLE SLUGGER"?
YEH..?
IT'S IN HIS CLOSET
GRR!!
WELL, SHOOT..
WHY DON'T WE JUST GO AND GET IT?
!
OH, LIKE THEY'D JUST GO ON VACATION AND LEAVE THE DOOR UNLOCKED!
THEY DIDN'T!
SO?
HOLD, PLEASE
POUF

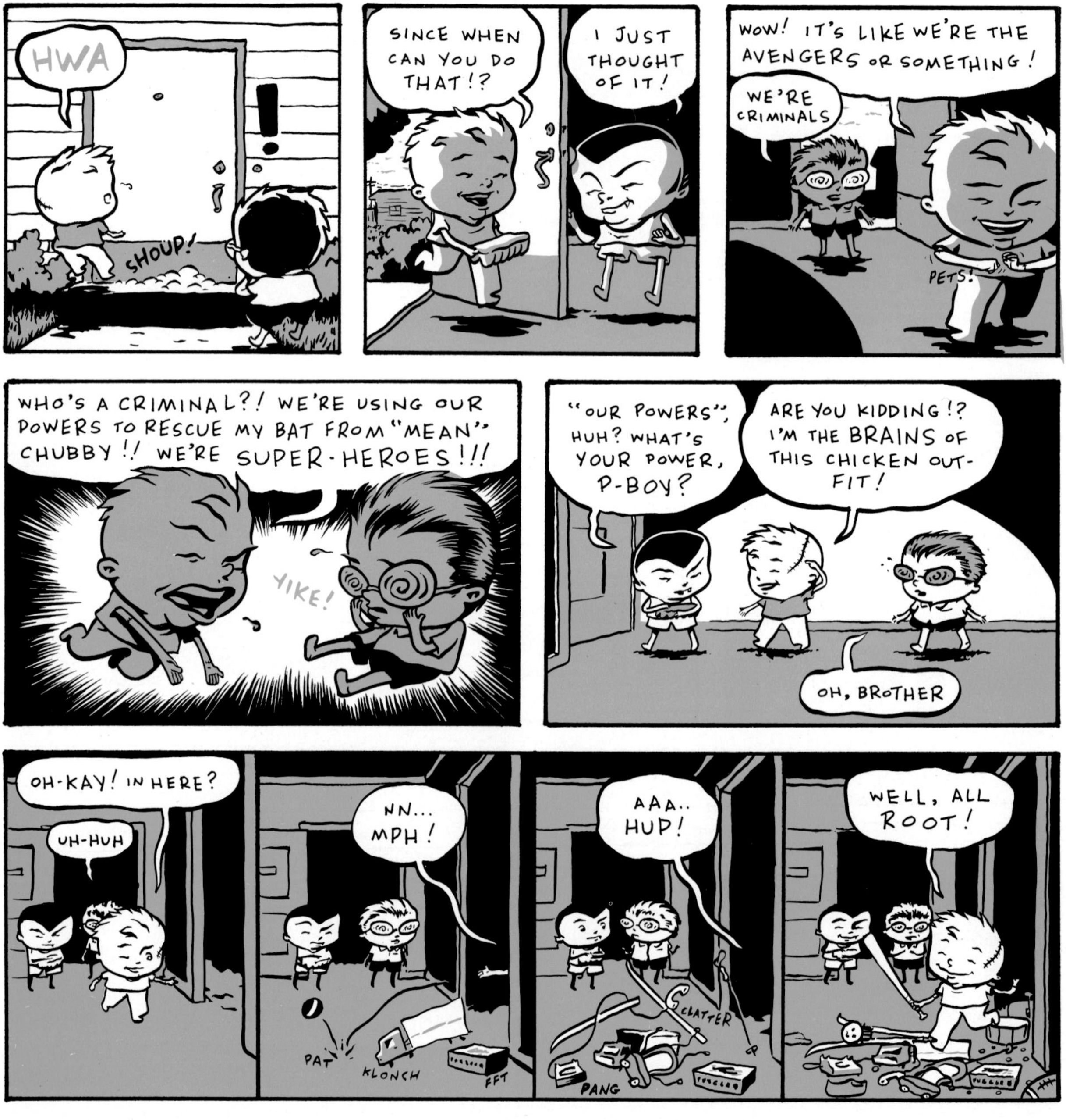
HWA
SHOUP!
SINCE WHEN CAN YOU DO THAT!?
I JUST THOUGHT OF IT!
WOW! IT'S LIKE WE'RE THE AVENGERS OR SOMETHING!
WE'RE CRIMINALS
PETS!
WHO'S A CRIMINAL?! WE'RE USING OUR POWERS TO RESCUE MY BAT FROM "MEAN" CHUBBY!! WE'RE SUPER-HEROES!!!
YIKE!
"OUR POWERS", HUH? WHAT'S YOUR POWER, P-BOY?
ARE YOU KIDDING!? I'M THE BRAINS OF THIS CHICKEN OUT-FIT!
OH, BROTHER
OH-KAY! IN HERE?
UH-HUH
NN... MPH!
PAT
KLONCH
FFT
AAA.. HUP!
CLATTER
PANG
WELL, ALL ROOT!

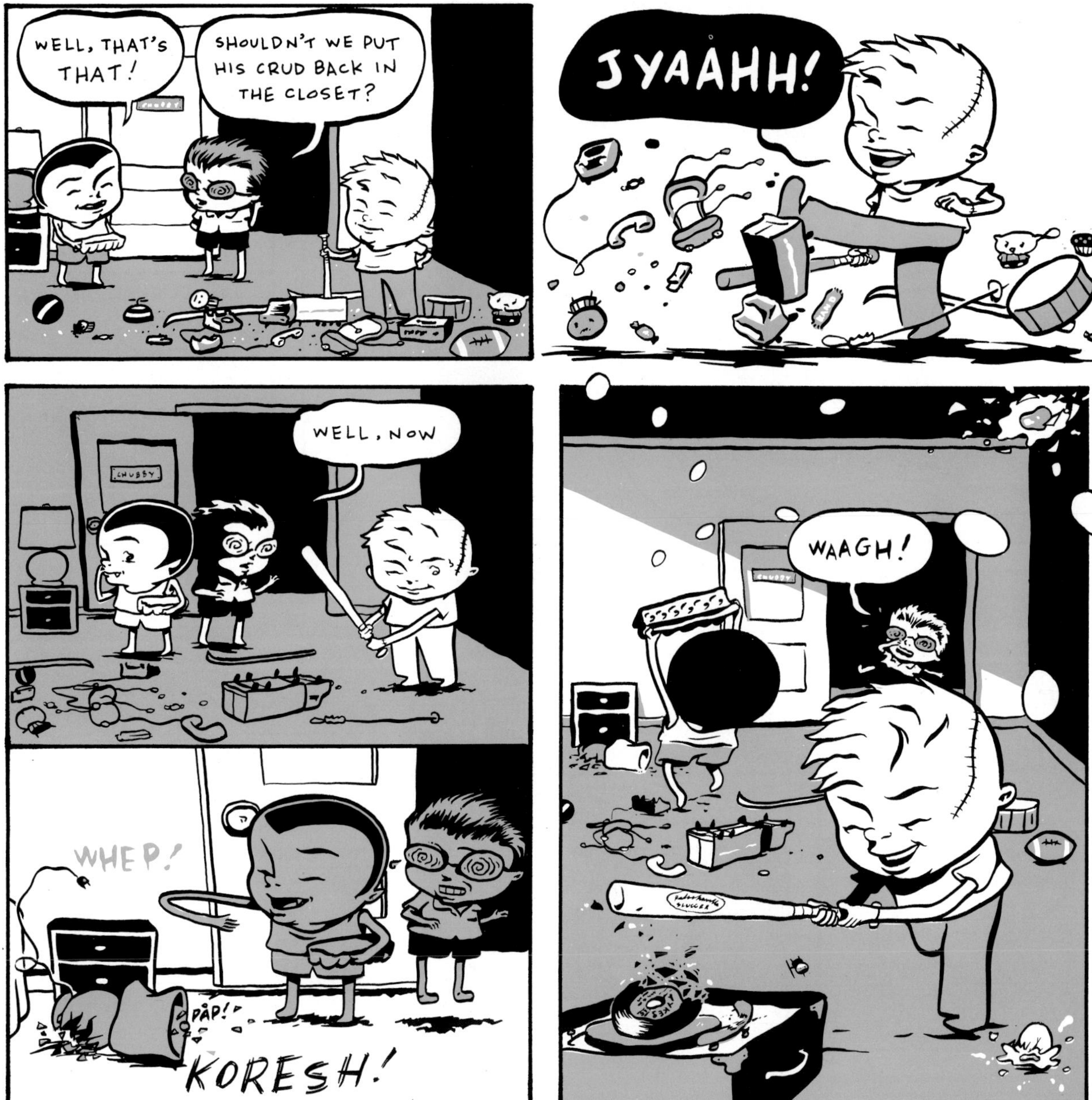
WELL, THAT'S THAT!
SHOULDN'T WE PUT HIS CRUD BACK IN THE CLOSET?
CHUBBY
JYAAHH!
WELL, NOW
CHUBBY
WHEP!
PÅP!
KORESH!
WAAGH!
CHUBBY

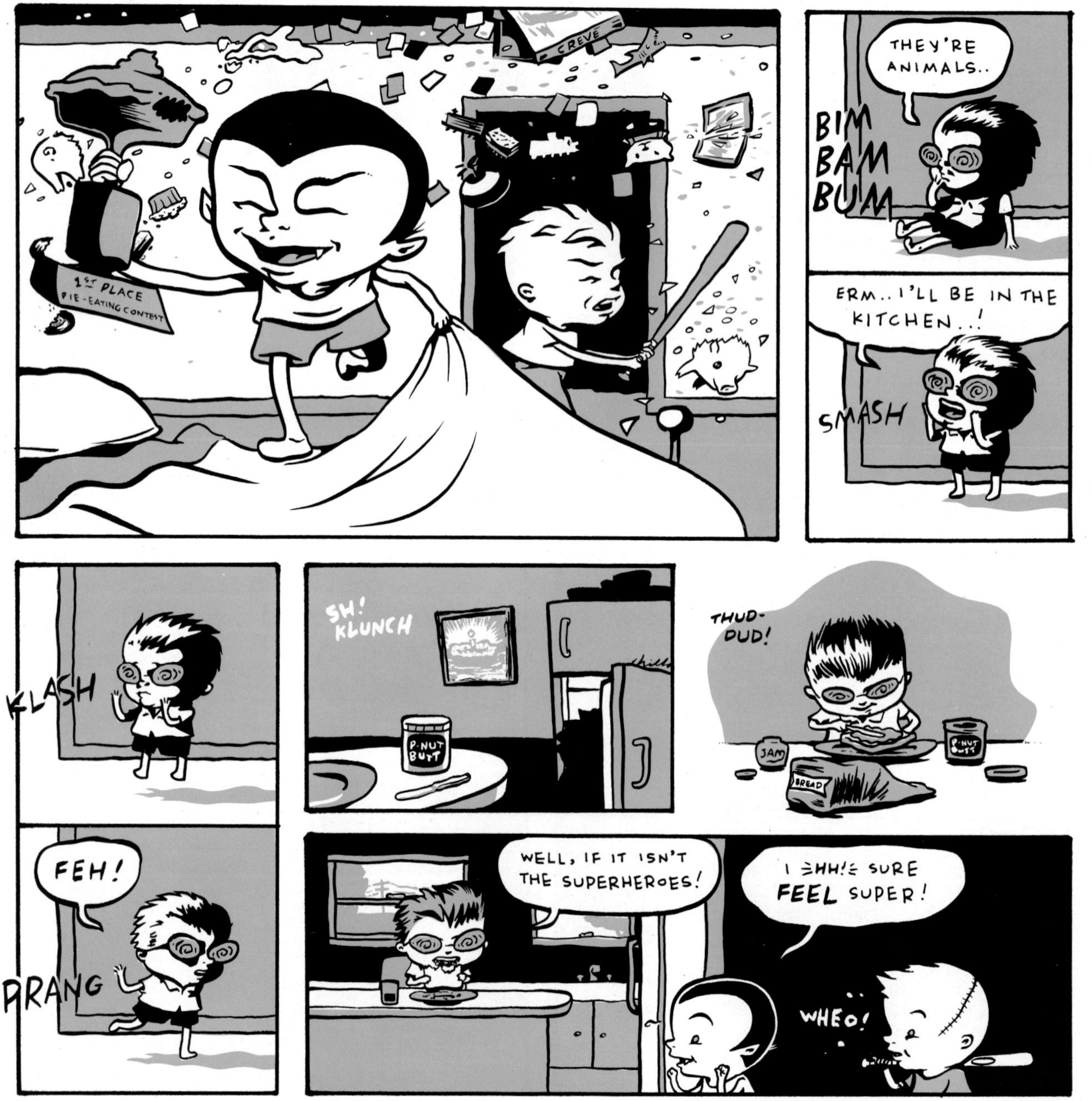
1ST PLACE PIE-EATING CONTEST
CREVE
THEY'RE ANIMALS..
BIM BAM BUM
ERM.. I'LL BE IN THE KITCHEN..!
SMASH
KLASH
SH! KLUNCH
P-NUT BUTT
THUD-DUD!
JAM
P-NUT BUTT
BREAD
FEH!
PRANG
WELL, IF IT ISN'T THE SUPERHEROES!
I ƎHH!Ɛ SURE FEEL SUPER!
WHEO!

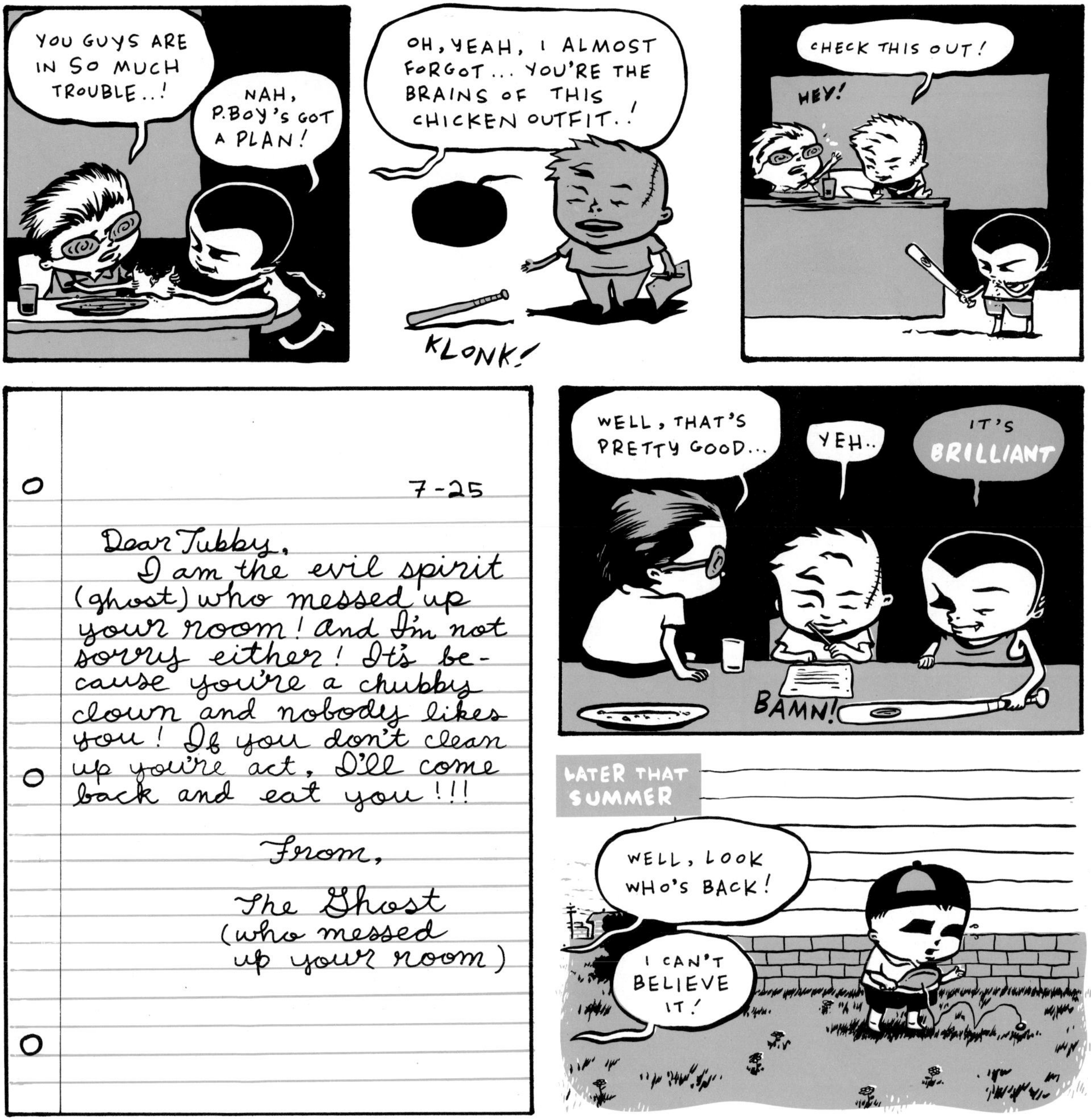
YOU GUYS ARE IN SO MUCH TROUBLE..!
NAH, P.BOY'S GOT A PLAN!
OH, YEAH, I ALMOST FORGOT... YOU'RE THE BRAINS OF THIS CHICKEN OUTFIT..!
KLONK!
CHECK THIS OUT!
HEY!
7-25
Dear Tubby,
I am the evil spirit (ghost) who messed up your room! And I'm not sorry either! It's be-cause you're a chubby clown and nobody likes you! If you don't clean up you're act, I'll come back and eat you!!!
From,
The Ghost (who messed up your room)
WELL, THAT'S PRETTY GOOD...
YEH..
IT'S BRILLIANT
BAMN!
LATER THAT SUMMER
WELL, LOOK WHO'S BACK!
I CAN'T BELIEVE IT!

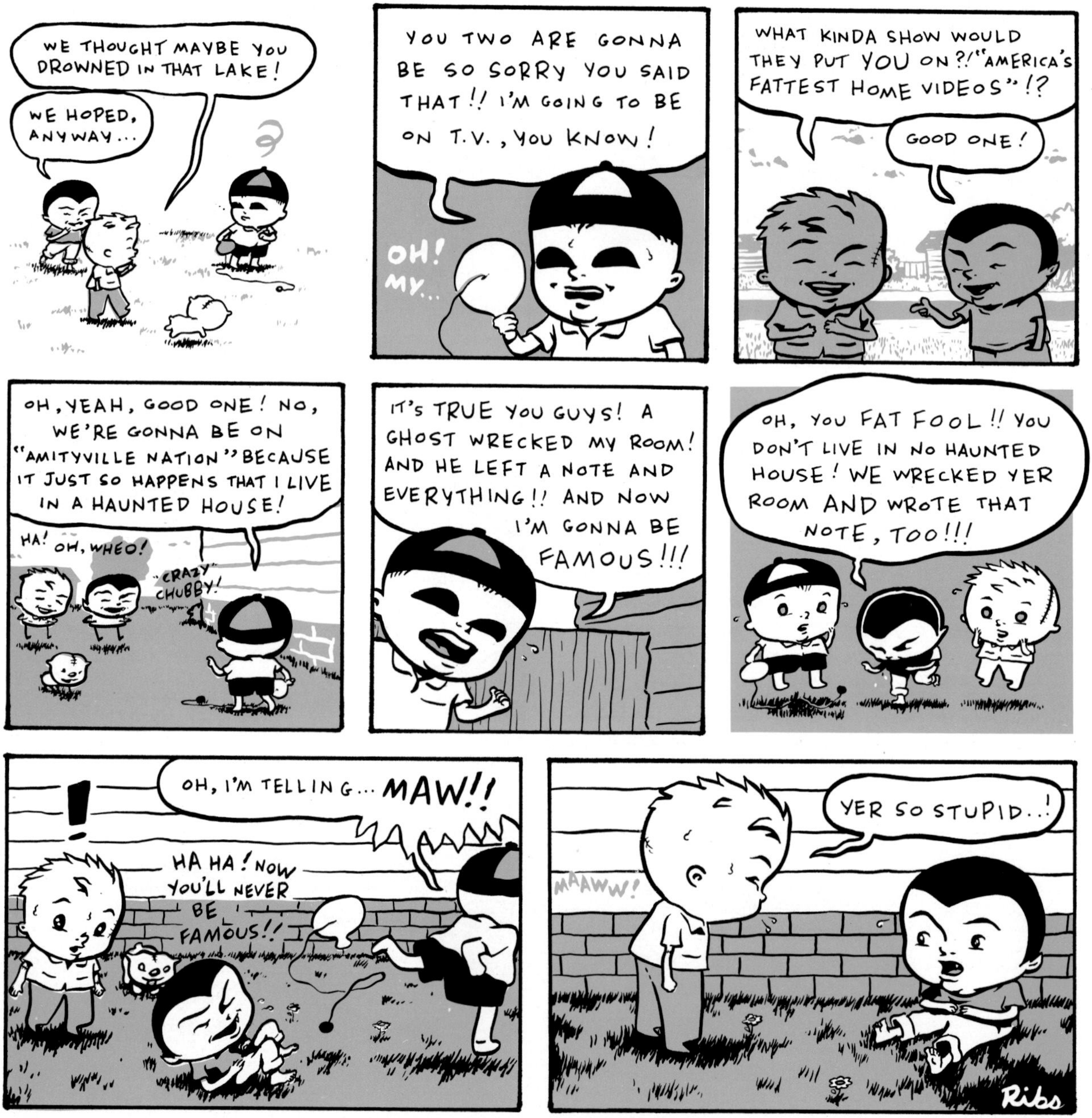

WE THOUGHT MAYBE YOU DROWNED IN THAT LAKE!
WE HOPED, ANYWAY...
YOU TWO ARE GONNA BE SO SORRY YOU SAID THAT!! I'M GOING TO BE ON T.V., YOU KNOW!
OH! MY...
WHAT KINDA SHOW WOULD THEY PUT YOU ON?! "AMERICA'S FATTEST HOME VIDEOS"!?
GOOD ONE!
OH, YEAH, GOOD ONE! NO, WE'RE GONNA BE ON "AMITYVILLE NATION" BECAUSE IT JUST SO HAPPENS THAT I LIVE IN A HAUNTED HOUSE!
HA! OH, WHEO!
CRAZY CHUBBY!
IT'S TRUE YOU GUYS! A GHOST WRECKED MY ROOM! AND HE LEFT A NOTE AND EVERYTHING!! AND NOW I'M GONNA BE FAMOUS!!!
OH, YOU FAT FOOL!! YOU DON'T LIVE IN NO HAUNTED HOUSE! WE WRECKED YER ROOM AND WROTE THAT NOTE, TOO!!!
!
OH, I'M TELLING... MAW!!
HA HA! NOW YOU'LL NEVER BE FAMOUS!!
MAAWW!
YER SO STUPID..!
Ribs

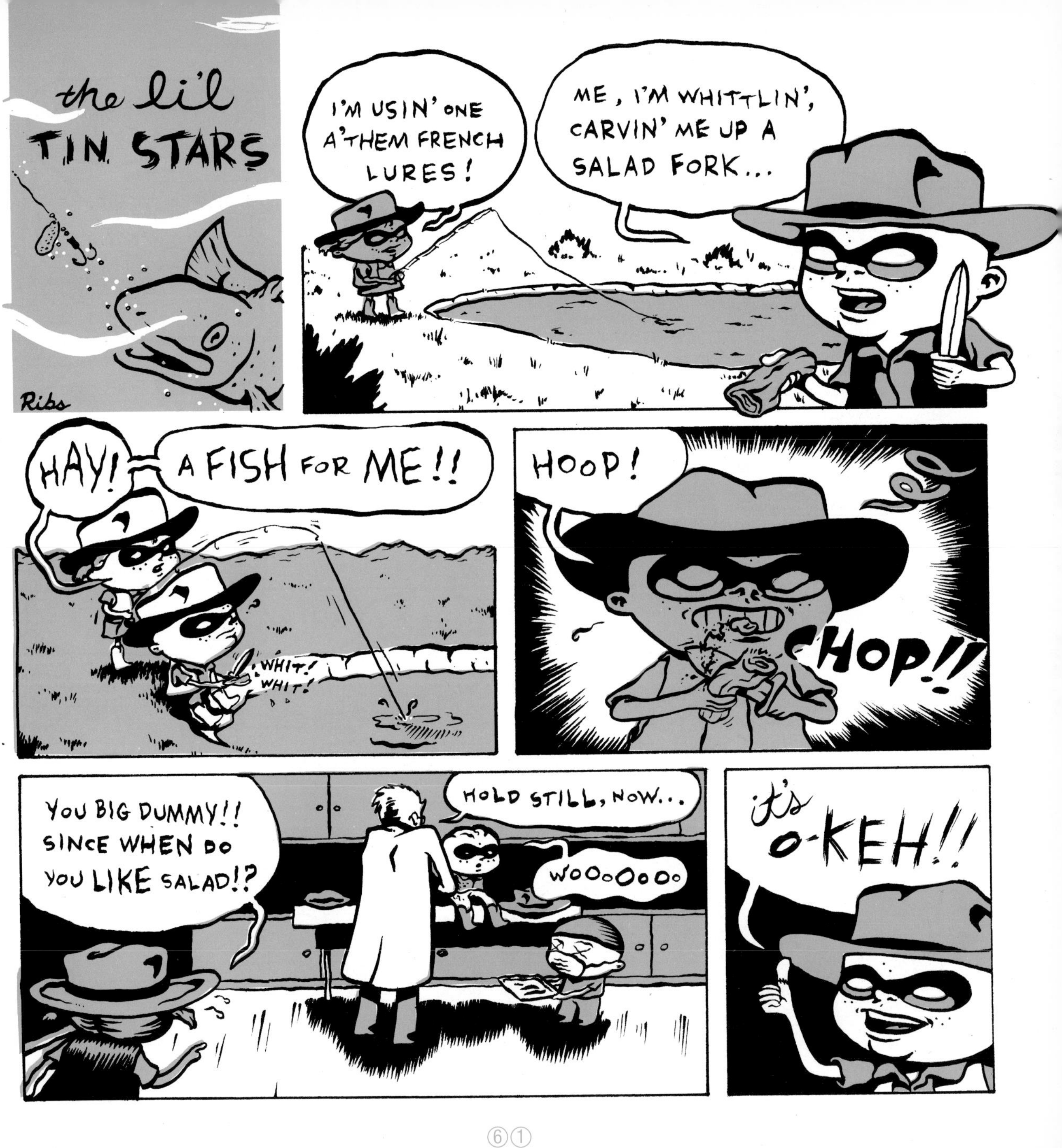
the li'l
TIN STARS
Ribs
I'M USIN' ONE A'THEM FRENCH LURES!
ME, I'M WHITTLIN', CARVIN' ME UP A SALAD FORK...
HAY!
A FISH FOR ME!!
WHIT! WHIT!
HOOP!
CHOP!!
YOU BIG DUMMY!! SINCE WHEN DO YOU LIKE SALAD!?
HOLD STILL, NOW...
WOOoOOOo
it's O-KEH!!

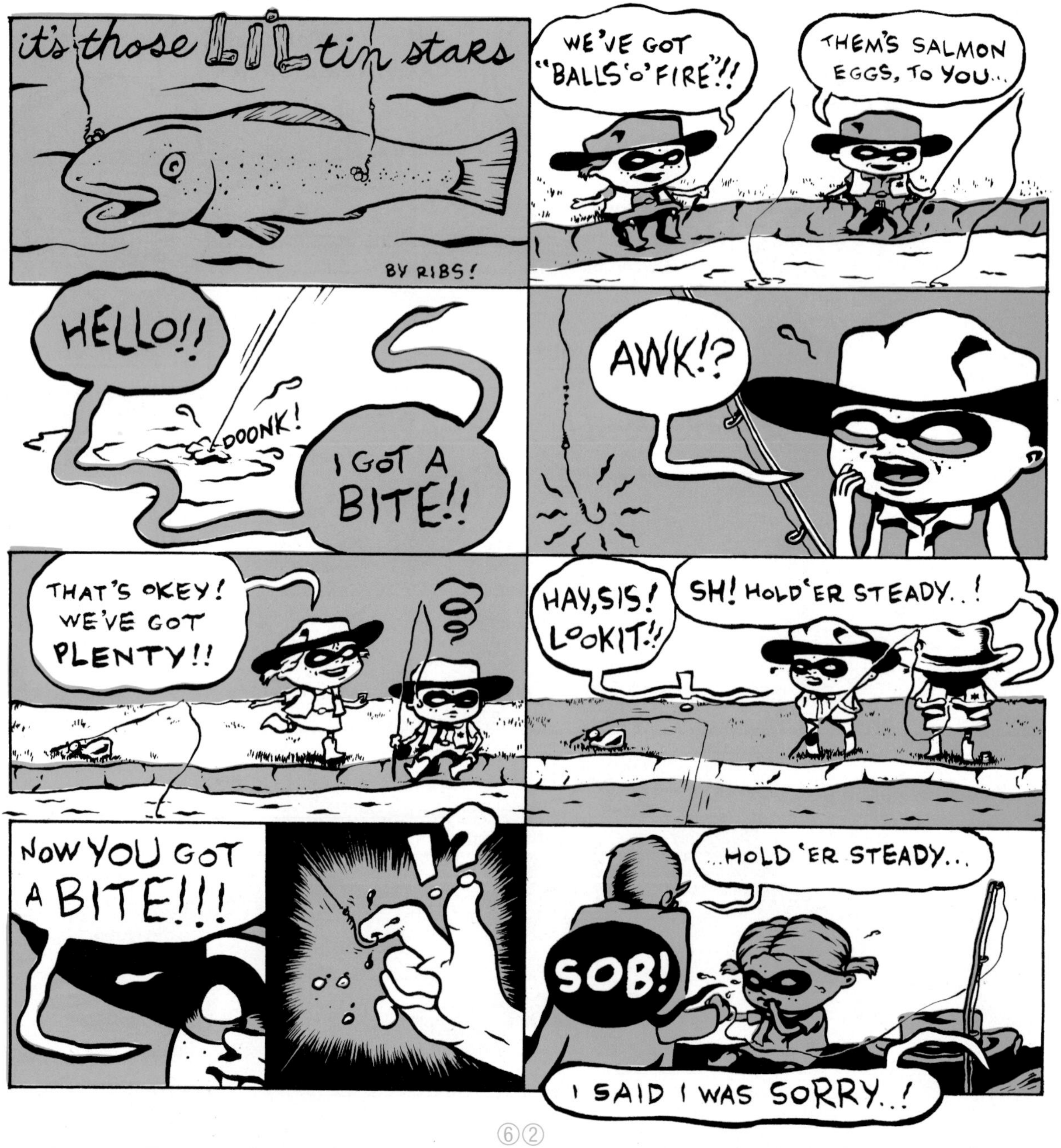
it's those LIL tin stars
BY RIBS!
WE'VE GOT "BALLS 'o' FIRE"!!
THEM'S SALMON EGGS, TO YOU...
HELLO!!
DOONK!
I GOT A BITE!!
AWK!?
THAT'S OKEY! WE'VE GOT PLENTY!!
HAY, SIS! LOOKIT!!
SH! HOLD 'ER STEADY..!
NOW YOU GOT A BITE!!!
!?
...HOLD 'ER STEADY...
SOB!
I SAID I WAS SORRY..!

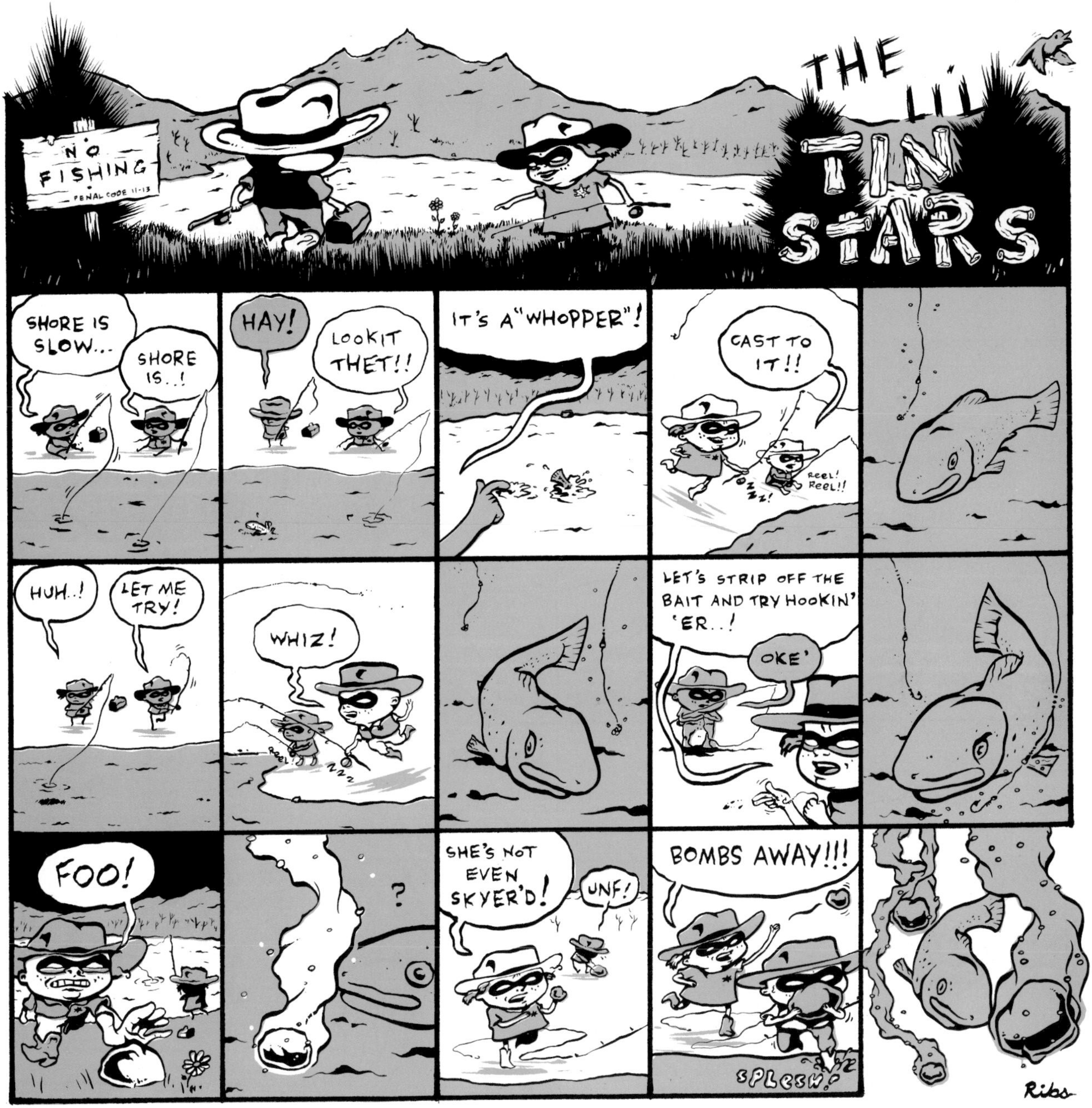
NO FISHING
PENAL CODE 11-13
THE LI'L TIN STARS
SHORE IS SLOW...
SHORE IS..!
HAY!
LOOKIT THET!!
IT'S A "WHOPPER"!
CAST TO IT!!
REEL! REEL!!
HUH..!
LET ME TRY!
WHIZ!
LET'S STRIP OFF THE BAIT AND TRY HOOKIN' 'ER..!
OKE'
FOO!
?
SHE'S NOT EVEN SKYER'D!
UNF!
BOMBS AWAY!!!
SPLESH!
Ribs

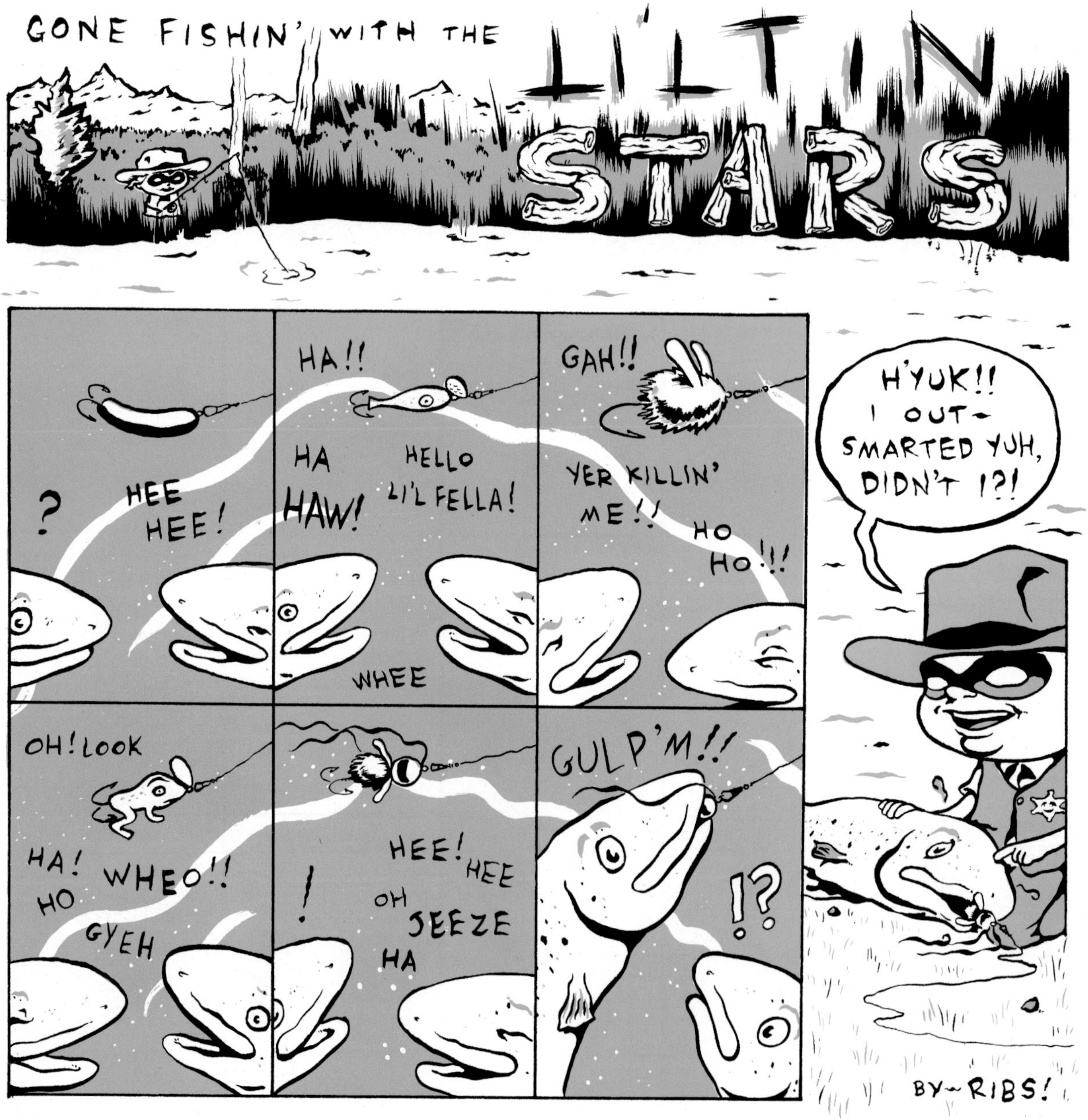
GONE FISHIN' WITH THE LI'L TIN STARS
?
HEE HEE!
HA!!
HA HAW!
HELLO LI'L FELLA!
WHEE
GAH!!
YER KILLIN' ME!!
HO HO!!!
OH! LOOK
HA! HO
WHEO!!
GYEH
!
HEE! HEE
OH JEEZE HA
GULP'M!!
!?
H'YUK!! I OUT-SMARTED YUH, DIDN'T I?!
BY~RIBS!

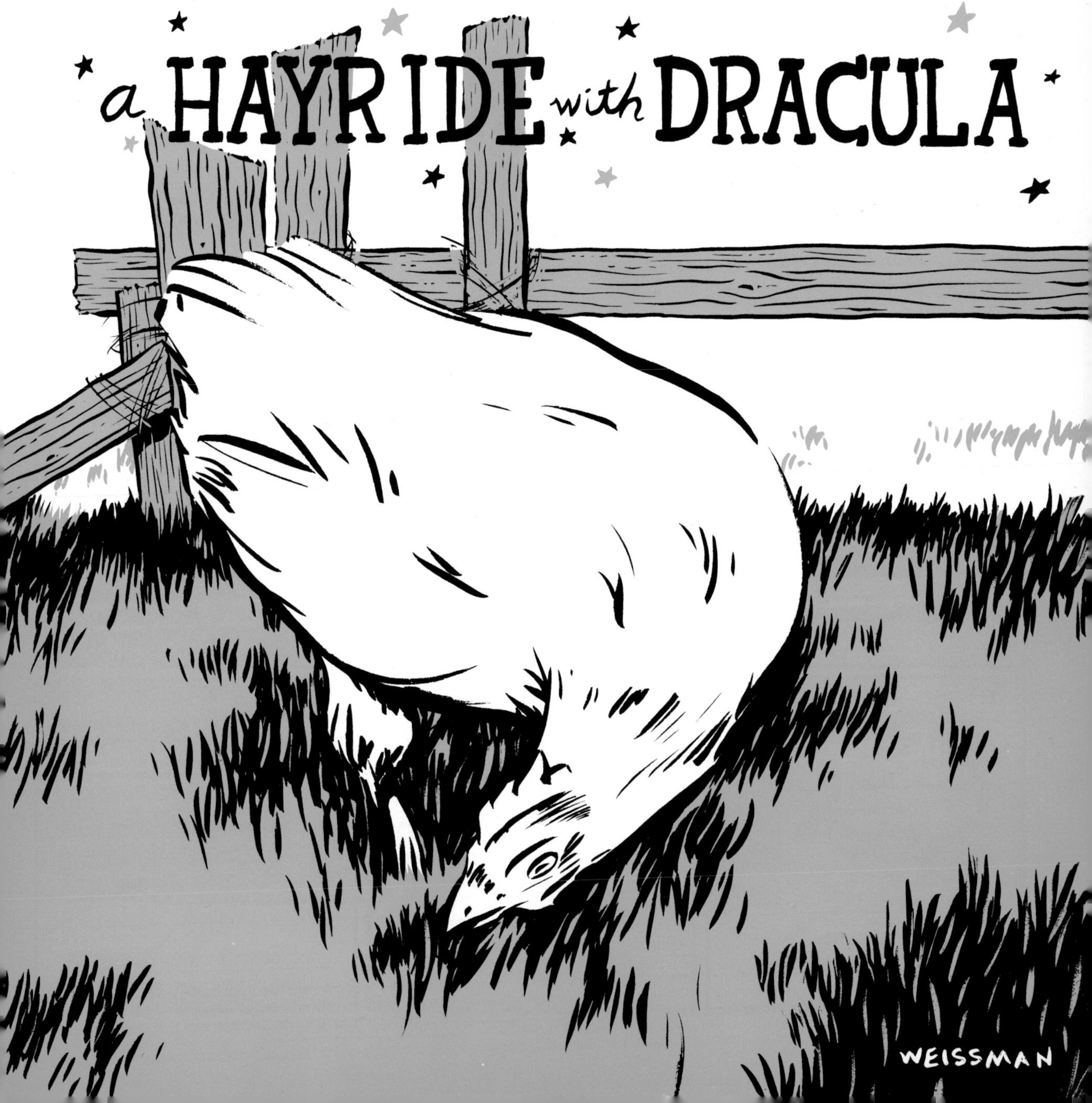
a HAYRIDE with DRACULA
WEISSMAN

ONE DAY

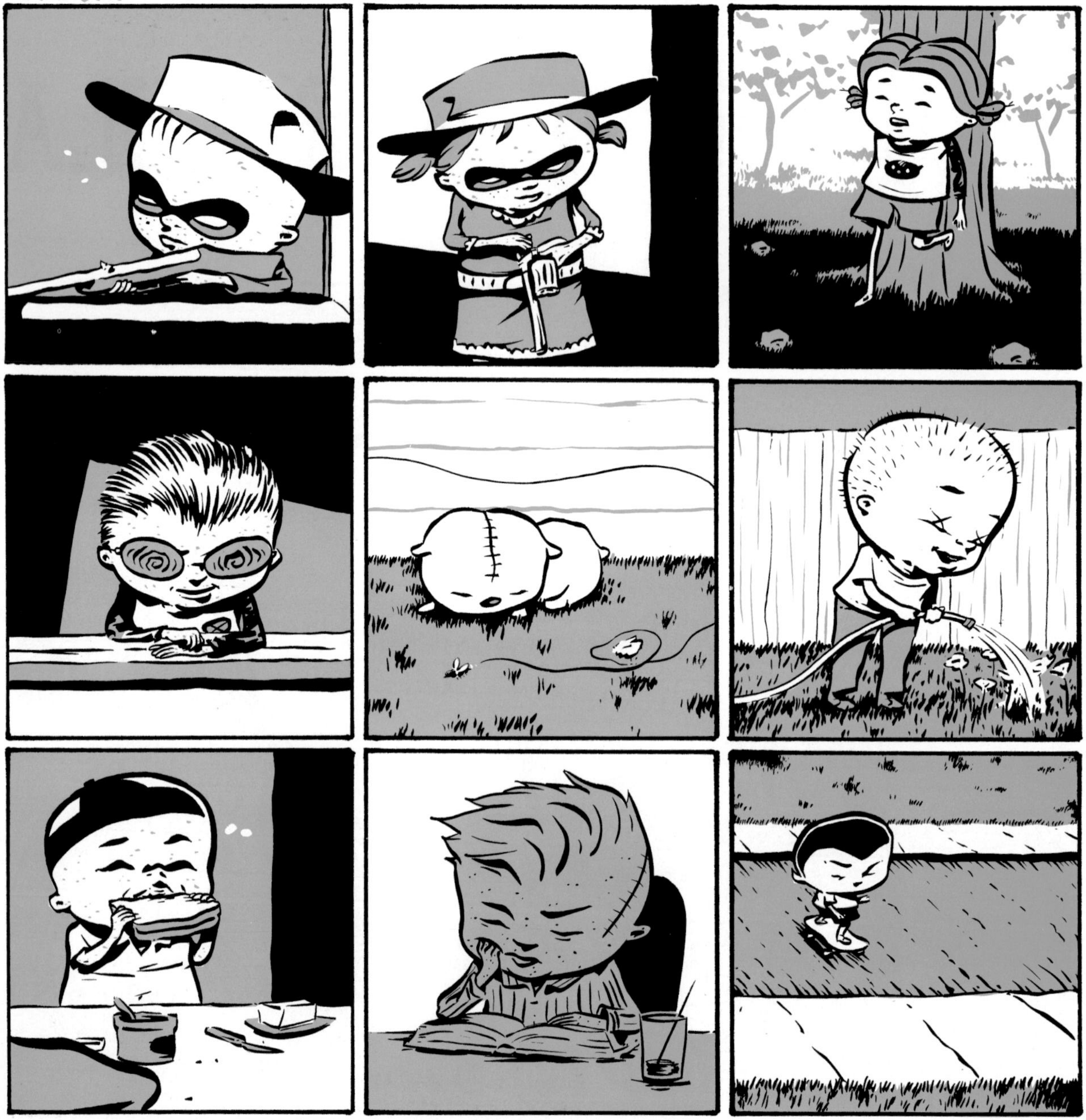

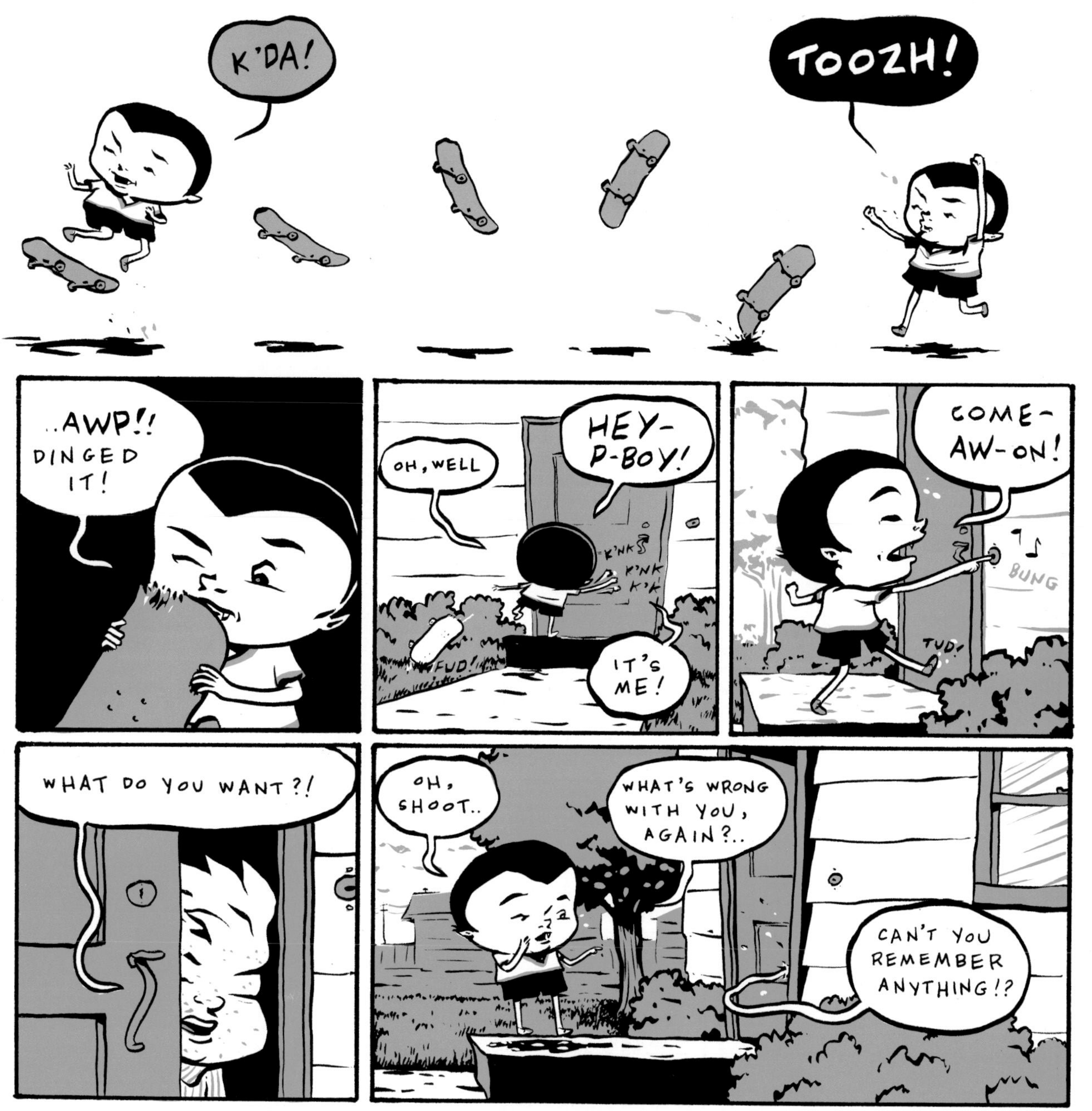
K'DA!
TOOZH!
..AWP!! DINGED IT!
OH, WELL
HEY- P-BOY!
K'NK K'NK K'K
FUD!
IT'S ME!
COME- AW-ON!
BUNG
TUD
WHAT DO YOU WANT?!
OH, SHOOT..
WHAT'S WRONG WITH YOU, AGAIN?..
CAN'T YOU REMEMBER ANYTHING!?

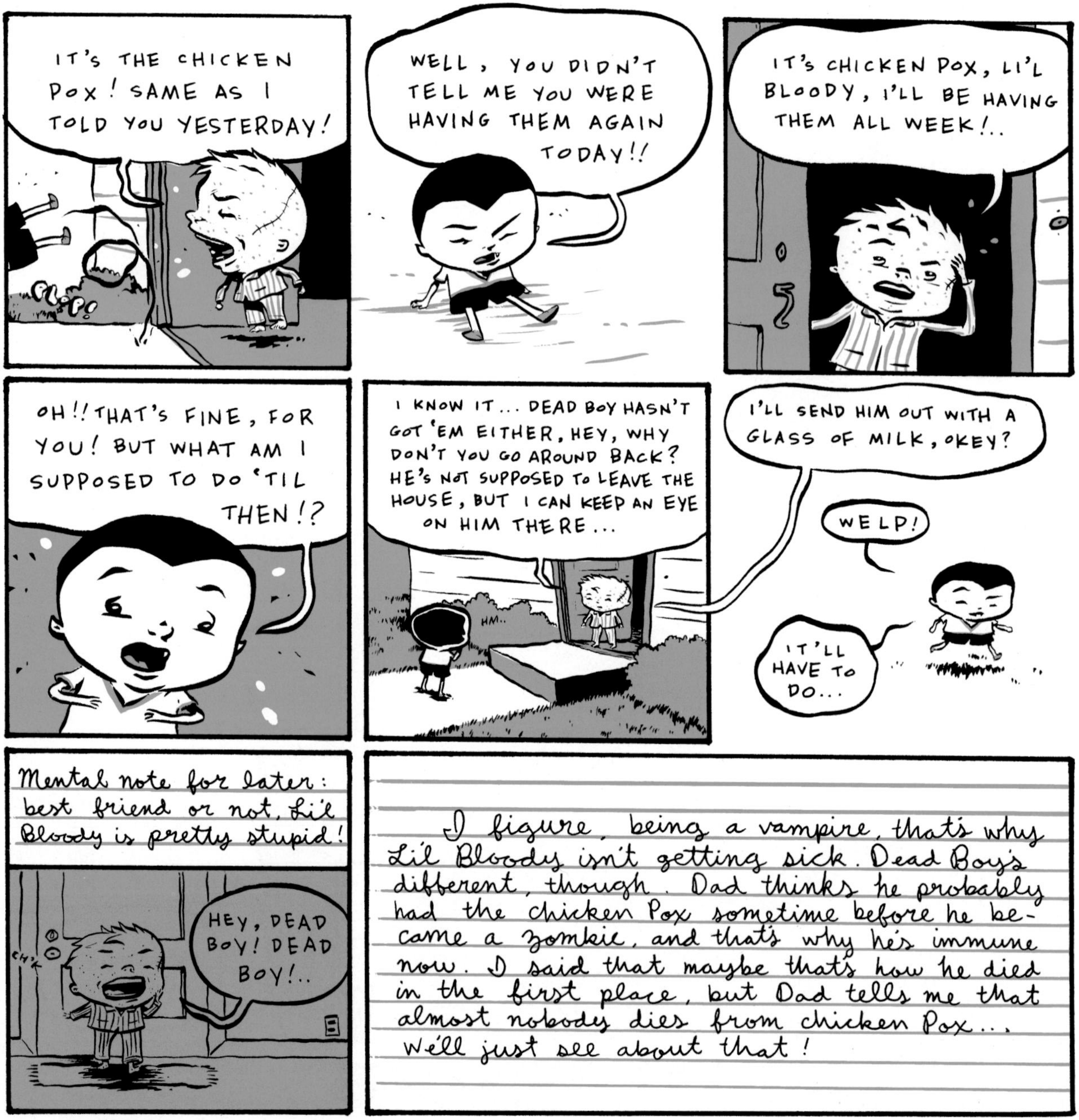
IT'S THE CHICKEN POX! SAME AS I TOLD YOU YESTERDAY!
FLOP!
WELL, YOU DIDN'T TELL ME YOU WERE HAVING THEM AGAIN TODAY!!
IT'S CHICKEN POX, LI'L BLOODY, I'LL BE HAVING THEM ALL WEEK!..
OH!! THAT'S FINE, FOR YOU! BUT WHAT AM I SUPPOSED TO DO 'TIL THEN!?
I KNOW IT... DEAD BOY HASN'T GOT 'EM EITHER, HEY, WHY DON'T YOU GO AROUND BACK? HE'S NOT SUPPOSED TO LEAVE THE HOUSE, BUT I CAN KEEP AN EYE ON HIM THERE...
HM..
I'LL SEND HIM OUT WITH A GLASS OF MILK, OKEY?
WELP!
IT'LL HAVE TO DO...
Mental note for later: best friend or not, Li'l Bloody is pretty stupid!
CHK
HEY, DEAD BOY! DEAD BOY!..
I figure, being a vampire, that's why Li'l Bloody isn't getting sick. Dead Boy's different, though. Dad thinks he probably had the chicken Pox sometime before he became a zombie, and that's why he's immune now. I said that maybe that's how he died in the first place, but Dad tells me that almost nobody dies from chicken Pox... We'll just see about that!

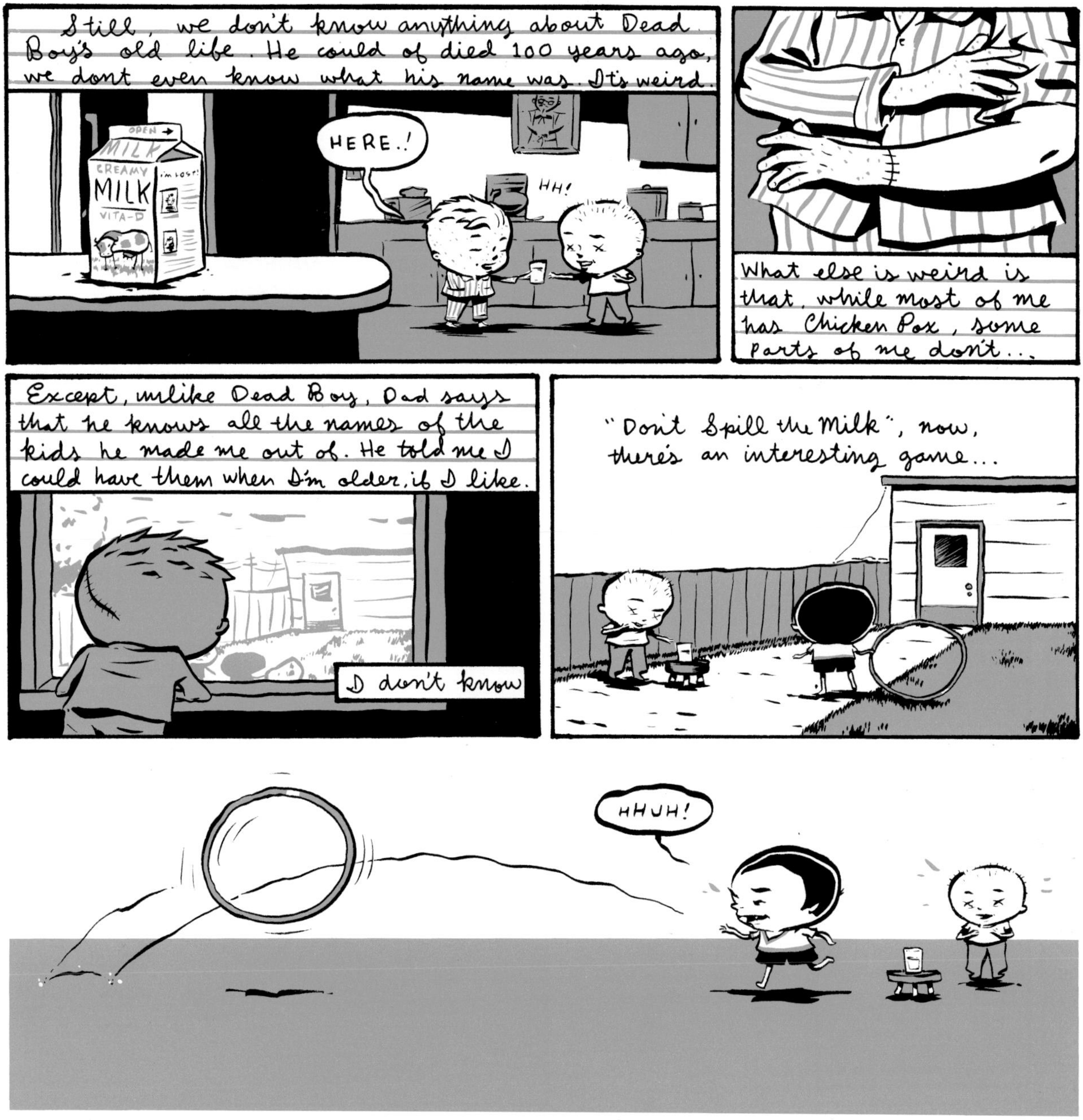
Still, we don't know anything about Dead Boy's old life. He could of died 100 years ago, we dont even know what his name was. It's weird.
OPEN →
MILK
CREAMY
MILK
VITA-D
I'm LOST!
HERE.!
HH!
What else is weird is that, while most of me has Chicken Pox, some Parts of me don't...
Except, unlike Dead Boy, Dad says that he knows all the names of the kids he made me out of. He told me I could have them when I'm older, if I like.
I don't know
"Don't Spill the Milk", now, there's an interesting game...
HHUH!

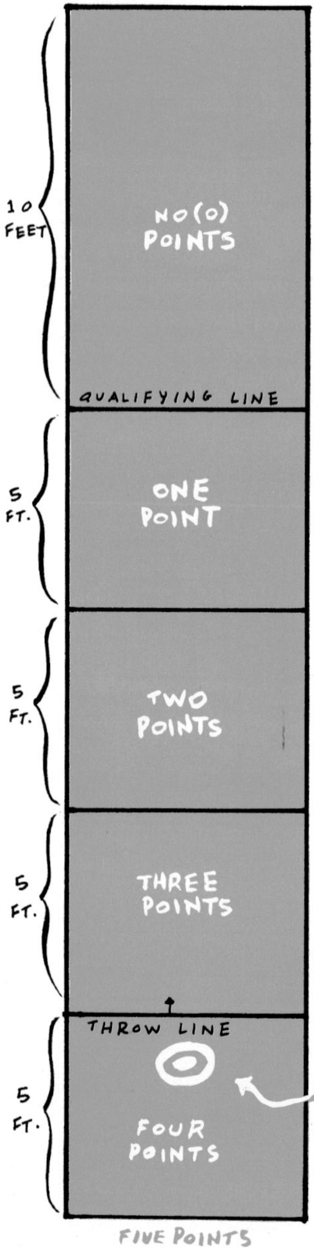

10 FEET
NO (0) POINTS
QUALIFYING LINE
5 FT.
ONE POINT
5 FT.
TWO POINTS
5 FT.
THREE POINTS
THROW LINE
5 FT.
FOUR POINTS
FIVE POINTS

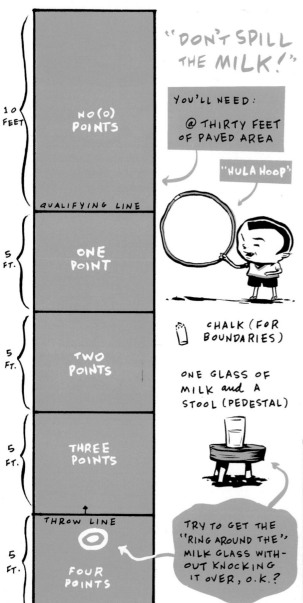

"DON'T SPILL THE MILK!"

YOU'LL NEED:

@ THIRTY FEET OF PAVED AREA

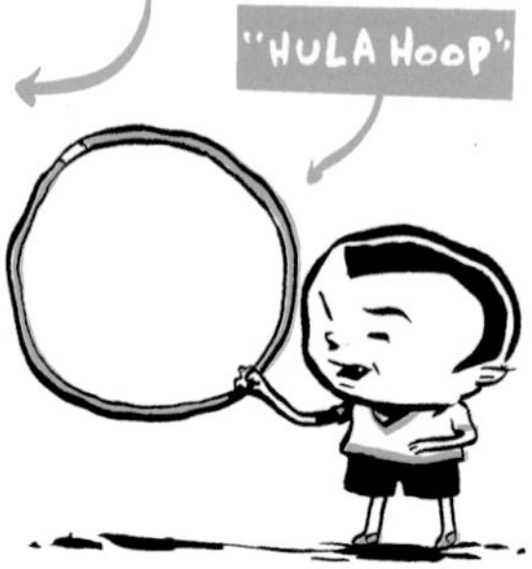

"HULA HOOP"

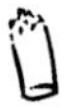

CHALK (FOR BOUNDARIES)

ONE GLASS OF MILK *and* A STOOL (PEDESTAL)

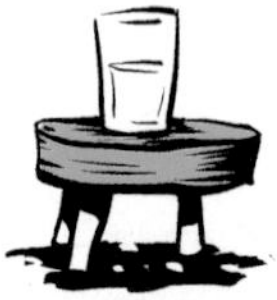

TRY TO GET THE "RING AROUND THE" MILK GLASS WITHOUT KNOCKING IT OVER, O.K.?

OBJECT OF PLAY: "DON'T SPILL THE MILK" IS A CHALLENGING GAME OF SKILL - AND NERVE - FOR TWO OR MORE PLAYERS. PARTICIPANTS TAKE TURNS THROWING A "HULA HOOP" FROM THE THROW-LINE OVER THE QUALIFYING LINE. THE HOOP IS THROWN WITH AN UNDER-HANDED TECHNIQUE, WITH ENOUGH BACKSPIN TO (HOPEFULLY) RETURN IT TO THE THROW LINE, AND BEYOND. POINTS ARE AWARDED BASED ON WHERE THE HOOP LANDS, WITH MOST GAMES BEING PLAYED UP TO FIFTY (50) POINTS. GAMES CAN BE WON OR LOST ON ONE THROW, HOWEVER, WHEN THE HOOP COMES INTO CONTACT WITH THE GLASS OF MILK, AND/OR IT'S PEDESTAL. SHOULD THE THROWER "RING" THE GLASS OF MILK, WITHOUT KNOCKING IT OVER, THE GAME IS WON AND THE THROWER MAY SELECT AN OPPONENT (IF THERE IS MORE THAN ONE) TO DRAIN THE CUP (IN ONE GULP, EVEN!). IF, HOWEVER, THE GLASS IS SPILLED, THE GAME IS LOST, AND THE LOSING THROWER TAKES THE BLAME! SHOULD THE HOOP COME INTO CONTACT WITH THE GLASS (OR PEDESTAL) WITHOUT INCIDENT, THE THROWER IS AWARDED TEN (10) POINTS.

RULES: 1) HOOP MUST BE THROWN FROM BEHIND THROW-LINE.
2) ALL THROWS MUST CROSS QUALIFYING-LINE.

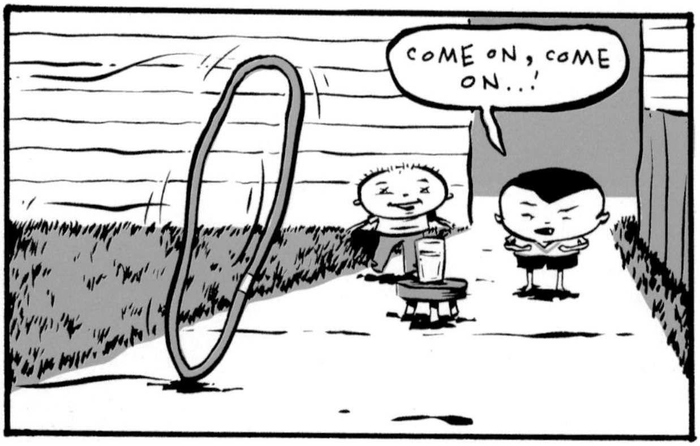

COME ON, COME ON...!

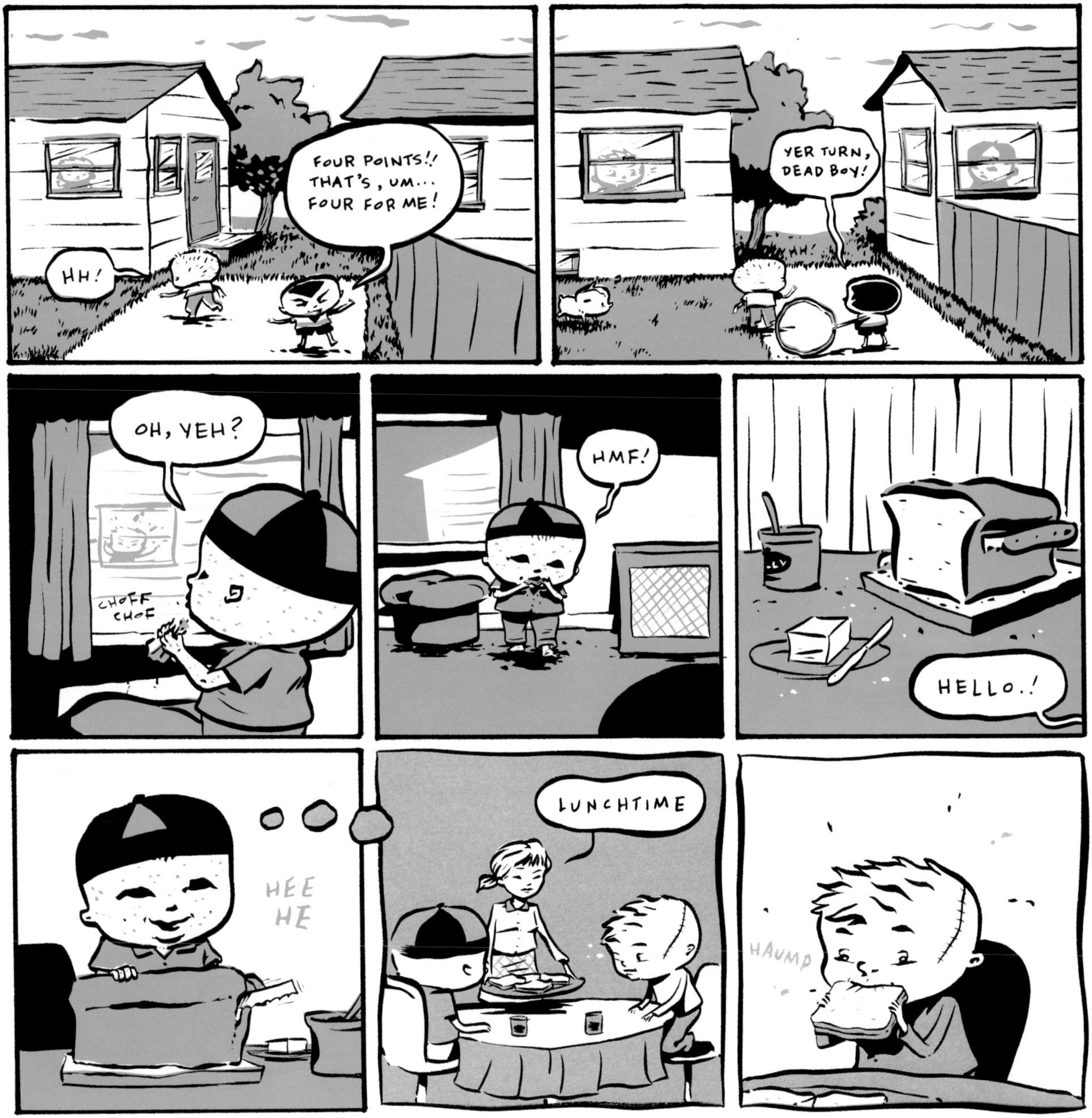
HH!
FOUR POINTS!!
THAT'S, UM...
FOUR FOR ME!
YER TURN,
DEAD BOY!
OH, YEH?
CHOFF
CHOF
HMF!
HELLO..!
HEE
HE
LUNCHTIME
HAUMP

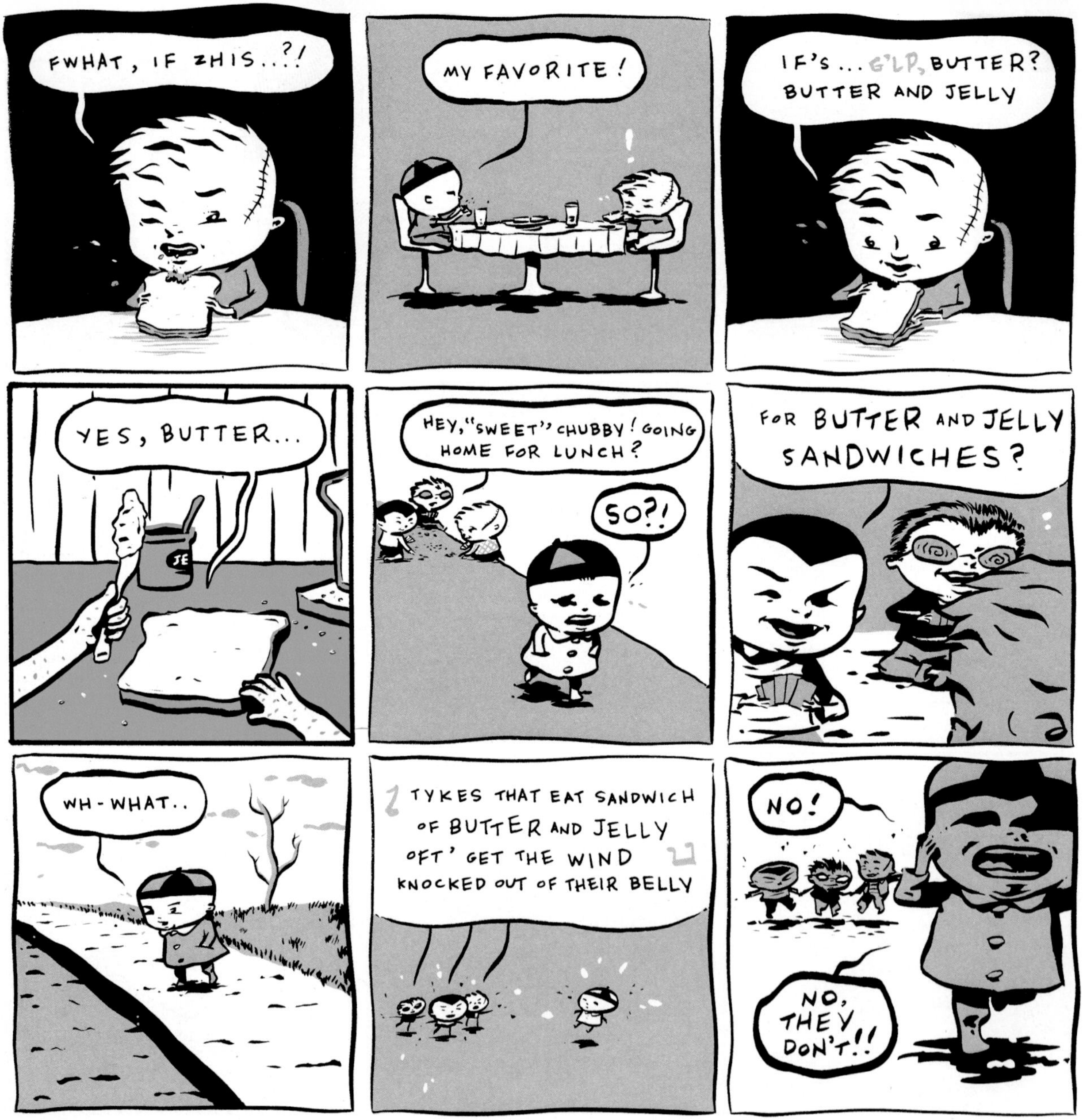
FWHAT, IF ZHIS...?!
MY FAVORITE!
IF'S... G'LP, BUTTER? BUTTER AND JELLY
YES, BUTTER...
HEY, "SWEET" CHUBBY! GOING HOME FOR LUNCH?
SO?!
FOR BUTTER AND JELLY SANDWICHES?
WH-WHAT..
TYKES THAT EAT SANDWICH OF BUTTER AND JELLY OFT' GET THE WIND KNOCKED OUT OF THEIR BELLY
NO!
NO, THEY DON'T!!

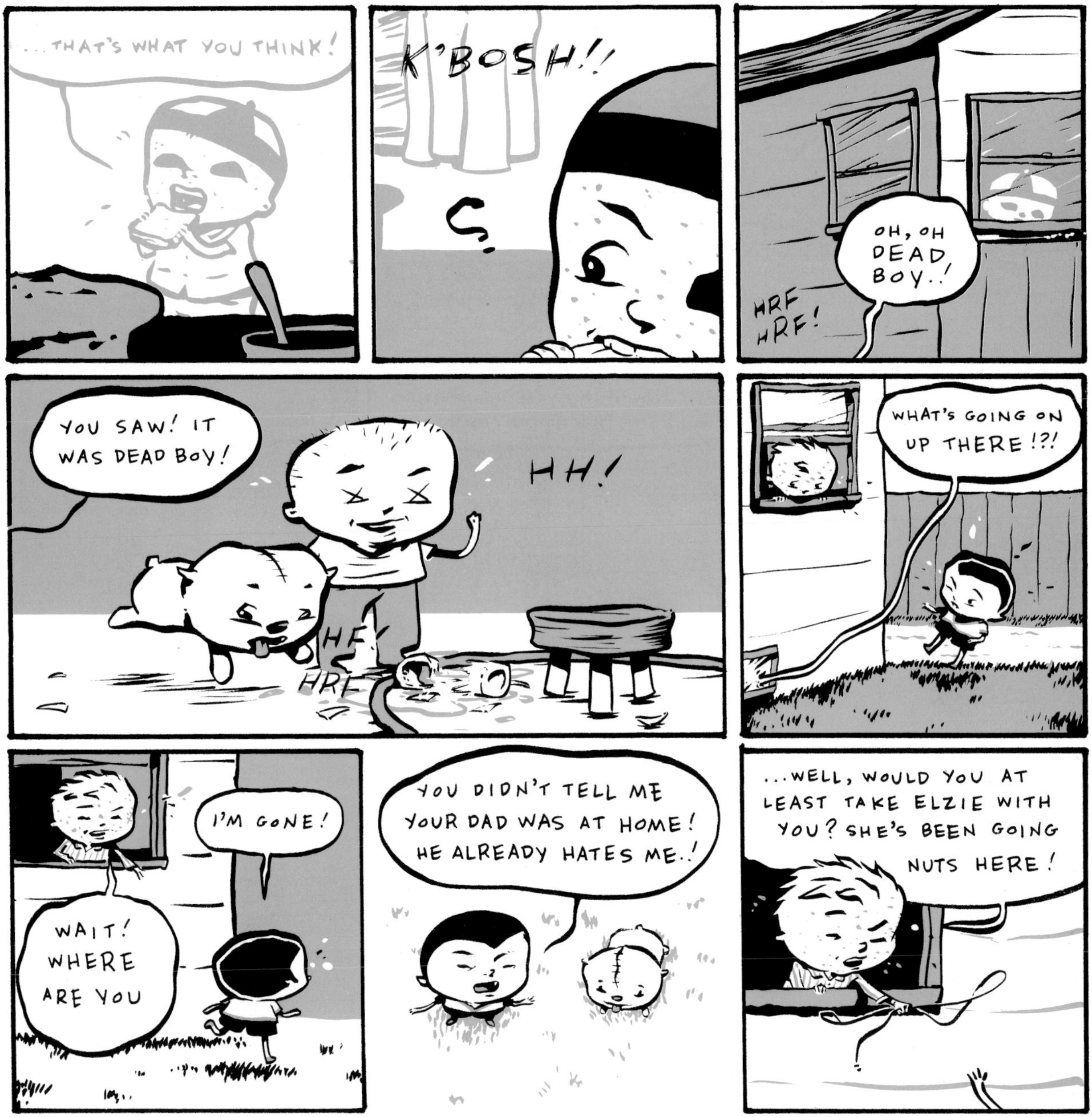
...THAT'S WHAT YOU THINK!
K'BOSH!!
OH, OH DEAD BOY..!
HRF HRF!
YOU SAW! IT WAS DEAD BOY!
HH!
HF HRF
WHAT'S GOING ON UP THERE!?!
I'M GONE!
WAIT! WHERE ARE YOU
YOU DIDN'T TELL ME YOUR DAD WAS AT HOME! HE ALREADY HATES ME..!
...WELL, WOULD YOU AT LEAST TAKE ELZIE WITH YOU? SHE'S BEEN GOING NUTS HERE!

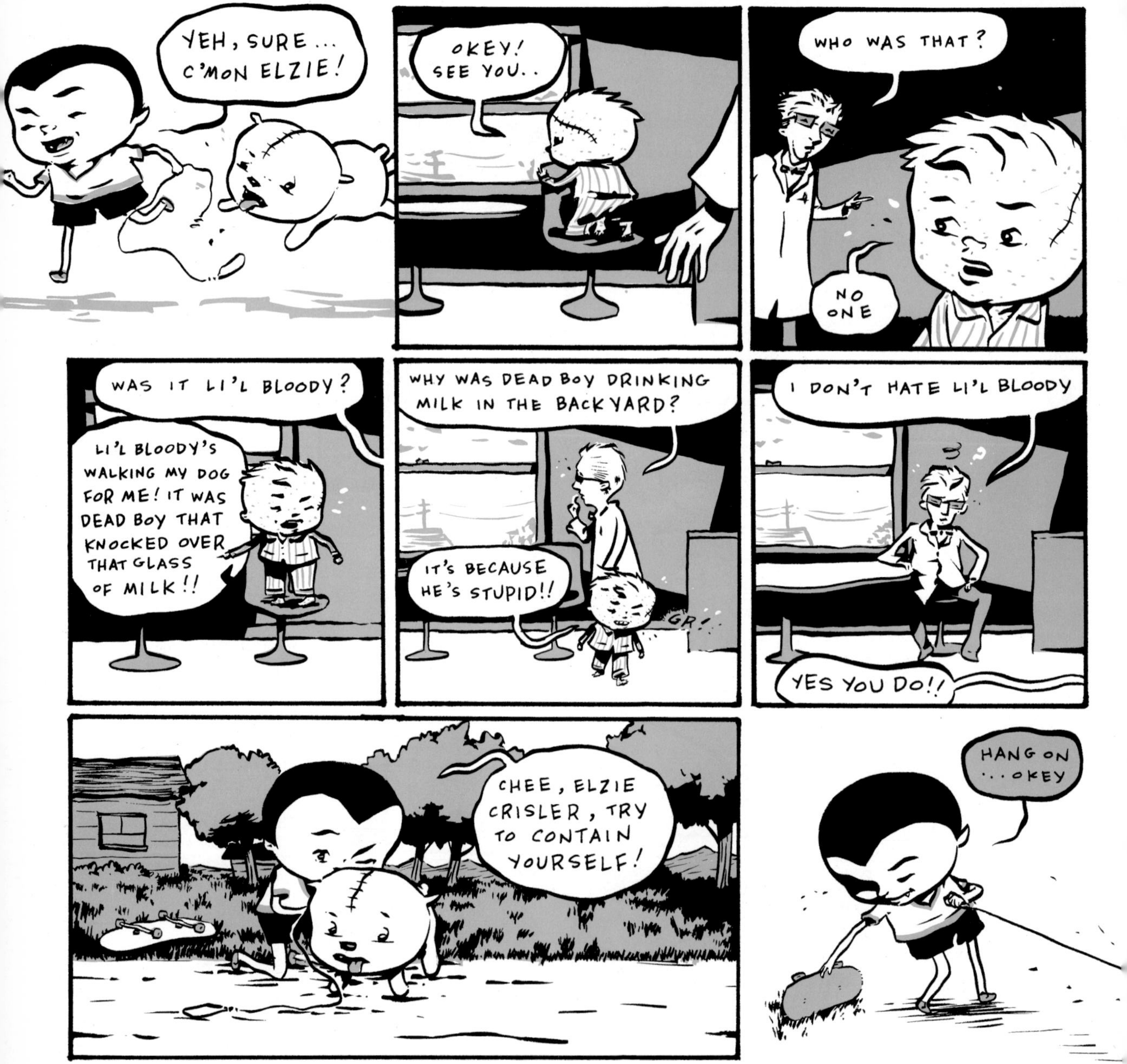
YEH, SURE... C'MON ELZIE!
OKEY! SEE YOU..
WHO WAS THAT?
NO ONE
WAS IT LI'L BLOODY?
LI'L BLOODY'S WALKING MY DOG FOR ME! IT WAS DEAD BOY THAT KNOCKED OVER THAT GLASS OF MILK!!
WHY WAS DEAD BOY DRINKING MILK IN THE BACKYARD?
IT'S BECAUSE HE'S STUPID!!
GR!
I DON'T HATE LI'L BLOODY
YES YOU DO!!
CHEE, ELZIE CRISLER, TRY TO CONTAIN YOURSELF!
HANG ON ...OKEY

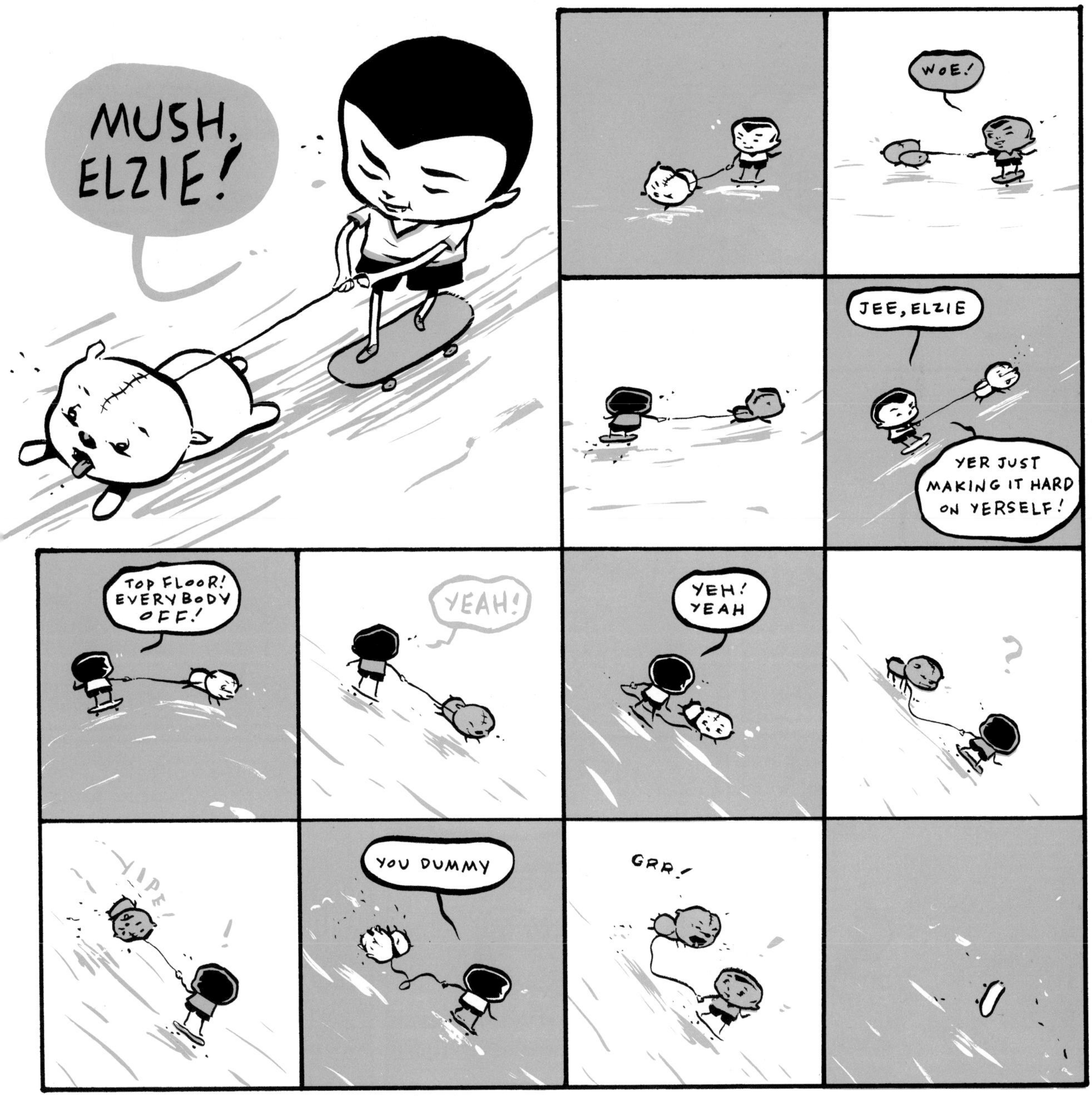
MUSH, ELZIE!
WOE!
JEE, ELZIE
YER JUST MAKING IT HARD ON YERSELF!
TOP FLOOR! EVERYBODY OFF!
YEAH!
YEH! YEAH
?
YIPE!
!
YOU DUMMY
GRR!

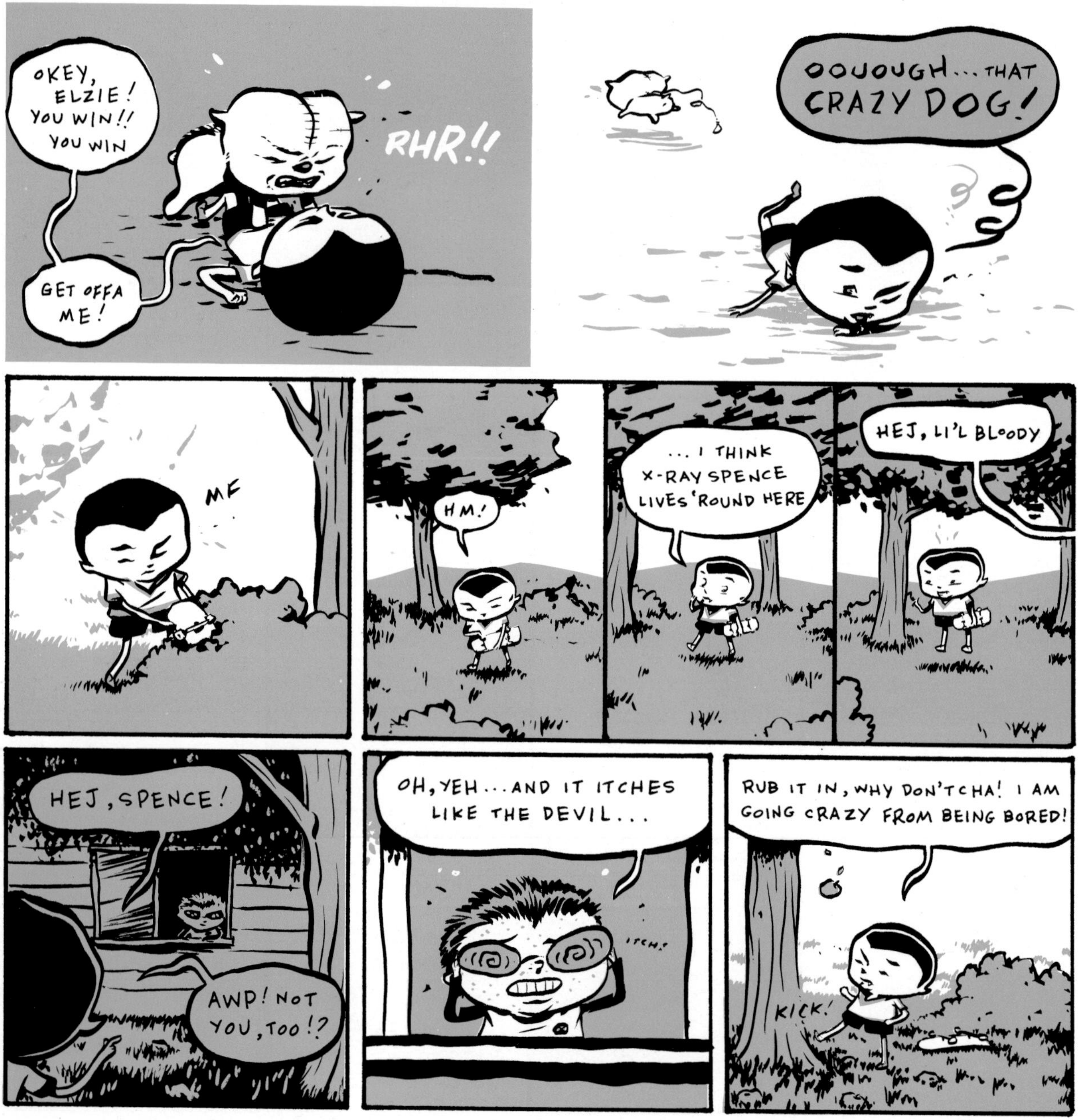
OKEY, ELZIE! YOU WIN!! YOU WIN
GET OFFA ME!
RHR!!
OOUOUGH... THAT CRAZY DOG!
MF
HM!
... I THINK X-RAY SPENCE LIVES 'ROUND HERE
HEJ, LI'L BLOODY
HEJ, SPENCE!
AWP! NOT YOU, TOO!?
OH, YEH... AND IT ITCHES LIKE THE DEVIL...
ITCH!
RUB IT IN, WHY DON'TCHA! I AM GOING CRAZY FROM BEING BORED!
KICK!

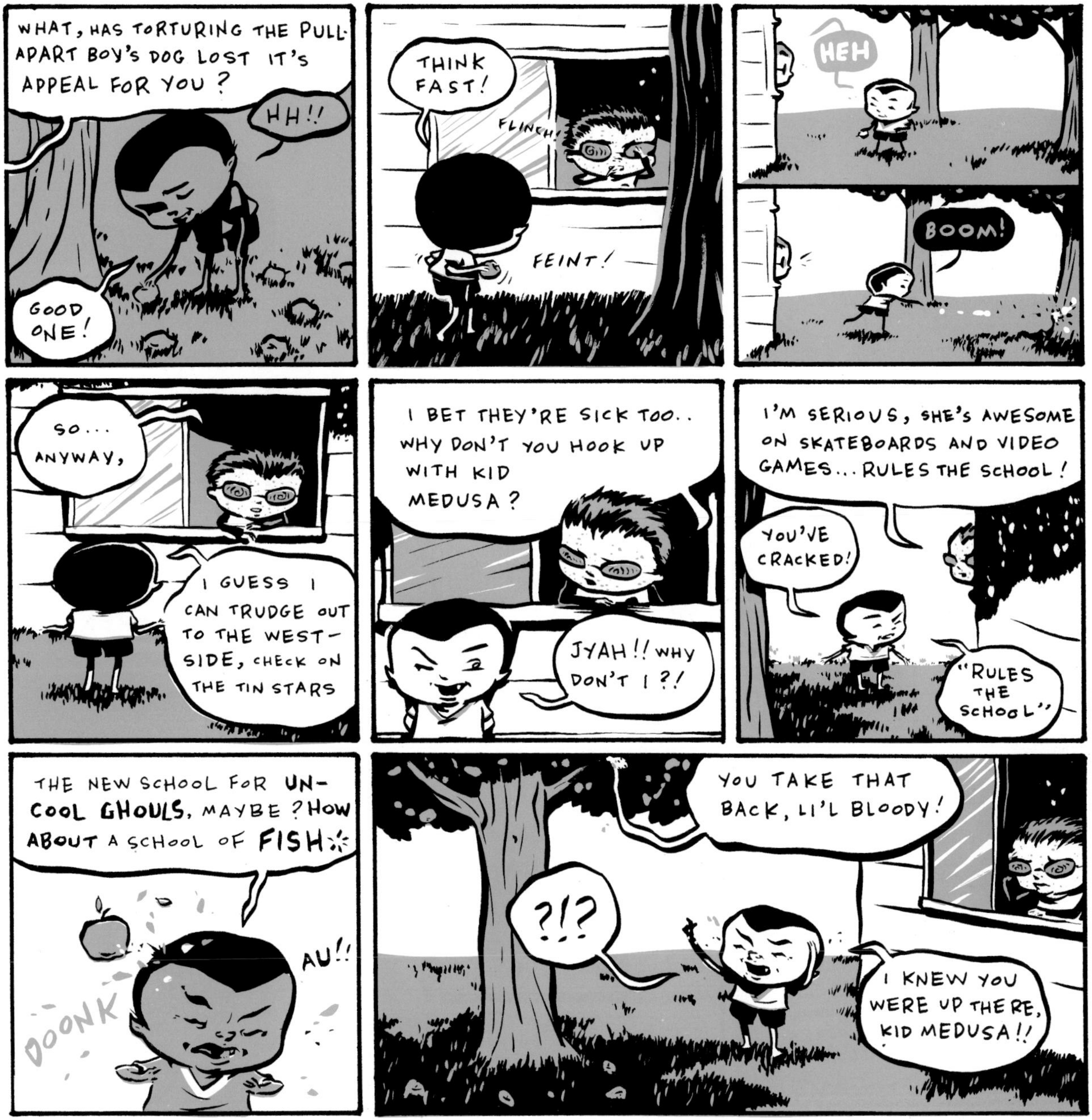
WHAT, HAS TORTURING THE PULL-APART BOY'S DOG LOST IT'S APPEAL FOR YOU ?
HH!!
GOOD ONE!
THINK FAST!
FLINCH!
FEINT!
HEH
BOOM!
SO... ANYWAY,
I GUESS I CAN TRUDGE OUT TO THE WEST-SIDE, CHECK ON THE TIN STARS
I BET THEY'RE SICK TOO.. WHY DON'T YOU HOOK UP WITH KID MEDUSA ?
JYAH!! WHY DON'T I ?!
I'M SERIOUS, SHE'S AWESOME ON SKATEBOARDS AND VIDEO GAMES... RULES THE SCHOOL !
YOU'VE CRACKED!
"RULES THE SCHOOL"
THE NEW SCHOOL FOR UN-COOL GHOULS, MAYBE ? HOW ABOUT A SCHOOL OF FISH
AU!!
DOONK
YOU TAKE THAT BACK, LI'L BLOODY!
?!?
I KNEW YOU WERE UP THERE, KID MEDUSA!!

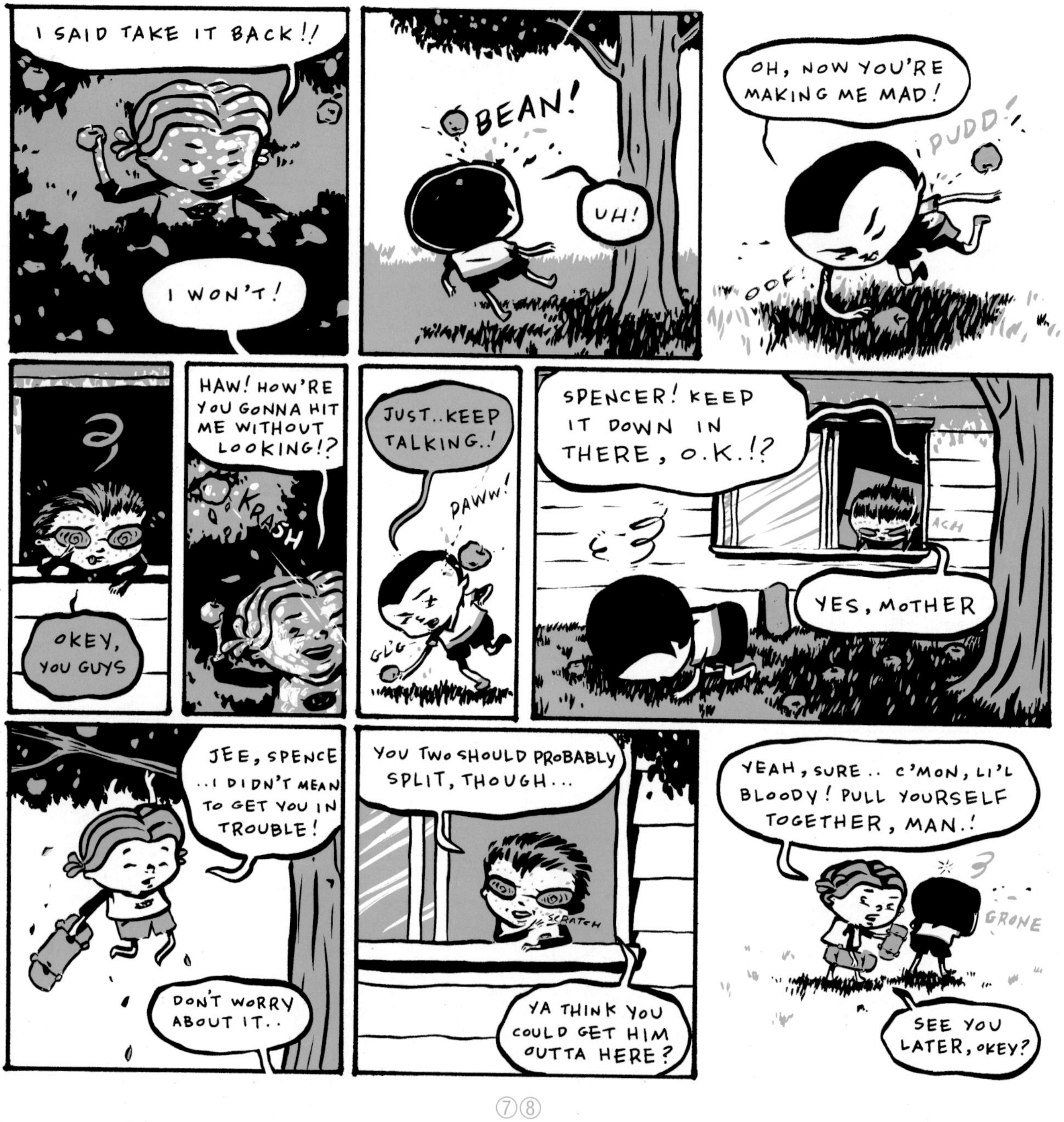
I SAID TAKE IT BACK!!
I WON'T!
BEAN!
UH!
OH, NOW YOU'RE MAKING ME MAD!
PUDD
OOF
OKEY, YOU GUYS
HAW! HOW'RE YOU GONNA HIT ME WITHOUT LOOKING!?
KRASH
JUST..KEEP TALKING..!
PAWW!
SPENCER! KEEP IT DOWN IN THERE, O.K.!?
ACH
YES, MOTHER
JEE, SPENCE ..I DIDN'T MEAN TO GET YOU IN TROUBLE!
DON'T WORRY ABOUT IT..
YOU TWO SHOULD PROBABLY SPLIT, THOUGH...
SCRATCH
YA THINK YOU COULD GET HIM OUTTA HERE?
YEAH, SURE.. C'MON, LI'L BLOODY! PULL YOURSELF TOGETHER, MAN.!
GRONE
SEE YOU LATER, OKEY?

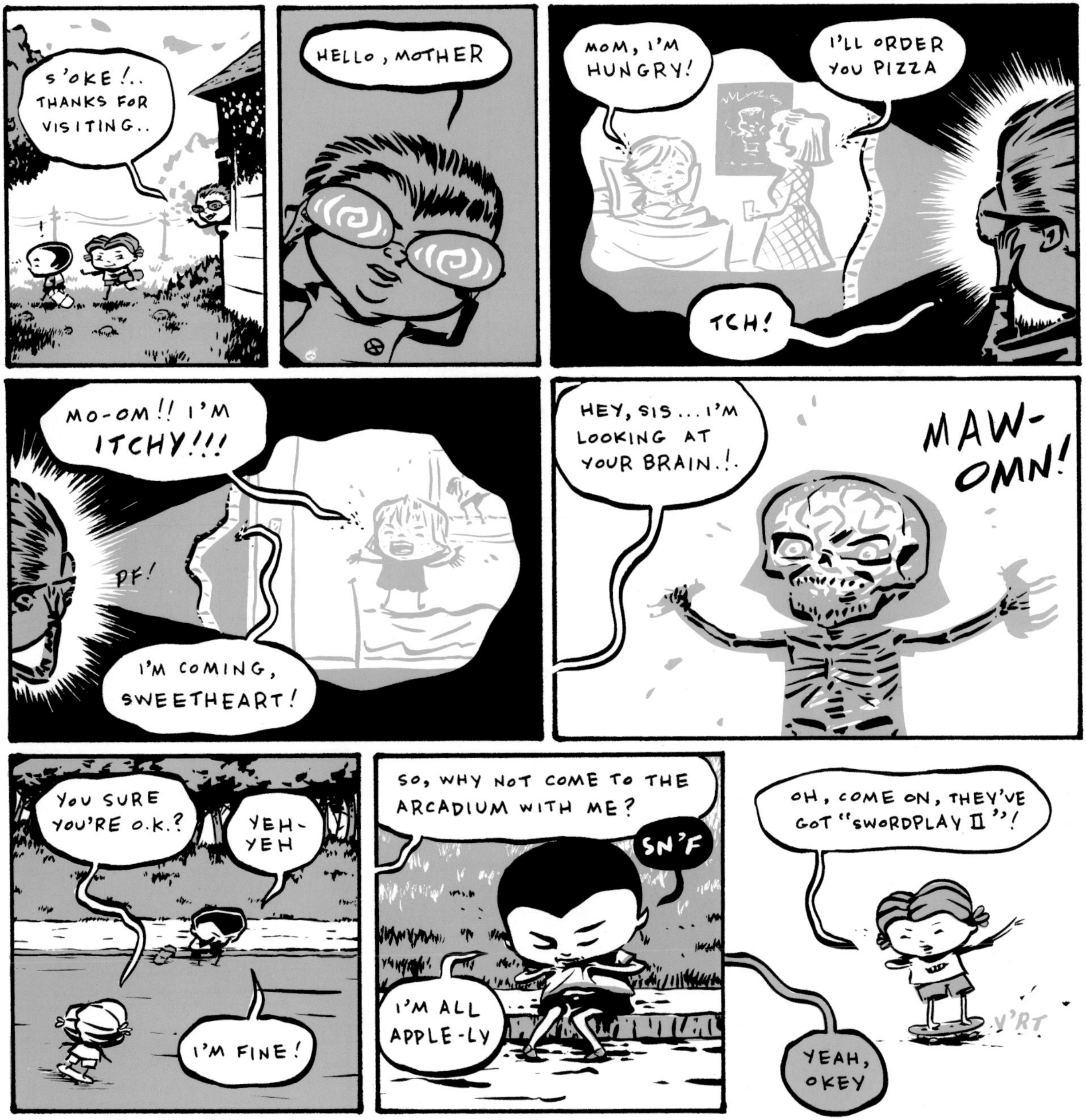
S'OKE!..
THANKS FOR VISITING..
HELLO, MOTHER
MOM, I'M HUNGRY!
I'LL ORDER YOU PIZZA
TCH!
MO-OM!! I'M ITCHY!!!
PF!
I'M COMING, SWEETHEART!
HEY, SIS... I'M LOOKING AT YOUR BRAIN.!.
MAW-OMN!
YOU SURE YOU'RE O.K.?
YEH-YEH
I'M FINE!
SO, WHY NOT COME TO THE ARCADIUM WITH ME?
SN'F
I'M ALL APPLE-LY
OH, COME ON, THEY'VE GOT "SWORDPLAY II"!
YEAH, OKEY
V'RT

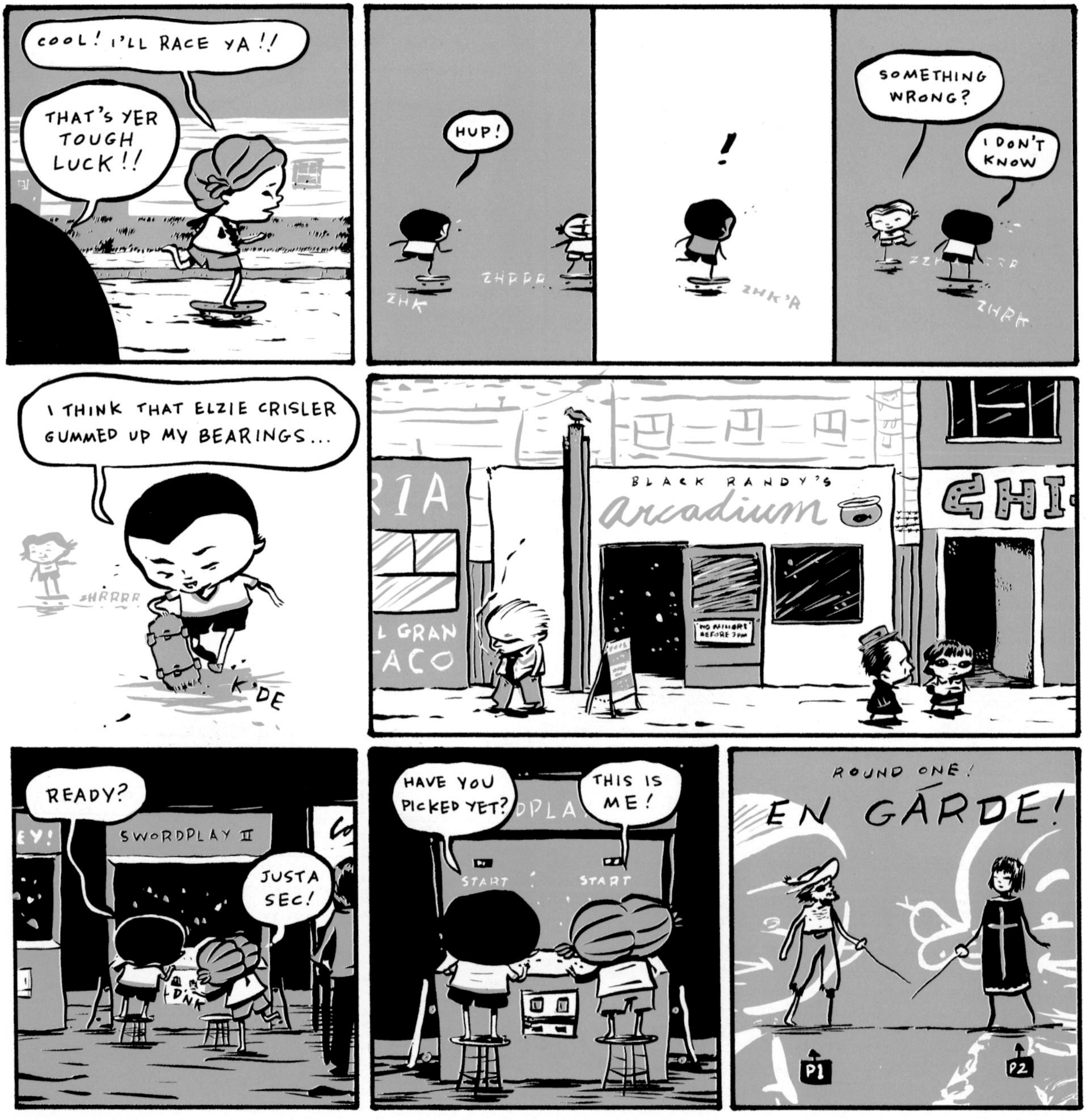
COOL! I'LL RACE YA!!
THAT'S YER TOUGH LUCK!!
HUP!
ZHK
ZHRRR
!
ZHK'R
SOMETHING WRONG?
I DON'T KNOW
ZHRK
I THINK THAT ELZIE CRISLER GUMMED UP MY BEARINGS...
ZHRRRR
K'DE
RIA
L GRAN
TACO
BLACK RANDY'S
arcadium
"NO MINORS" BEFORE 3PM
GHI
READY?
SWORDPLAY II
JUSTA SEC!
DNK
HAVE YOU PICKED YET?
THIS IS ME!
START
START
ROUND ONE!
EN GARDE!
P1
P2

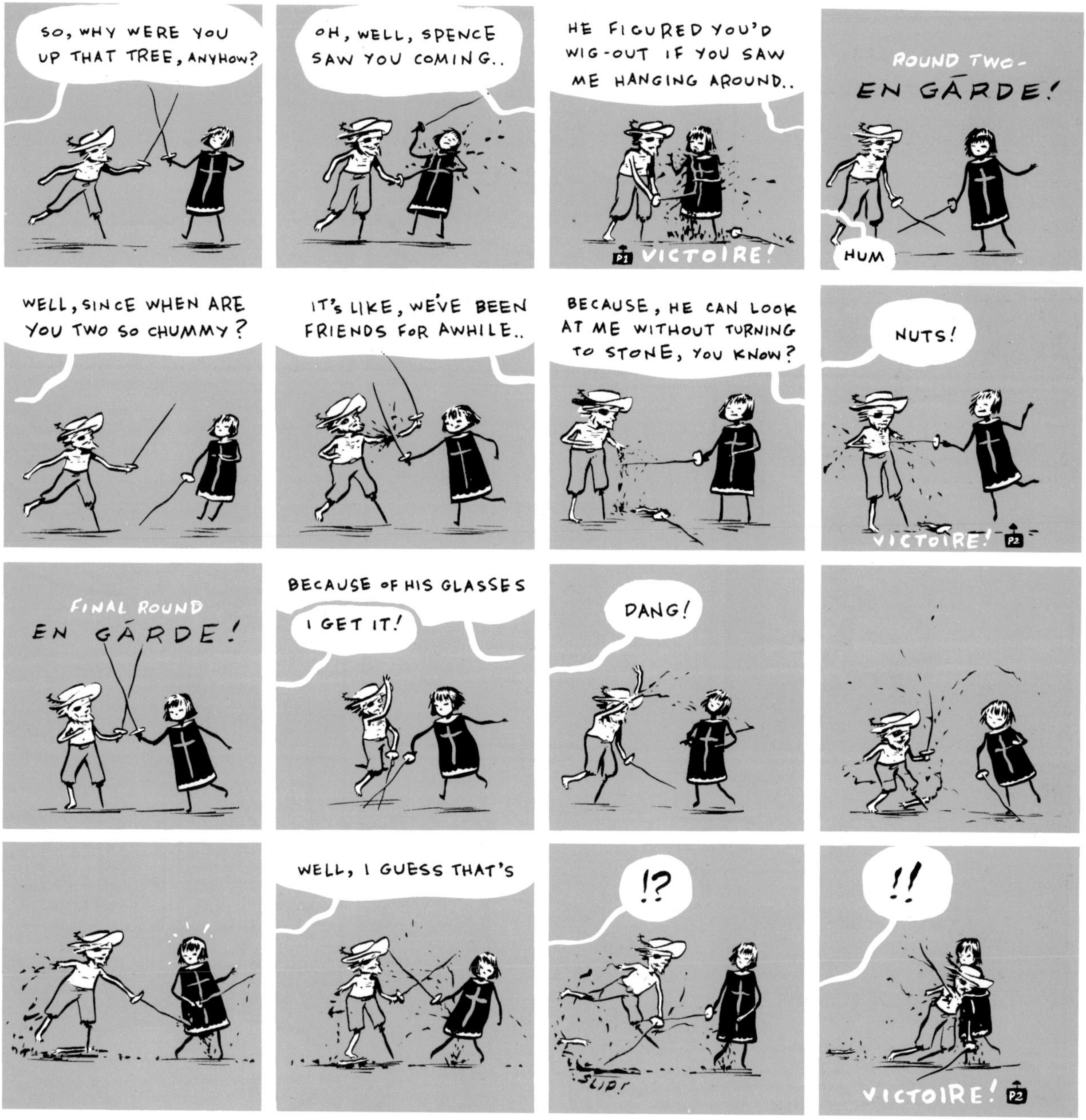
SO, WHY WERE YOU UP THAT TREE, ANYHOW?
OH, WELL, SPENCE SAW YOU COMING..
HE FIGURED YOU'D WIG-OUT IF YOU SAW ME HANGING AROUND..
P2 VICTOIRE!
ROUND TWO-
EN GÁRDE!
HUM
WELL, SINCE WHEN ARE YOU TWO SO CHUMMY?
IT'S LIKE, WE'VE BEEN FRIENDS FOR AWHILE..
BECAUSE, HE CAN LOOK AT ME WITHOUT TURNING TO STONE, YOU KNOW?
NUTS!
VICTOIRE! P2
FINAL ROUND
EN GÁRDE!
BECAUSE OF HIS GLASSES
I GET IT!
DANG!
WELL, I GUESS THAT'S
!?
SLIP!
!!
VICTOIRE! P2

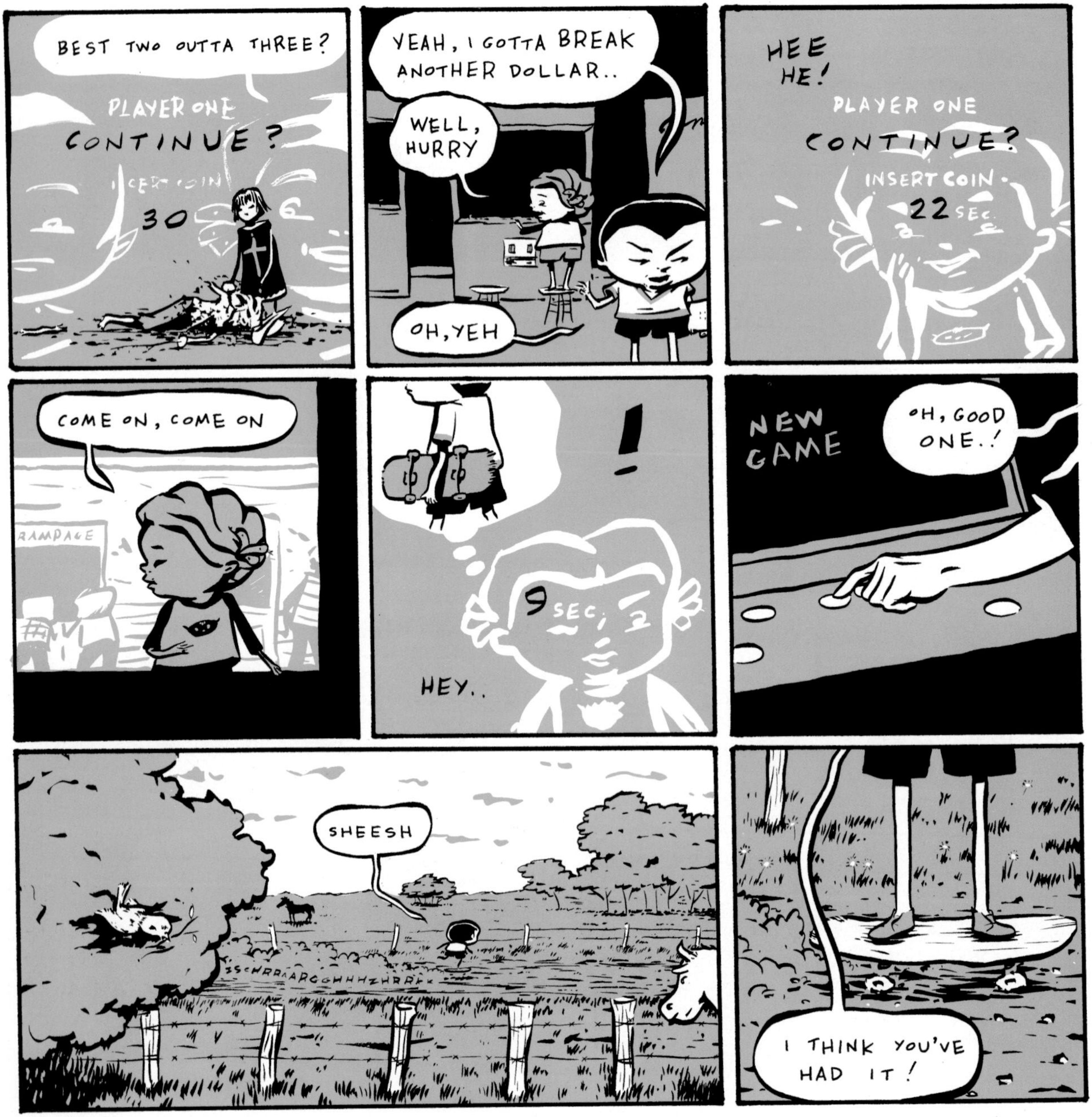
BEST TWO OUTTA THREE?
PLAYER ONE
CONTINUE?
30
YEAH, I GOTTA BREAK ANOTHER DOLLAR..
WELL, HURRY
OH, YEH
HEE HE!
PLAYER ONE
CONTINUE?
INSERT COIN
22 SEC.
COME ON, COME ON
RAMPAGE
!
9 SEC.
HEY..
NEW GAME
OH, GOOD ONE..!
SHEESH
I THINK YOU'VE HAD IT!

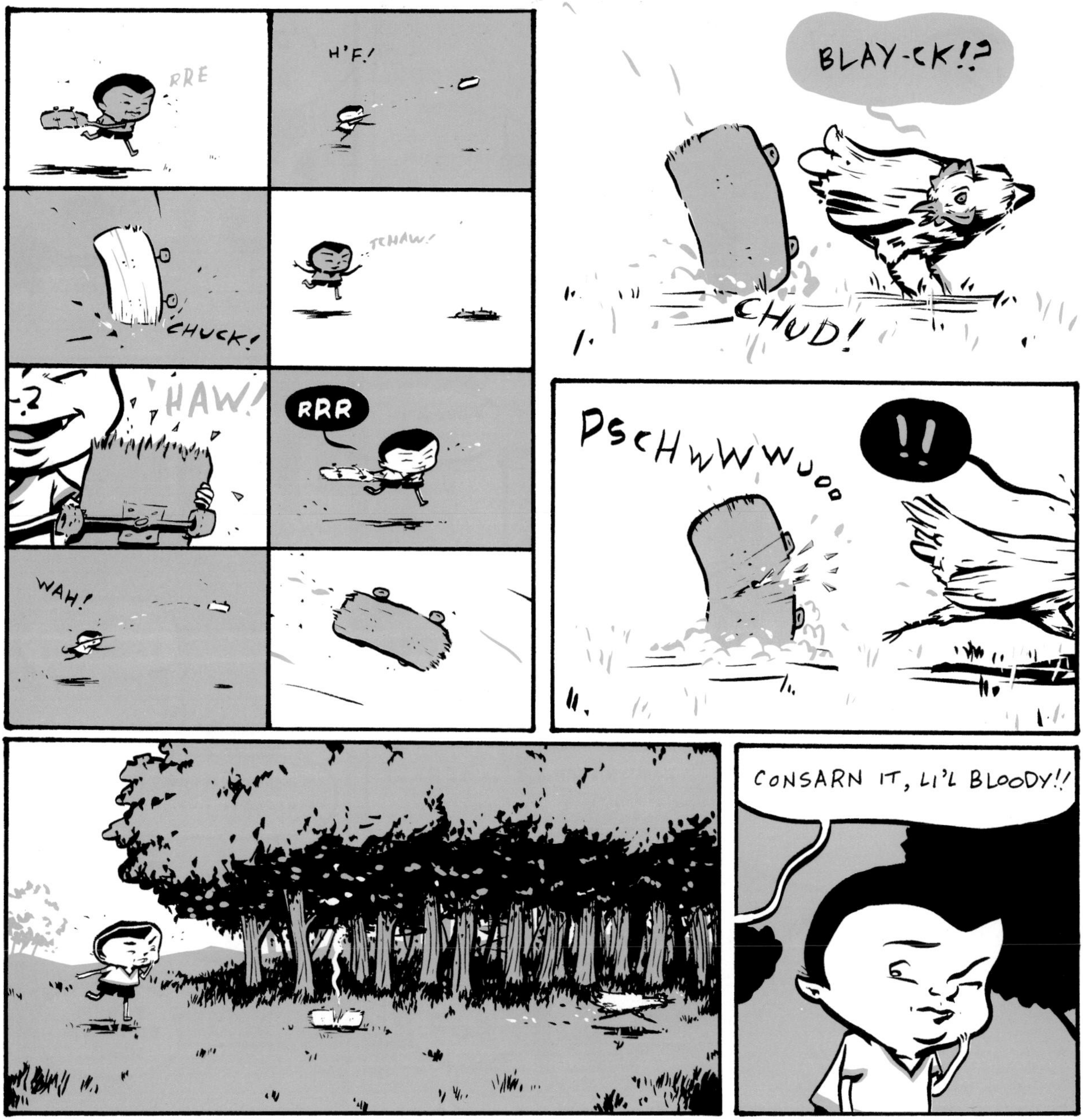
RRE
H'F!
CHUCK!
TCHAW!
HAW!
RRR
WAH!
BLAY-CK!?
CHUD!
PSCHWWWWUOO
!!
CONSARN IT, LI'L BLOODY!!

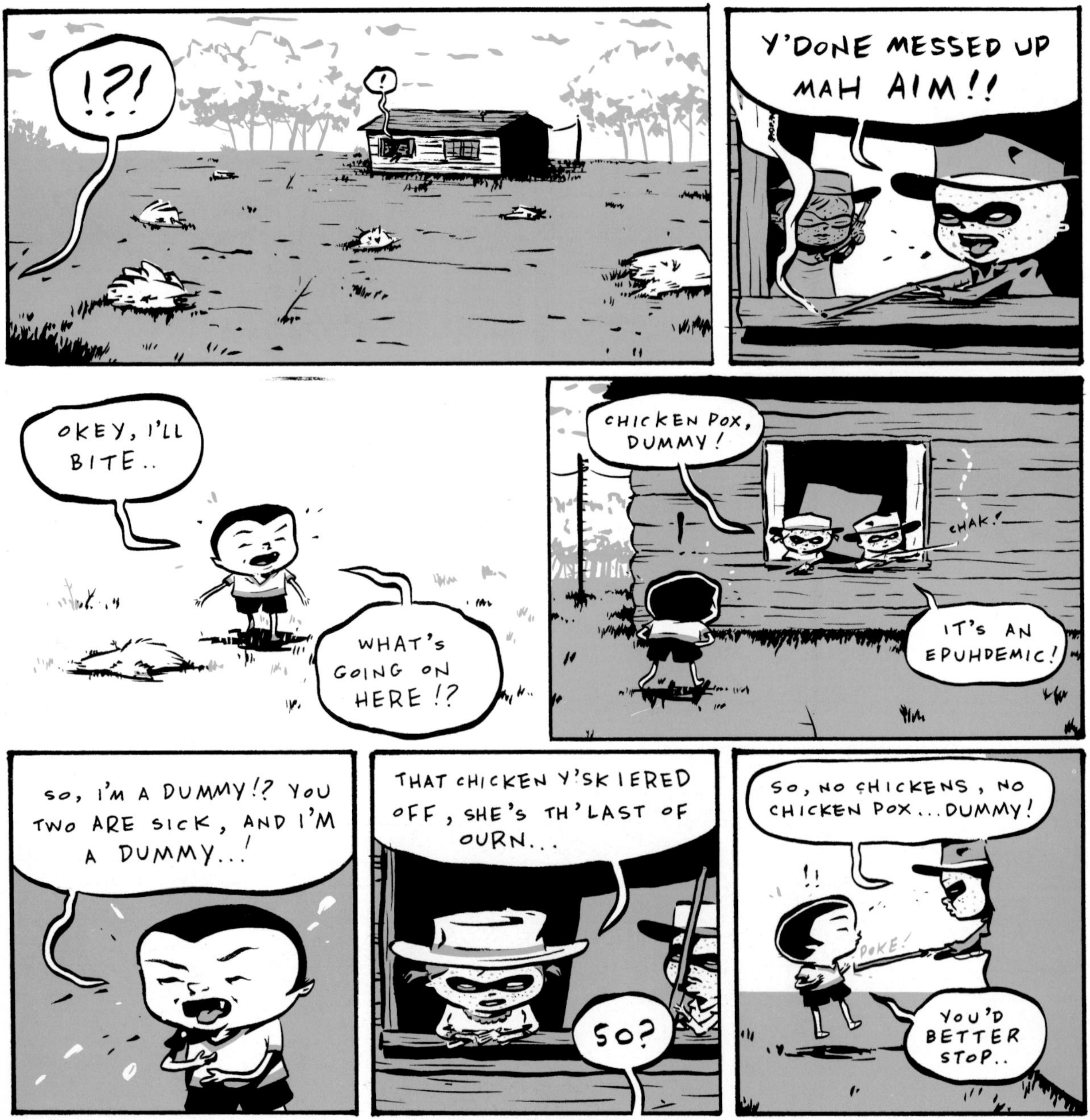
!?!
!
Y'DONE MESSED UP MAH AIM!!
OKEY, I'LL BITE..
WHAT'S GOING ON HERE!?
CHICKEN POX, DUMMY!
!
CHAK!
IT'S AN EPUHDEMIC!
SO, I'M A DUMMY!? YOU TWO ARE SICK, AND I'M A DUMMY...!
THAT CHICKEN Y'SKIERED OFF, SHE'S TH'LAST OF OURN...
SO?
SO, NO CHICKENS, NO CHICKEN POX...DUMMY!
!!
POKE!
YOU'D BETTER STOP..

LOOKIT, LI'L BLOODY, WE AIN'T MAD AT YEW.. BUT WE'RE GONNA NEED YORE HELP...

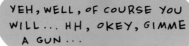

YEH, WELL, OF COURSE YOU WILL... HH, OKEY, GIMME A GUN...

"GIMME A GUN"- YOH!! SERIOUSLY, LI'L BLOODY, AH NEED YA T'GO INTO TH' SCRUB THERE AND FLUSH THAT HEN OUT!

WHADDAYA TAKE ME FOR!? ONE OF YER MANGY HOUND DOGS!?

OH, MANGY ARE THEY?!

HAY!! Y'ALL'RE CRAZY! FIGHTIN' OVER HOUND DOGS WE AIN'T EVEN GOT!

BANG! BANG!

GHRR

NOW, C'MON, LI'L BLOODY, KIN'T YUH SEE YER WAY CLEAR T'HELPIN' US OUT?

WILL YOU GUYS TEACH ME HOW TO SHOOT A GUN, AT LEAST?

LI'L BLOODY, YEW KNOW WE KIN'T DO THAT..

RATS..

WE KIN'T GIVE A GUN TO A KNOWN KILLER, IT'S AGIN' REGULATIONS

HANG ON, SIS! AH GOT SOMETHIN'

STRAIGHT UP, LI'L DUDE! Y'KIN HAVE THIS HERE DAISY JR. BUCK-KNIFE, WITH GENUINE COW-HIDE SHEATH!

OH!

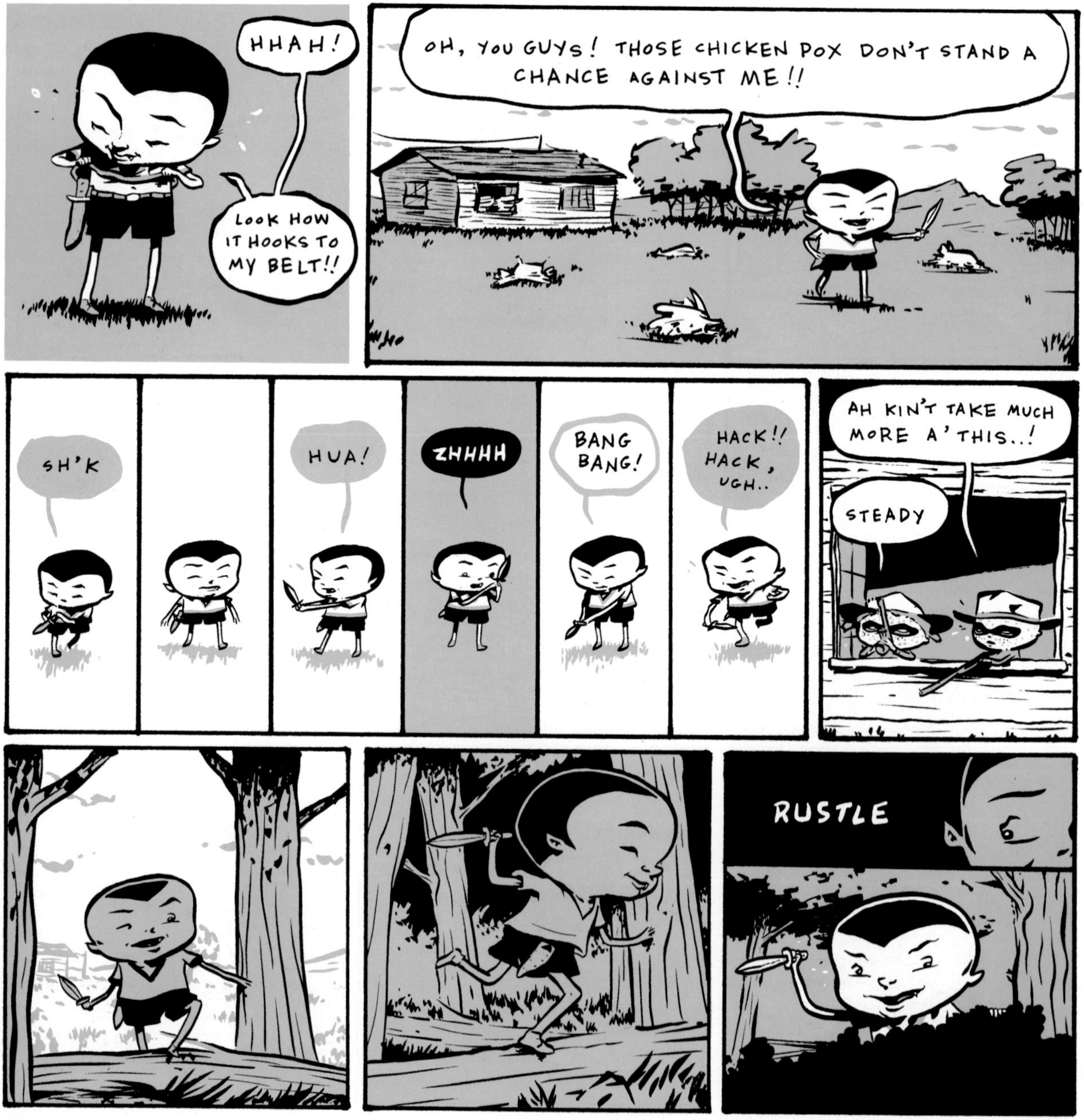
HHAH!
LOOK HOW IT HOOKS TO MY BELT!!
OH, YOU GUYS! THOSE CHICKEN POX DON'T STAND A CHANCE AGAINST ME!!
SH'K
HUA!
ZHHHH
BANG BANG!
HACK!! HACK, UGH..
AH KIN'T TAKE MUCH MORE A' THIS..!
STEADY
RUSTLE

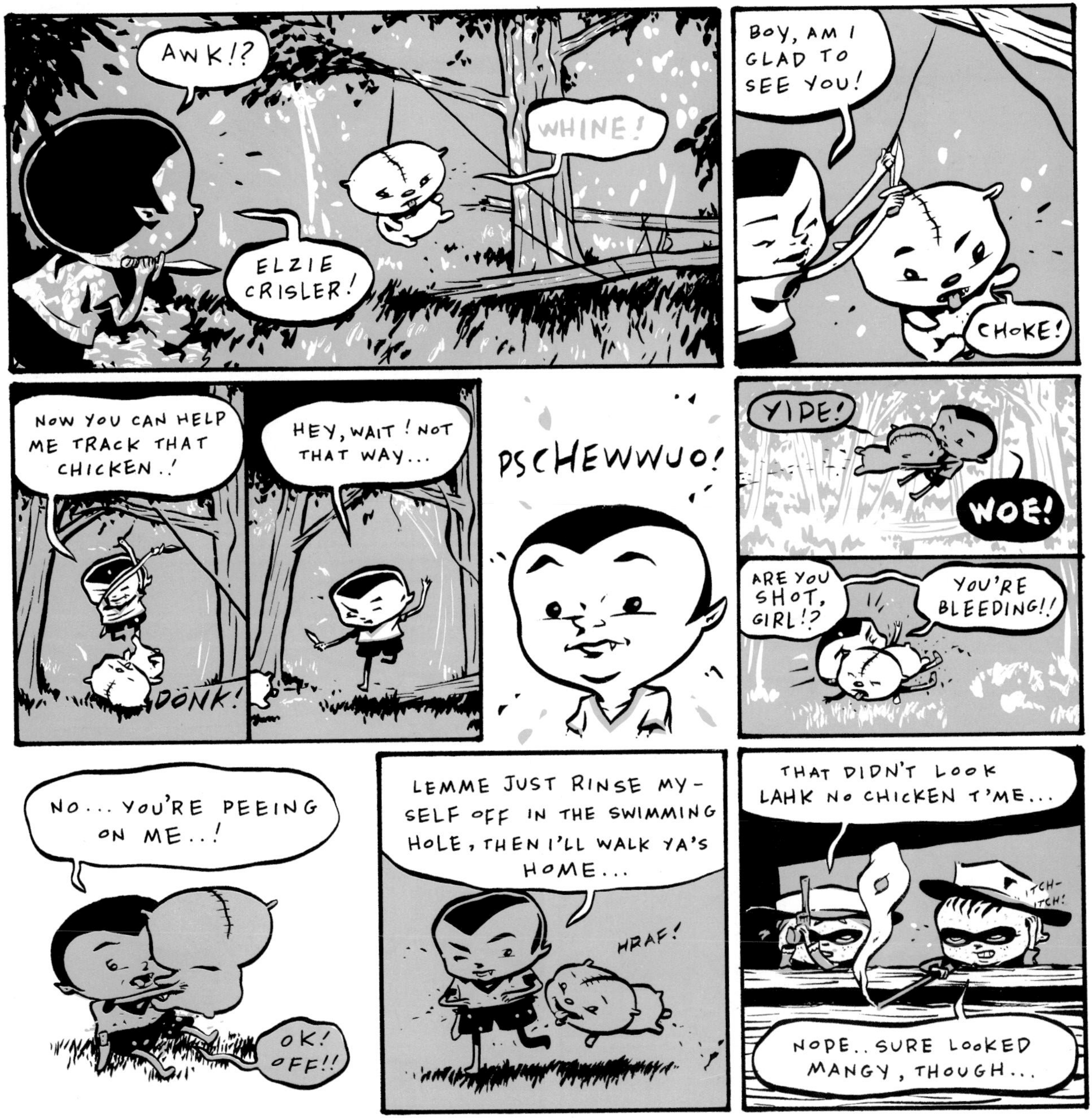
AWK!?
WHINE!
ELZIE CRISLER!
BOY, AM I GLAD TO SEE YOU!
CHOKE!
NOW YOU CAN HELP ME TRACK THAT CHICKEN..!
DONK!
HEY, WAIT! NOT THAT WAY...
PSCHEWWUO!
YIPE!
WOE!
ARE YOU SHOT, GIRL!?
YOU'RE BLEEDING!!
NO... YOU'RE PEEING ON ME..!
OK! OFF!!
LEMME JUST RINSE MY-SELF OFF IN THE SWIMMING HOLE, THEN I'LL WALK YA'S HOME...
HRAF!
THAT DIDN'T LOOK LAHK NO CHICKEN T'ME...
NOPE.. SURE LOOKED MANGY, THOUGH...

100 YEARS LATER

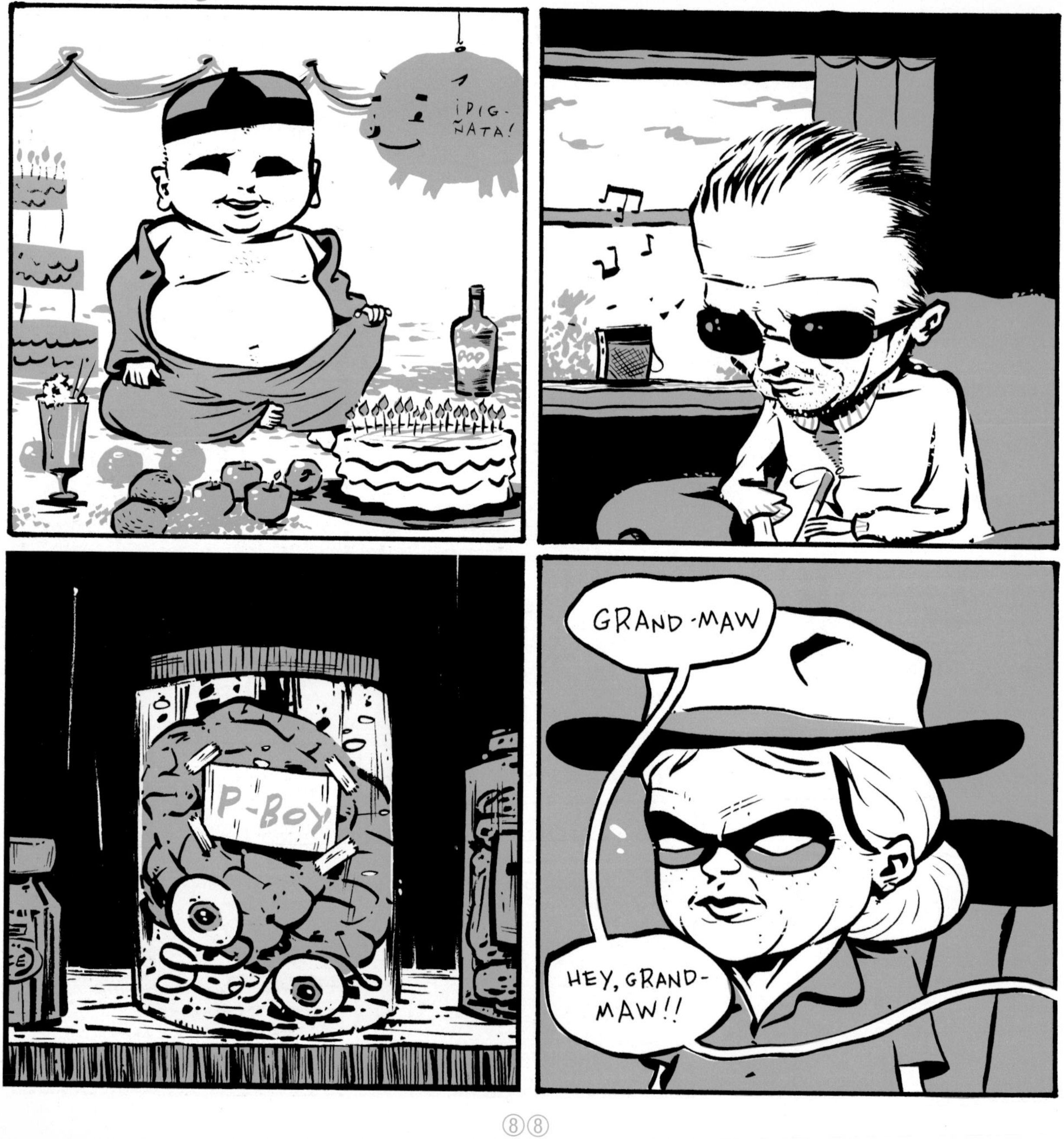
¡DIG-ÑATA!
POP
P-BOY
GRAND-MAW
HEY, GRAND-MAW!!

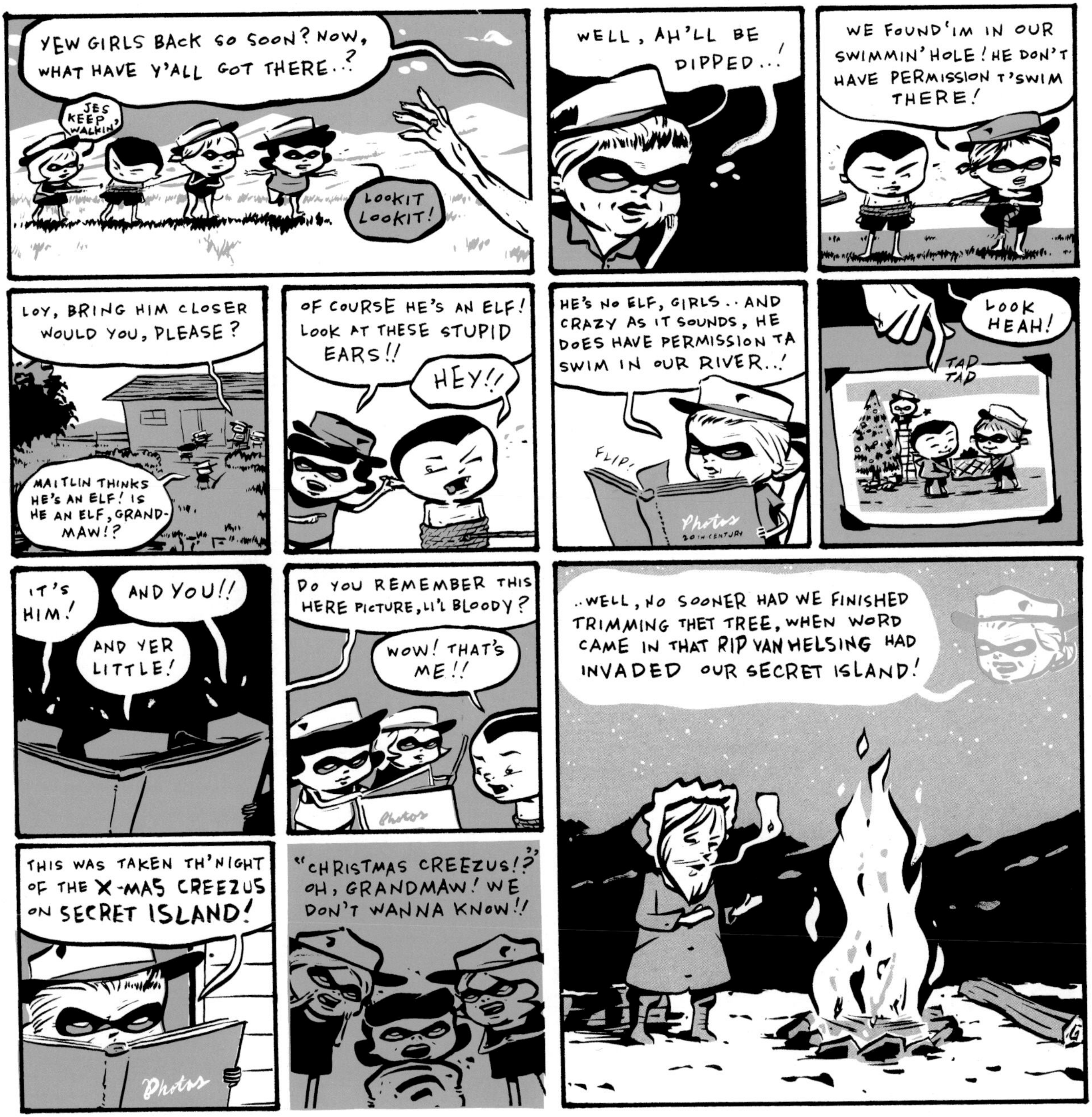
YEW GIRLS BACK SO SOON? NOW, WHAT HAVE Y'ALL GOT THERE..?
JES KEEP WALKIN'
LOOKIT LOOKIT!
WELL, AH'LL BE DIPPED...!
WE FOUND 'IM IN OUR SWIMMIN' HOLE! HE DON'T HAVE PERMISSION T'SWIM THERE!
LOY, BRING HIM CLOSER WOULD YOU, PLEASE?
MAITLIN THINKS HE'S AN ELF! IS HE AN ELF, GRAND-MAW!?
OF COURSE HE'S AN ELF! LOOK AT THESE STUPID EARS!!
HEY!!
HE'S NO ELF, GIRLS.. AND CRAZY AS IT SOUNDS, HE DOES HAVE PERMISSION TA SWIM IN OUR RIVER..!
FLIP!
Photos
20TH CENTURY
LOOK HEAH!
TAP TAP
IT'S HIM!
AND YOU!!
AND YER LITTLE!
DO YOU REMEMBER THIS HERE PICTURE, LI'L BLOODY?
WOW! THAT'S ME!!
Photos
..WELL, NO SOONER HAD WE FINISHED TRIMMING THET TREE, WHEN WORD CAME IN THAT RIP VAN HELSING HAD INVADED OUR SECRET ISLAND!
THIS WAS TAKEN TH'NIGHT OF THE X-MAS CREEZUS ON SECRET ISLAND!
Photos
"CHRISTMAS CREEZUS!?" OH, GRANDMAW! WE DON'T WANNA KNOW!!

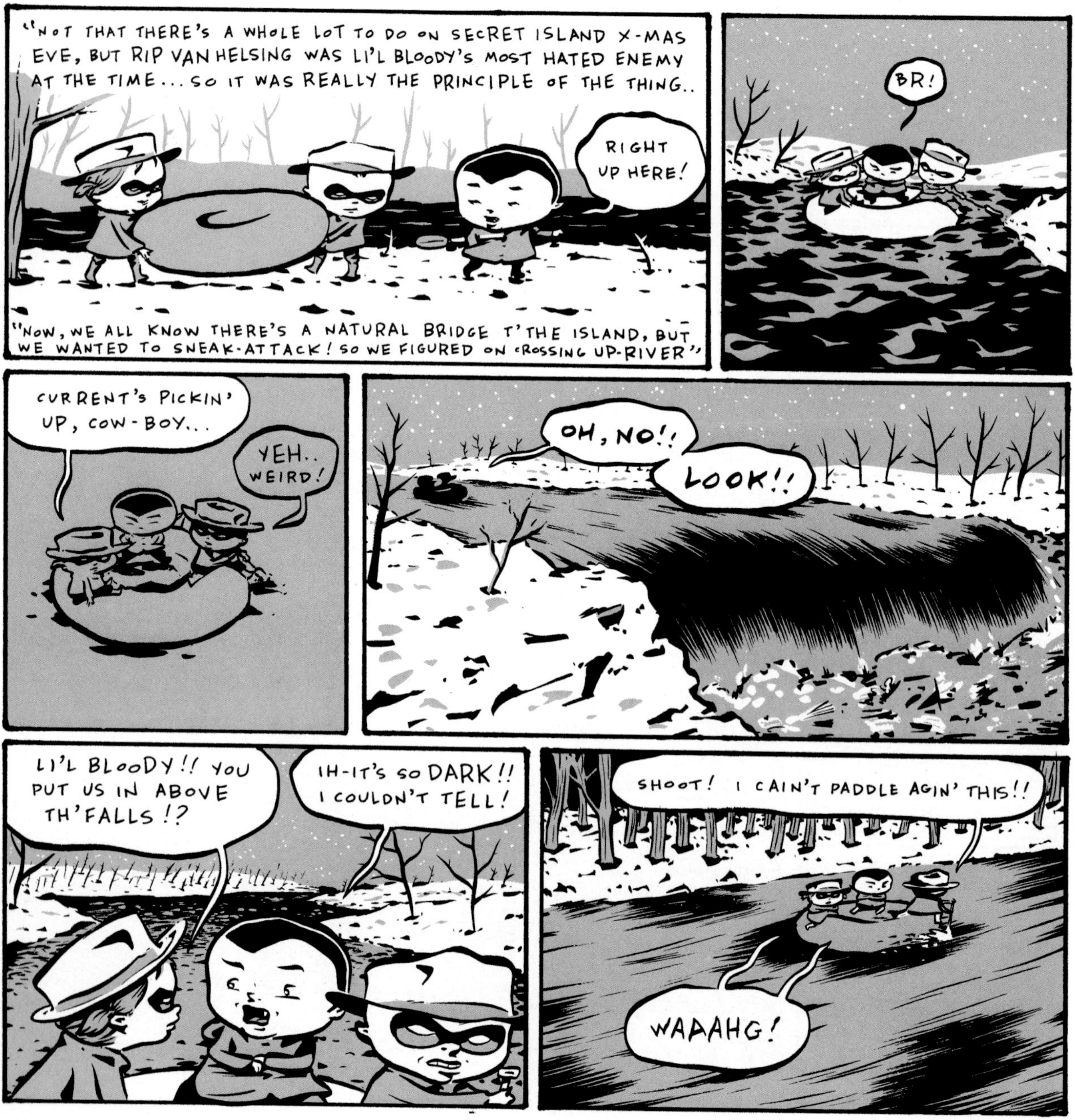
"NOT THAT THERE'S A WHOLE LOT TO DO ON SECRET ISLAND X-MAS EVE, BUT RIP VAN HELSING WAS LI'L BLOODY'S MOST HATED ENEMY AT THE TIME... SO IT WAS REALLY THE PRINCIPLE OF THE THING..
RIGHT UP HERE!
"NOW, WE ALL KNOW THERE'S A NATURAL BRIDGE T'THE ISLAND, BUT WE WANTED TO SNEAK-ATTACK! SO WE FIGURED ON CROSSING UP-RIVER"
BR!
CURRENT'S PICKIN' UP, COW-BOY...
YEH.. WEIRD!
OH, NO!!
LOOK!!
LI'L BLOODY!! YOU PUT US IN ABOVE TH'FALLS!?
IH-IT'S SO DARK!! I COULDN'T TELL!
SHOOT! I CAIN'T PADDLE AGIN' THIS!!
WAAAHG!

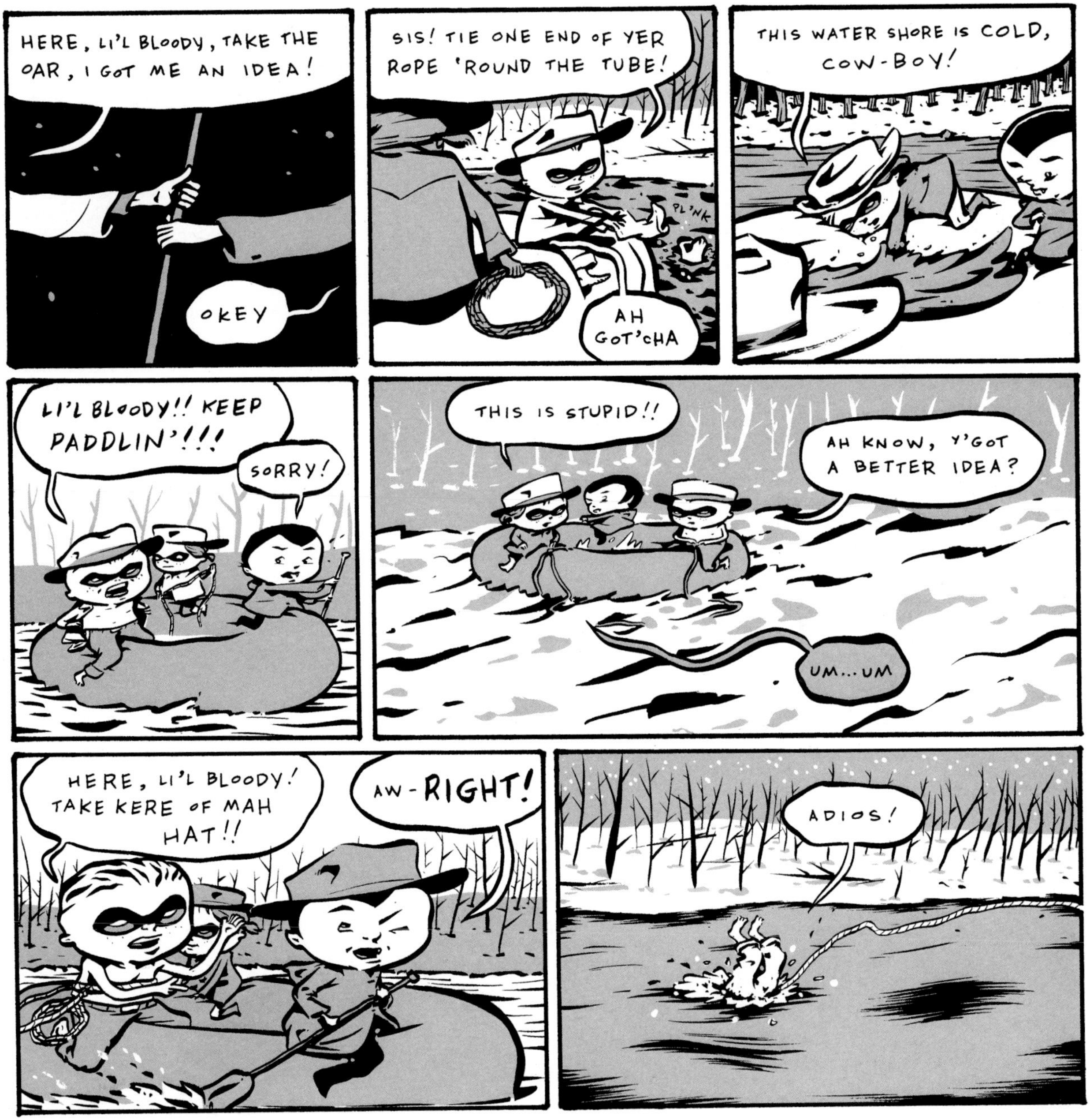
HERE, LI'L BLOODY, TAKE THE OAR, I GOT ME AN IDEA!
OKEY
SIS! TIE ONE END OF YER ROPE 'ROUND THE TUBE!
PL'NK
AH GOT'CHA
THIS WATER SHORE IS COLD, COW-BOY!
LI'L BLOODY!! KEEP PADDLIN'!!!
SORRY!
THIS IS STUPID!!
AH KNOW, Y'GOT A BETTER IDEA?
UM...UM
HERE, LI'L BLOODY! TAKE KERE OF MAH HAT!!
AW-RIGHT!
ADIOS!

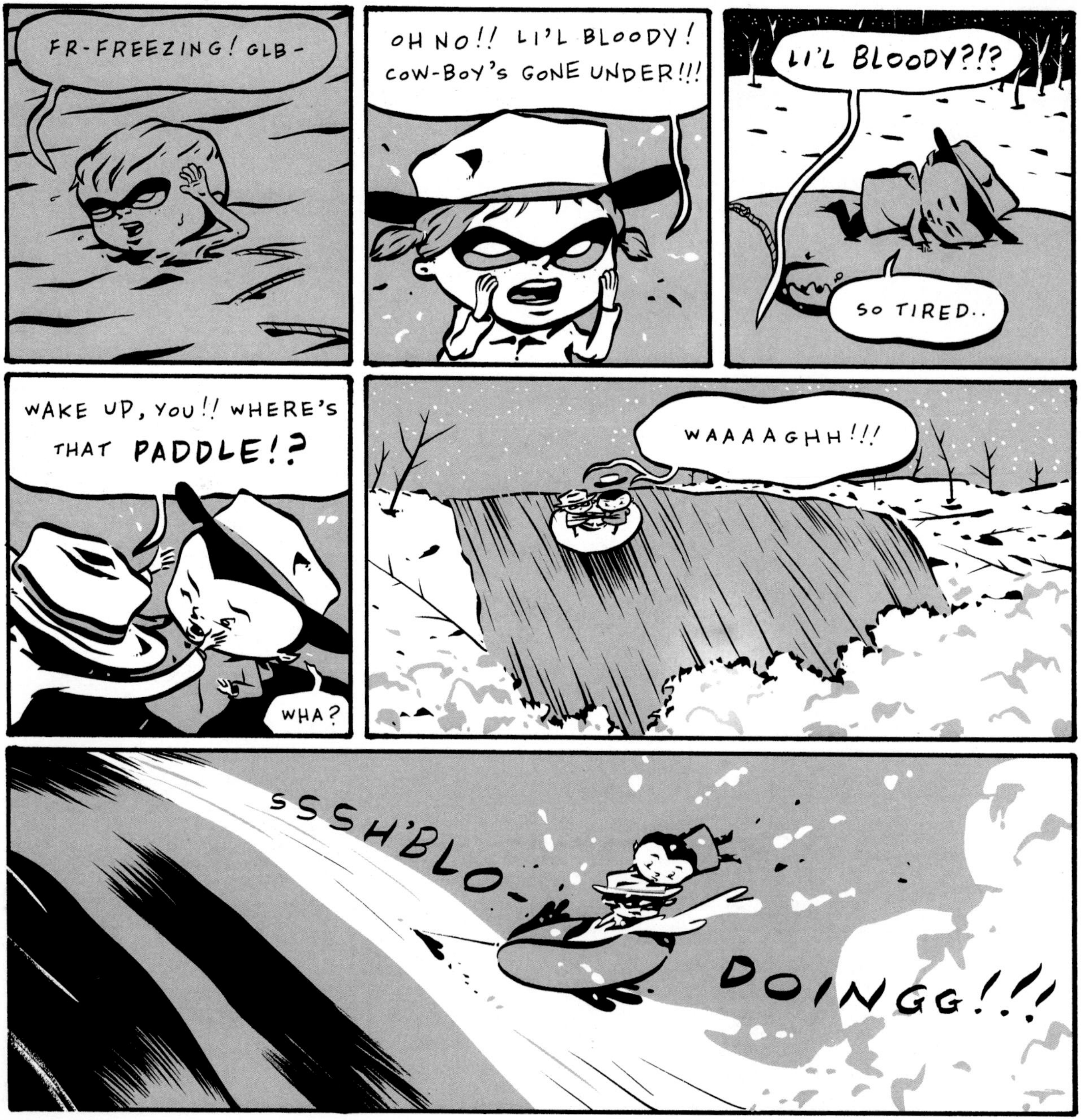
FR-FREEZING! GLB-
OH NO!! LI'L BLOODY! COW-BOY'S GONE UNDER!!!
LI'L BLOODY?!?
SO TIRED..
WAKE UP, YOU!! WHERE'S THAT PADDLE!?
WHA?
WAAAAGHH!!!
SSSH'BLO-
DOINGG!!!

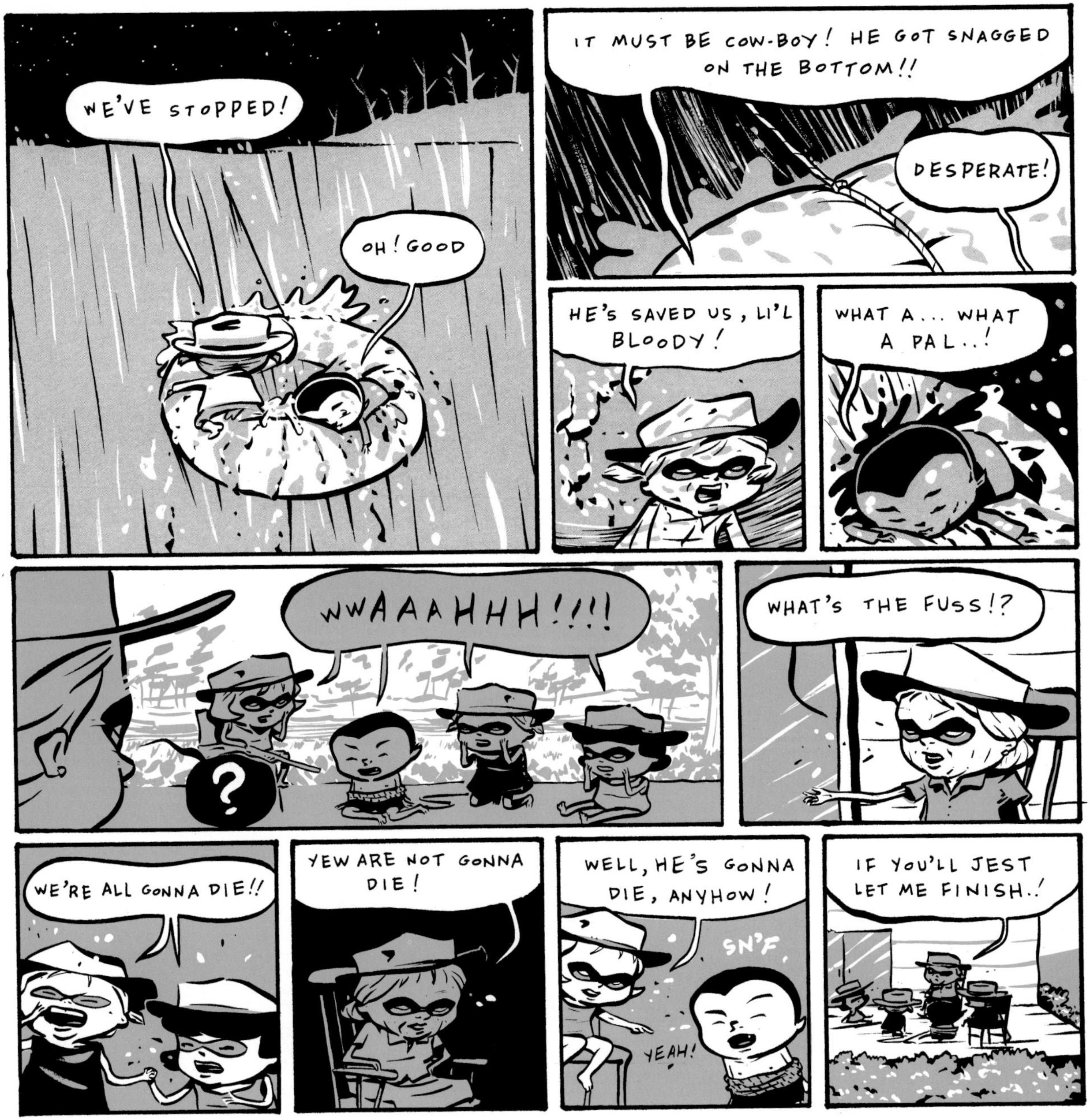
WE'VE STOPPED!
OH! GOOD
IT MUST BE COW-BOY! HE GOT SNAGGED ON THE BOTTOM!!
DESPERATE!
HE'S SAVED US, LI'L BLOODY!
WHAT A... WHAT A PAL..!
WWAAAHHH!!!!
WHAT'S THE FUSS!?
WE'RE ALL GONNA DIE!!
YEW ARE NOT GONNA DIE!
WELL, HE'S GONNA DIE, ANYHOW!
SN'F
YEAH!
IF YOU'LL JEST LET ME FINISH..!

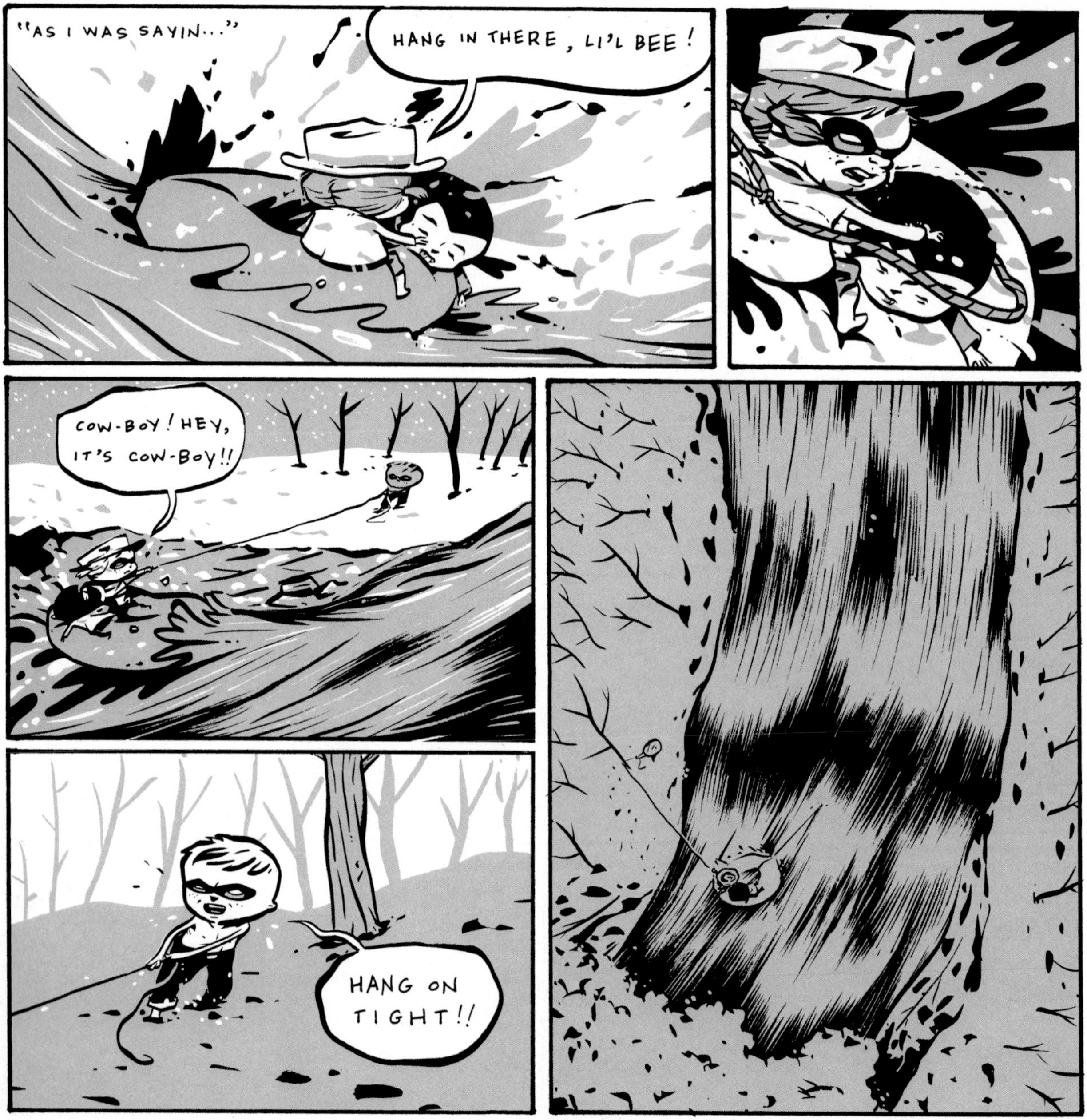
"AS I WAS SAYIN..."
HANG IN THERE, LI'L BEE!
COW-BOY! HEY, IT'S COW-BOY!!
HANG ON TIGHT!!

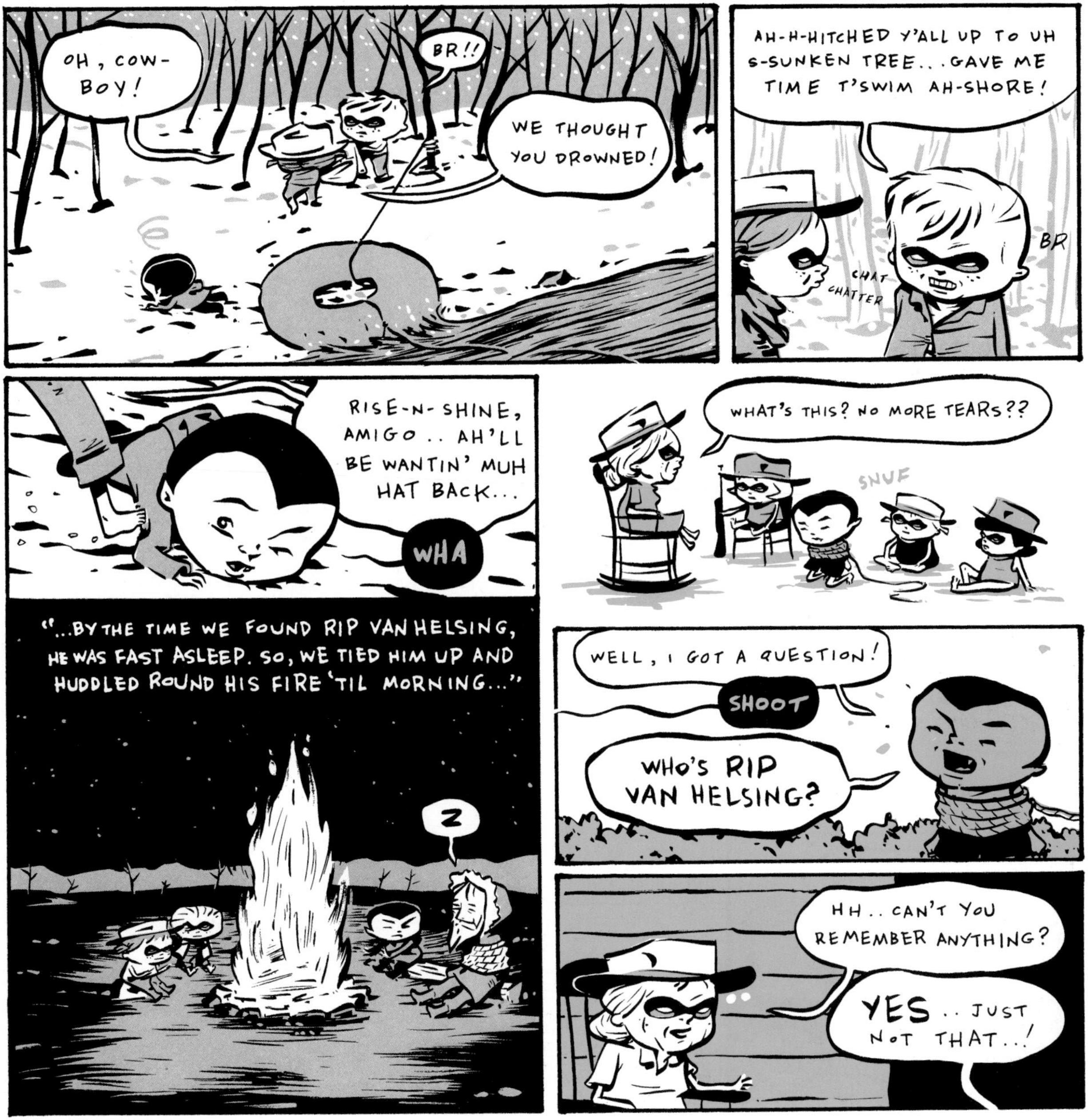
OH, COW-BOY!
BR!!
WE THOUGHT YOU DROWNED!
AH-H-HITCHED Y'ALL UP TO UH S-SUNKEN TREE...GAVE ME TIME T'SWIM AH-SHORE!
BR
CHAT CHATTER
RISE-N-SHINE, AMIGO.. AH'LL BE WANTIN' MUH HAT BACK...
WHA
WHAT'S THIS? NO MORE TEARS??
SNUF
"...BY THE TIME WE FOUND RIP VAN HELSING, HE WAS FAST ASLEEP. SO, WE TIED HIM UP AND HUDDLED ROUND HIS FIRE 'TIL MORNING..."
Z
WELL, I GOT A QUESTION!
SHOOT
WHO'S RIP VAN HELSING?
HH.. CAN'T YOU REMEMBER ANYTHING?
YES.. JUST NOT THAT..!

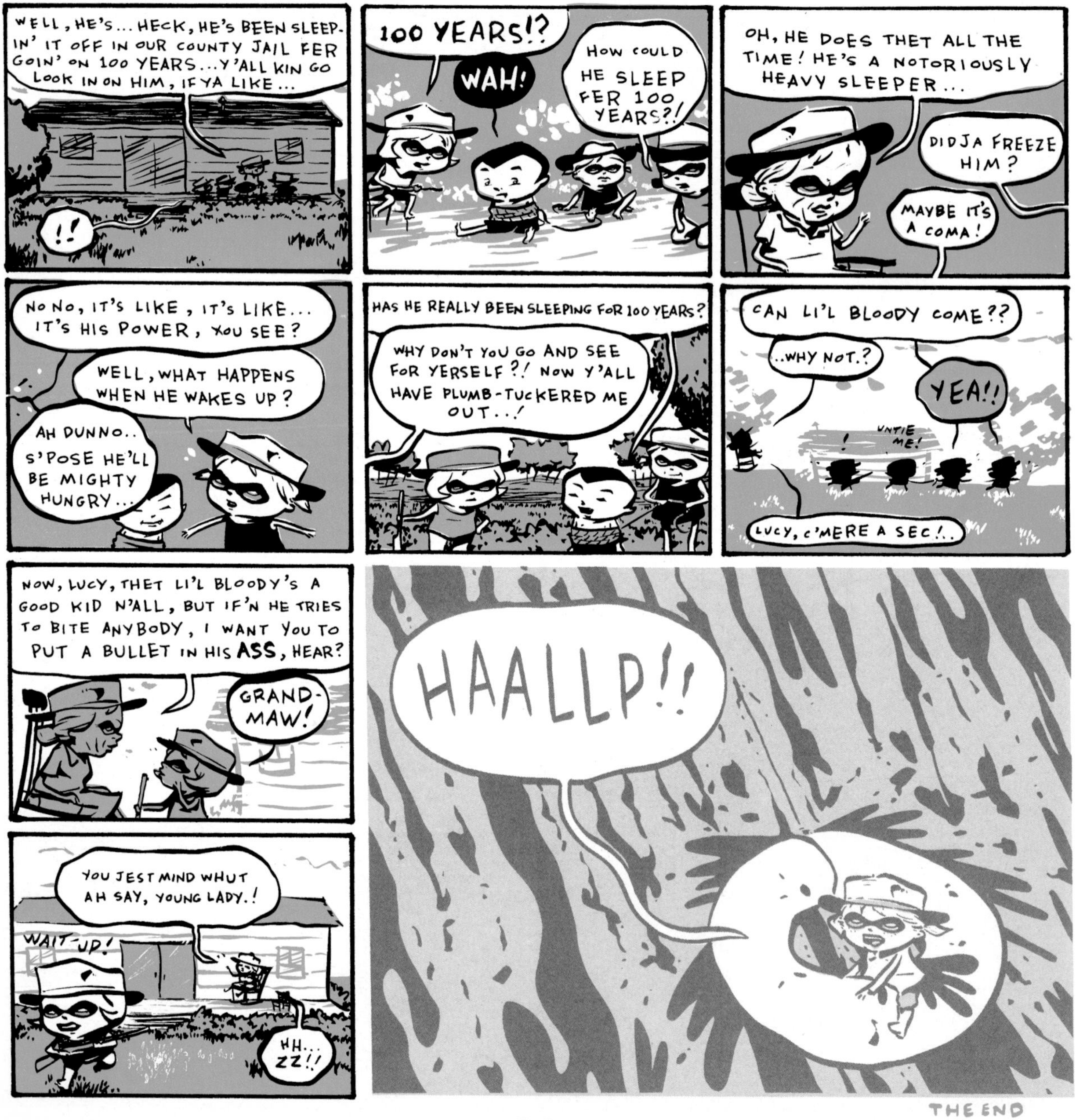

WELL, HE'S... HECK, HE'S BEEN SLEEP-IN' IT OFF IN OUR COUNTY JAIL FER GOIN' ON 100 YEARS... Y'ALL KIN GO LOOK IN ON HIM, IF YA LIKE...
!!
100 YEARS!?
WAH!
HOW COULD HE SLEEP FER 100 YEARS?!
OH, HE DOES THET ALL THE TIME! HE'S A NOTORIOUSLY HEAVY SLEEPER...
DIDJA FREEZE HIM?
MAYBE IT'S A COMA!
NO NO, IT'S LIKE, IT'S LIKE... IT'S HIS POWER, YOU SEE?
WELL, WHAT HAPPENS WHEN HE WAKES UP?
AH DUNNO.. S'POSE HE'LL BE MIGHTY HUNGRY...
HAS HE REALLY BEEN SLEEPING FOR 100 YEARS?
WHY DON'T YOU GO AND SEE FOR YERSELF?! NOW Y'ALL HAVE PLUMB-TUCKERED ME OUT..!
CAN LI'L BLOODY COME??
..WHY NOT.?
YEA!!
!
UNTIE ME!
LUCY, C'MERE A SEC!.
NOW, LUCY, THET LI'L BLOODY'S A GOOD KID N'ALL, BUT IF'N HE TRIES TO BITE ANYBODY, I WANT YOU TO PUT A BULLET IN HIS ASS, HEAR?
GRAND-MAW!
YOU JEST MIND WHUT AH SAY, YOUNG LADY.!
WAIT-UP!
HH... ZZ!!
HAALLP!!

THE END